PRAISE FOR SARAH SMITH AND *BROKEN BEAUTY*

"So many of us have been touched by the ripple effect of a loved one being diagnosed with Alzheimer's disease or dementia. *Broken Beauty* is a story of fighting for a life given a terminal diagnosis, living one day and moment at a time, and proof that with God, anything is possible. Sarah's journey, outlined in these pages, brings hope and light to what, from a distance, might seem hopeless and dark. Love always wins."

—Michael W. Smith, Singer/Songwriter

"There are few subjects that compel us to look into the broken heart of human existence as this one does. But this marvelous book shows that it is precisely because of this that our deepest need for God—and His willingness to meet that need—can also be gloriously revealed, if we are willing."

—Eric Metaxas, *New York Times* best-selling author of *Bonhoeffer* and *Miracles*, and nationally syndicated radio host

"A beautifully written book by Sarah Smith. Having lost my mom to Alzheimer's many years ago, it was as if I were living my own journey all over again. It touched all the same emotions that I'm sure every son or daughter has gone through with a loved one. A step-by-step story of a tragic disease and how the good Lord carried this family through it."

—Lee Majors, film and television actor of *The Big Valley*, *The Six Million Dollar Man*, and *The Fall Guy*

"In a culture where our value is measured by our looks, our income, and our talent, we need reminders of the beauty of sacrificial love and the truth of the inherent worth every human has because they are made in God's image. *Broken Beauty* is a reminder that is beautifully written and full of grace and truth."

—John Stonestreet, president, the Chuck Colson
Center for Christian Worldview

"*Broken Beauty* provides a rare, authentic look into the challenges and triumphs of a family walking the journey with Alzheimer's disease. The story speaks to the need for a community of support, compassionate and competent professionals, and eyes that continue to see and embrace beauty *in the midst of a challenging diagnosis.*"

—Audette Rackley, MS/CCC-SLP, Head of Special Programs at
The University of Texas at Dallas, Center for BrainHealth,
and author of *I Can Still Laugh: Stories of Inspiration
and Hope from People Living with Alzheimer's*

"Heartfelt, heartbreaking, ultimately hopeful, *Broken Beauty* is the kind of book you buy for friends and then a week later, get together and talk about it over a cappuccino."

—Ron Hall, author of the #1 *New York Times* bestseller,
Same Kind of Different as Me, and producer and writer
of the Paramount film of the same name

BROKEN BEAUTY

BROKEN
BEAUTY

Piecing Together Lives Shattered by
Early-Onset Alzheimer's

SARAH B. SMITH

GREENLEAF
BOOK GROUP PRESS

This publication is designed to provide accurate and authoritative information in regard to the subject matter covered. It is sold with the understanding that the publisher and author are not engaged in rendering legal, accounting, or other professional services. If legal advice or other expert assistance is required, the services of a competent professional should be sought.

Some names and identifying characteristics referenced in this book have been changed to protect their privacy.

Published by Greenleaf Book Group Press
Austin, Texas
www.gbgpress.com

Distributed by Greenleaf Book Group

For ordering information or special discounts for bulk purchases, please contact Greenleaf Book Group at PO Box 91869, Austin, TX 78709, 512.891.6100.

Design and composition by Greenleaf Book Group and Kim Lance
Cover design by Greenleaf Book Group and Kim Lance
Cover bowl photograph: ©Shutterstock / Zapylaiev Kostiantyn

Publisher's Cataloging-in-Publication data is available.

Print ISBN: 978-1-62634-597-3

eBook ISBN: 978-1-62634-598-0

Part of the Tree Neutral® program, which offsets the number of trees consumed in the production and printing of this book by taking proactive steps, such as planting trees in direct proportion to the number of trees used: www.treeneutral.com

TreeNeutral®

Printed in the United States of America on acid-free paper

18 19 20 21 22 23   10 9 8 7 6 5 4 3 2 1

First Edition

This book is dedicated to caregivers of every shape and form, professional or not. This disease doesn't just belong to the person who has been afflicted. It is your disease also. You face it with dignity and grace, and you enhance the quality of life as you do. Your hearts are full of love, and you do whatever it takes to make our loved ones feel safe. You are patient, courageous, strong, selfless, compassionate, and tolerant. You are the real heroes, and to me, you are our earthly angels.

--⊷⊱✕⊰⊶--

To Mom and Dad, who have been married fifty-two years and whose love continues to grow stronger.

"Those who abandon ship the first time it enters a storm miss the calm beyond. And the rougher the storms weathered together, the deeper and stronger real love grows." —Ruth Bell Graham

--⊷⊱✕⊰⊶--

And to my loving husband, Thad, and our three children: Frensley, Emery, and Elijah. You gave me the courage to believe in myself and gifted me the opportunity to spend more time with Beauty and Pop so that I could strive to be the best daughter possible. Thank you for your support in sharing our story with the world.

Foreword by Ron Hall

RECENTLY, I DISCOVERED THAT MY friend Sarah and I are the *same kind of different*.

She may disagree, but I don't believe God put us here on earth to be authors. Storytellers perhaps. We were traveling down similar paths of two distinctly separate yet beautiful lives when life began to look not so beautiful. But through brokenness, great stories are birthed, and when put on the page, are like salve for sore hearts—stories that bless untold millions and give hope to even more. *Broken Beauty* is such a story.

I love the title. It intrigues me and causes me to search for the deeper meaning behind the two simple words. Hopefully, as you dive into this story, which is much deeper than wide, you'll agree. However, in full disclosure, I'll admit that the title came to me in quiet, prayerful, and reflective moments after reading Sarah's manuscript. I reluctantly shared it.

As you join Sarah and her family on their journey to love and care for Beauty, your heart, like mine, will become velcroed to theirs. Page by page, together we find love, compassion, and ultimately hope and reassurance from the faith we share. The trials are many, and the victories few—but so, so sweet.

By now, most everyone has been affected by Alzheimer's disease. I know it well, as my late wife, Debbie, and I cared for both her parents, who suffered nearly ten years with Alzheimer's. The arrest, the trials, the tragedies, and the indignities were heartbreaking, as they never realized what happened to their beautiful world. They didn't even remember who they were. The victory in their case was to die just one week apart in their mid-eighties. Theirs was not *early-onset* like Beauty's. Early-onset Alzheimer's seems much more cruel, as it takes a greater toll on families once they realize a still young, vitally engaged family member has become a child once again.

Sarah's journey is real, and her honesty is often gripping. Even if you have miraculously avoided knowing people with this disease, you should begin turning the pages now, as the home you are about to enter could one day be yours. God doesn't give you more than you can handle, but he prepares you to handle what he gives you. That, I believe, is Sarah's testimony.

This story may not ring with familiarity today, but statistics prove it will become familiar to everyone who reads this beautifully rendered tale of a broken beauty. Grab your readers and a warm blanket, stretch out on the couch, turn the pages, and be blessed.

RON HALL
Author of the #1 *New York Times* bestseller,
Same Kind of Different as Me
Producer and writer of the
Paramount film of the same name

BROKEN BEAUTY

--◦❁◦--

I'LL NEVER FORGET THE DAY my mom almost ate glass.

After her diagnosis, my parents moved from Houston to Dallas and bought a beautiful home a few blocks away from my family. I was thrilled to have them closer, and for the first time in years, Mom and I spent so much more time together. Whether we were sitting in carpool lines to pick up my kids or driving to Starbucks to order her favorite drink, an iced soy chai, we were inseparable.

One morning I was folding my parents' laundry while Dad poured Mom a bowl of cereal. He carried it into the living room so she could eat it in her favorite chair. He'd just come back into the kitchen to fix her a hot cup of coffee when we both heard the sound of breaking glass.

"Ahhh!" Mom yelled. "Shoot!"

Dad and I ran into the living room to see what had happened. Mom had dropped her cereal, and the rim and one side of the bowl had broken into pieces. The main part of the bowl, however, was still intact.

She picked up several pieces of glass and put them back in the bowl, and then she scooped up another spoonful of raisin bran and brought it to her mouth.

"Becky!" Dad shouted. "Don't eat that!"

"What?" Mom asked. "It's fine. It's just a few pieces. I can still eat out of it."

"It's broken, Becky. If you eat a piece of glass, you could choke or kill yourself."

Dad couldn't grasp why she didn't understand this. It was common sense, after all.

Still, he was patient and loving and regained his composure quickly. "Here," he said gently. "Let me get you a new bowl."

She looked up at him and back down at what she thought was a perfectly fine bowl of cereal and caved. "Okay. I think it's a waste, but fine." She held out the bowl, which shook in her hands, splashing more milk onto the floor. Because of her disease, she couldn't grip things well anymore. Whenever she held a coffee cup, a drinking glass, or a bowl, it leaned sideways. We continually followed her around with a paper towel to clean up her spills.

"Oh, Mama," I said, trying to keep the mood light. "What are you doing here? Are you stirring up trouble and making messes again?"

She chuckled, then cleared her throat. "I guess so. I'm always doing something." She knew something was wrong with her, but she was still trying to cover it up.

As she stood to help me clean up, I noticed a tiny piece of glass sticking out of her ring finger.

"Mom, hang on. Let me get that glass out of your skin."

She sat back down and, holding her finger steady, I carefully pinched the glass with my fingernails and pulled it out. On my knees, I looked up at her. She looked back into my eyes.

"Mom, I love you. You know that, don't you?"

"Yes, Daughter. I know."

She smiled softly and continued to stare into my eyes with complete trust, believing that I would take care of her and help her get through this journey. I smiled back, blissfully unaware how hard that journey would soon become.

IT ALL HAPPENED SO FAST. One moment, my mom was the funny, strong, opinionated woman she'd always been, blowing air through the gap in her front teeth to make a whistle you could hear for blocks. Then, seemingly overnight, not only had she forgotten how to whistle, but she also had a hard time stringing together coherent sentences.

Early-onset Alzheimer's disease (EOAD) is the cruelest disease I have ever seen. Unpredictable and uncontrollable, it follows its own rules. The disease lives in the moment. It had taken over my mom like a Category 5 hurricane, but sometimes the storm would pass, the clouds would part, and she would be lucid again. During these moments of calm, we'd have beautiful conversations.

Even in these brief exchanges, I'd find myself savoring every word—good or bad, positive or negative—spoken from my mom's lips. And when words were nonexistent, her eyes never failed to express love.

MY JOURNEY WITH MY MOM has been wonderful, painful, terrifying, life-affirming, crazy-making, and beautiful. Every day is different, and there is no consistency. I'm only forty-two, but over the past several years, I've walked through a lifetime's worth of heartache and hope—as have my dad, my husband, my children, and the many friends who've walked beside me. There is so much brokenness all around us, but there's beauty too. With every new crack or fissure, I peek through to see the light. With every new break, I cup my hands around an even greater love.

God gives me glimpses and moments of hope. He teaches me to trust Him along the way. He shows me, through Mom's eyes, how much He loves me. And when I touch her face and hands, I feel a softness and a sense of peace within me. Mom knows how much I love her. Although she can't express her love for me the way she once did, I know that when we are together, our love only grows stronger.

Don't get me wrong: This situation is painful and not at all pretty. There are days that break my heart. But then some of it is so very beautiful, like when I get to dance with Mom. She may not remember what a chai latte is or have any recollection of all the times we went to Star-bucks together, but when I dance with her for twenty minutes, it is amazing. We lock eyes, the disease temporarily disappears, and we feel the connection we have had since she carried me on her hip during my toddler years.

As I've walked beside Mom through her incurable disease, I've begun to see love with a clearer, deeper understanding. There are so many kinds of love—love between spouses, parents, children, caretakers, friends, sib-lings, and, of course, God's abiding love. I wouldn't be where I am today without those kinds of love.

THIS BOOK IS MY LOVE letter to my mom and God's abiding love. It's a story about how love can turn even a tragic, heartbreaking battle into a daily testimony of redemption and grace. Although I recognize that I have lived a life of privilege, my story is no different than that of any-one else facing the travesty of EOAD or any other debilitating disease.

This book is for anyone who has ever felt broken; anyone who has ever struggled with a painful, earth-shattering loss; anyone who has a hunger to know God and witness His daily miracles; and anyone who wants to know whether love can mend our human brokenness and heal all our wounds.

I'm here to tell you: It can.

ONE

HOME SWEET HOME

Thanksgiving and Christmas 2009

⚬•❈•⚬

THE THANKSGIVING AND CHRISTMAS HOLIDAYS were the highlight of my parents' year, especially because Mom loved to entertain guests. It was Thanksgiving 2009, and other than their Sunday-morning church services, nothing brought Mom and Dad greater joy than opening the front door of their Houston home to greet their kids and grandkids.

My daughters, Frensley and Emery, jumped out of the car as soon as we parked in the driveway and ran to Mom. Frensley was almost six years old, and Emery was four.

"*Beauty!*"

The girls had called her Beauty since they could talk. Mom made it up because she did not want to be called Grandma. She also thought it would be funny for the kids to call her Beauty when she was old and feeble. Dad simply settled on "Pop." The funny thing is, when Mom tried to teach the girls her grandma name, they kept pronouncing it "booty." Mom would laugh and say, "No. Beau-u-u-u-ty!" She would stress the "u" sound over and over until they finally got it. Following my children's lead, I often called my parents Beauty and Pop.

The girls looked up at Beauty with excitement. "We made it!"

Mom hugged the girls close. "We're so happy you are here. Now where's my little grandson?"

Elijah was asleep, still strapped into the car seat for the long ride from Dallas. As Thad, my husband, got the luggage and gear out of our car,

I wandered inside and breathed in the smells of the holidays. The candles were lit, music was playing over the speakers, and the fireplaces were burning. The kids' tables were already set with new plates and place mats, and their room was decked out with toys, stuffed animals, and beanbags. My parents' home was decorated beautifully, and I loved walking around to see if there were any new purchases peeking out.

"How do you like it?" Mom asked. "Did you see my new table runner? I love the fall colors, don't you?"

"Oh, Mom." I hugged her. "The house looks amazing, as always. How long have you been decorating, anyway?"

She shrugged. "Just a few weeks. This Thanksgiving couldn't get here soon enough—I'm over the moon that everyone will be here this year."

David, my older brother, lived in South Dakota; and my younger brother, Gabriel, lived in Lavon, just outside Dallas. Both their families were coming.

My dad peeked his head around the corner and made a funny face at the girls.

"Pop!" The girls jumped into my dad's arms. "Happy Thanksgiving, Pop!"

"Hey, Fufu and Wuwu! How are my girls? Have you been getting into any trouble or have you been good?"

"We're always good, Pop!"

My eyes filled with tears as I watched our girls with Dad. All the people I loved most in the world would be gathered under one roof for Thanksgiving. I was content and filled with gratitude.

Home sweet home.

WE HARDLY LEFT THE HOUSE all week. The cousins played, the adults conversed, and the food and desserts kept coming. Beauty and Pop had heated the swimming pool and hot tub, and they set out toys and bikes and balls in the back so the kids could play.

Mom would pour herself a cup of coffee at 8:00 p.m. and offer sweets and pies, and we adults would settle into a cozy room to chat about life. We talked about politics, faith, schools, funny things our kids said or did, and the Russian and Chinese missionaries Mom and Dad hosted in their home several times. Most of all, we enjoyed each other's presence.

My parents had done everything they wanted to do in life. In their early sixties, Dad had retired, and they didn't need or want anything more. They were in a place of contentment, and they wanted to enjoy their grandchildren while still young and active enough to do things with the kids and make an impact on their lives. They wanted to leave a legacy of their time, their love for family, and their love for the Lord. Their actions undoubtedly spoke louder than words. Their kids and grandkids knew how much Beauty and Pop loved them, and in the busyness of life there was nothing like being home for the holidays.

"Hey, Beauty?" I piped up over a slice of pecan pie when we were all chatting after dinner. "You want me to help wrap your Christmas gifts before I leave?"

"Oh yes," she said. "I can't believe all of my Christmas shopping is about done. Thank you, Sarah."

I beamed. This year I'd brought a car full of Christmas gifts for the family and grandchildren. Back in October, I'd offered to help Mom with her shopping, and she happily obliged. Usually she refused help because she was a very strong and independent woman, so I was surprised and pleased when she accepted. I also wanted to get ahead on my own shopping, especially if I could do it without taking along three small children.

Later that evening, she led me to the room where we'd hidden the presents and pulled out a big box of Christmas wrapping paper and ribbons. Together we began to wrap gifts. Suddenly, I noticed Mom struggling as she tied a bow on one of the gifts. She kept opening and closing her fingers, then grabbing her right forearm with her left hand and massaging the muscle as she clenched and unclenched her fist.

"Beauty? What's wrong? Is your arm bothering you?"

"Oh, it's nothing," she said, brushing me off. "It's been tingling on and off for a while now. It's numb sometimes, and all of a sudden I can't feel my fingers or move my hand. But it's nothing to worry about. I probably keep sleeping on it wrong."

"What do you mean by 'a while'? A few weeks or several months?"

"Probably a few months. It's fine, honey. I'll just let you tie the bows."

I chewed my lip. "Have you told Dad? Does he know?"

"He knows. I still work out with my trainer, so it's possible I've injured something. It will be fine. No big deal. It will go away."

"Well, I think I know the answer to this question, but have you considered seeing a doctor? Tingling and numbness can be a sign of something going on in your brain."

Mom looked frustrated. "You're right, Sarah. You know the answer to me seeing a doctor is no. *No doctors.* All a doctor would do is tell me I need to get in some machine and take pictures, and then they'd put me on some medication."

"Mom, you know I hate it when you say that. I wish you would be more open to seeing doctors. There's a reason we have them. You are so stubborn it makes me crazy."

"Blah, blah, blah," she said, mocking me. "I'm fine, honey. Now, what about this necklace? I got it for Patricia. Do you think she'll like it?"

My heart sank. Mom was very good at changing the subject. I looked at her hand—it did look normal. Physically, her hands and toned arms still looked young. She was sixty-four, but she was perfectly healthy and didn't look her age. Five-foot-eight and one hundred and thirty pounds, she walked four miles nearly every day, planted flowers in the yard, and swam in the pool. She also worked out with a trainer two or three days a week. Her nails were strong, long, and painted red. Just a few days earlier, she showed off high kicks from her Kilgore Rangerette dance team days to the girls. She had also lain on the floor that morning to play "Superman" with Emery. She placed her feet on Emery's tummy, clasped her granddaughter's hands, then spread their arms like wings. With a "Whee! Superman!" she hoisted Emery into the air. Emery loved it.

Emery was Mom's Mini-Me: She smiled like her, she was constantly moving, and she had Beauty's dark brown eyes. They had an instant bond—I call it the "English bond," for Mom's maiden name, because of their dark coloring and their strong wills. Mom especially didn't like to be told she couldn't do something, and she wouldn't take no for an answer.

I had to bring my worries up just one more time.

"Please at least think about going to see a doctor, Mom," I said.

She shook her head. "Trust me. I'm just sleeping on it wrong."

And I knew then that even if Mom wouldn't take no for an answer, she expected me to.

FROM THANKSGIVING ON, SOMETHING WASN'T right. I was concerned, and I wanted answers. I called Mom on the phone and occasionally asked, "How's that tingling in your arm? Is it any better?"

Her response, as expected, was, "Yeah, it seems much better. I'm fine!"

At Christmastime, my parents came up to Dallas.

Dad rang the doorbell, and I ran down the stairs to greet them.

"Y'all made it! Come on in."

We helped them carry their things to the third floor.

Beauty and Pop always slept in what we called the "in-law suite." We put a little refrigerator up there, and they had a sitting area with a TV in addition to the bedroom and bathroom. If they ever felt in the way, they would go up there and hide out, knowing it was their space.

Mom and I got some last-minute things at the grocery store for Christmas brunch, and as we loaded the car with bags, I noticed she was doing the same thing she'd done at Thanksgiving: opening and closing her fist, then rubbing her forearm with her left hand, massaging it. We got in the car, and she did it again. My fears screamed in my head.

Suddenly, she realized I'd seen her do it. Her fingers went still. As calmly as possible, I set my keys in the cup holder.

"Mom, I'm worried about your arm. I don't understand why you won't go see a doctor. Maybe it's nothing, but if it is something, wouldn't you rather catch it earlier than later?"

She angled her body away from me, and I sighed. "I know you hate doctors, Mom. But doctors can tell you if there is something wrong, and then you can choose if you want to do something about it. At least get someone to look at it."

She just looked down and continued to massage her arm.

"It went away for a while, and it just came back. I've been doing arm weights a lot with my trainer, and I think I've just pulled something. There isn't much you can do about a pulled muscle. It will heal, and I'm fine, honey—really, I am."

"All right then. But you aren't in your forties anymore, Mom. And if you catch something early, you can treat it. It just doesn't feel right."

I knew how much Mom didn't trust doctors. At that moment, I realized she would never see a doctor unless she'd fallen to the ground unconscious. In other words, I thought, unless she didn't have a choice.

Her distrust of doctors arose the moment her father died. I'll never forget that night in the hospital. It was just the two of us there, and she came in the small waiting room sobbing. She jabbed me in the shoulder and cried out, "They killed him! They're the reason he's gone." We hugged and cried for what felt like an eternity. She blamed her father's death on too much morphine toward the end. According to Mom, it was all the doctors' and hospital's fault. There wasn't much convincing her otherwise, no matter how hard I tried—her heart was broken to pieces.

"One more thing I am going to say," I said, "and then I will try not to say anything more. The 'no pain, no gain' attitude should not apply in this situation. Please don't be selfish. If something *is* wrong with you, it's not fair to keep it from Dad and your children and those who love you and can help take care of you. Dad especially. He would want to know if you had a brain tumor."

The thought that it was a brain tumor terrified me. I couldn't breathe. That night I cried as I told Thad how I couldn't stand how stubborn my mom was and asked him to remind me of my mother if I ever became like that. I, too, lived my life with the "no pain, no gain" mentality.

Growing up as a competitive gymnast, I constantly heard Mom say, "No pain, no gain, honey. No pain, no gain." So I powered through competitions with two broken toes, a jammed finger, terrible heel and knee pain, and eventually lower back pain. I would lie and say I was ready to go when I wasn't. I had a terrible back injury that took several months to heal, but I wasn't going to let the state meet pass me by. I had worked and trained way too hard to let that go. I was mentally prepared to compete sooner rather than later, no matter the cost.

It wasn't just my mom—it was the coaches. They were incredibly intimidating, and they would mentally (and occasionally verbally) abuse me in front of everyone. Mom didn't know, though. She was in the soundproof waiting room, talking with other mothers and watching practice. I didn't dare tell her because I would get in even more trouble with my coach—I feared I would not move up a level or get to compete. Or if I told her, she probably wouldn't believe me anyway. She got sucked into the manipulation as much as I did.

Little did I know then that the brokenness of keeping those secrets of abuse and embracing the "no pain, no gain" mentality would stare right back at me twenty-five years later through the eyes of my mother.

JUMBLED NUMBERS

2010

--◦✕◦--

MOM ALWAYS REMEMBERED PHONE NUMBERS, addresses, and the cost of things. She rarely used her address book or looked up a phone number, and it always amazed me.

Beauty and Pop would drive around and look at different properties—homes, lake houses, and even ranches—as potential investments and discuss pricing. Dad owned a construction company in Houston, so he dealt with numbers on a daily basis. A great team, they had fun estimating the value of houses and real estate.

One day as they were driving, Dad pointed to a property. "Hey, Beck, look at that one. It's seven acres. How much do you think that costs?"

Mom stared intently out the window, deep in thought. She confidently replied, "Fifty thousand."

Dad laughed. "Yeah, right! If that was fifty thousand, we would be in trouble with the land we own not too far from here."

"Well, you asked, and that's what I think. And you *know* I'm right."

Dad arched his eyebrow and gave the back of her neck an affectionate squeeze. "Oh, Beck. You make me laugh. It's more like five hundred thousand. You only missed a zero!"

Mom pulled away from him, questioning what he had just told her.

"No, I didn't. I said fifty thousand. You are just copying me, because you know I am right. Listen to yourself. You don't want to be wrong because you know I'll win this one!"

Mom had begun saying one number while thinking of another. This began a challenging time for Mom, Dad, and everyone around them, because while she thought she was speaking her thoughts, the words were coming out jumbled.

She didn't notice it, however. She didn't notice that "fifty thousand" did not sound like "five hundred thousand" and that they weren't the same number. Dad ignored it until she tried to persuade him she was right and repeated the number a second time.

He told me later he was thinking: "I wonder why her numbers aren't right? She must be tired. It's been a long day."

BEAUTY CALLED ME ONE FRIDAY morning and told me she was going shopping with her dear high school friend, Kelly Maness. When they were young, Kelly and Mom were often mistaken for twins. They looked alike, acted alike, and if a boy who wasn't very cute asked one of them out, she'd give the boy the other one's name. Kelly was from Beaumont, Texas, and had the most precious Southern accent. Mom lit up whenever Kelly walked in the room.

The phone rang, and I answered. "Hey, Daughter! Whatcha doin?"

I smiled. "Hey, Beauty! I just dropped the kids off at school, and I'm heading to the gym. What are you up to today?"

"I'm going shopping for makeup with Kelly. She's driving over from Beaumont. I wish you were here. She's so much fun."

I sighed with jealousy. "Awww, man. I love makeup shopping! I'm so glad you are doing that, Mom."

She quickly answered, "Yep!"

"You can let someone do your makeup and then buy whatever you like that they use. And buy several brands. It's fun to get a lipstick from one counter and mascara from another. I wish I could go."

Mom paused. "Me, too. I miss you, Sarah. I just wanted to say hi and tell you I get to see Kelly today. I'll call you later and tell you what

I bought. Maybe Kelly and I can get our picture taken once we are dolled up."

"That would be great. I can't wait to see. Give Kelly a hug for me."

Kelly's daughter, Gillian, texted me several hours later. Mom and Kelly were so close that I felt like Gillian was a long-lost sister. Her text was a beautiful picture of Mom and Kelly. They had shimmery, smoky eyes, soft pink lips, and bronze cheeks with a hint of pink. They looked stunning and so happy to be together.

Not long after that text, Mom called me.

"Hey, hey! We had so much fun. I got all sorts of makeup. But Sarah, I need to tell you something: I thought the makeup was only $150, but I think the lady overcharged me because the receipt says I spent $1,500! One thousand, five hundred dollars, Sarah."

I gasped. "What? What in the world did you buy? Why did you spend so much? Makeup can be expensive, but fifteen hundred bucks? Didn't you see the receipt before you signed it?"

She paused. "Well, yes, but I thought it read $150. I didn't think I got that much stuff."

I was in disbelief. "Mom, I want you to get all of your makeup out right now and tell me what you bought. There should be a price on your receipt for each item, so let's double-check that you did not get overcharged. And if you didn't, then you need to return some of it. I'm annoyed the makeup lady even let you buy that much."

"I should have paid closer attention, but I was having so much fun and letting them do whatever they wanted on my face."

Mom was not overcharged. She did, in fact, purchase two foundations, two mascaras, three blushes, three eyeliners, and the list went on and on. It was insane. My mom, usually content with buying cosmetics at the drugstore, would never spend that much money on makeup.

I told her she should keep one foundation, one blush, the black mascara, and the red lipstick. That's it. That was all Mom needed anyway. She was a natural beauty, which was another reason why I loved to call her Beauty.

• • •

ANOTHER WEEKEND THAT SUMMER, I drove to Houston with Ginny, Mom's other close friend who lived in Dallas. She wanted to spend some time with Mom, and I wanted to take the kids to see Beauty and Pop. All they wanted to do was swim, swim, and swim some more.

That Saturday afternoon, Ginny and Mom went to the Houstonian, a hotel with a private club, for a spa treatment. The kids and I would meet up with them later for an early dinner. When I arrived, Ginny seemed distracted.

Beauty took the kids to get a snow cone, and Ginny leaned over to me. "Sarah, I'm concerned about your mother. Have you noticed anything different about her? When I say different, I mean she's not as sharp as she's always been, and she seems a little confused with her numbers."

I hesitated but knew she was right. "Yes on the numbers, I guess. But I haven't noticed that she's lacking sharpness." I told her about the $1,500 makeup purchase.

Ginny pressed her lips together and stared over at Mom. She turned to me, and, with her deep stern voice, said, "I'm worried about her. I don't like to say that to you because I know how much you love her, and I don't want to scare you, but there is something not right with her. I've known her almost my entire life. We were roommates. She has always been right on with numbers and sharp as a tack, but she's not the same. Has your dad said anything to you? Probably not, because he wouldn't want you to worry either."

She paused, then said, "When we got to the Houstonian today, she couldn't remember the gate code to get in. Even she realized she should know it. It's been the same code all summer, and she couldn't recall the digits. We had to talk to the security guard. Luckily, he knew your mother."

As Ginny spoke, I watched Beauty with my children. She was smiling and laughing and holding Elijah on her right hip. She was in her element. She loved being with those kids. She would ask Thad and me,

"Sarah, when are y'all going on your next trip? We are ready for them to come stay with us!" Or, "Sarah, how about meeting us halfway to Houston and leaving the kids with us for a few days? It will give you and Thad some time together, and y'all can go on a date night and have a little break."

As I watched Beauty carrying Elijah with his rainbow-colored snow cone, I saw her acting like a child, not knowing that one day her mind would revert back to a child's forever.

GINNY, MOM, AND I WENT shopping for clothes while Dad took the kids fishing on some property they owned nearby. They loved fishing with Pop. Dad would let Emery and Frensley drive the pickup truck while Elijah napped in the car seat. The kids felt a sense of freedom out in the open fields as Pop let them have some fun. I trusted Dad and knew he would make sure they were safe. He let me drive at a young age, so I knew exactly what my girls were feeling.

While Mom was in the dressing room, Ginny brought a fuchsia silk top for Mom to try on.

"Becky, you have to try this on. It's to die for! It would look striking on you, and it's only $50."

Ginny could always find the bargains. She could put on a $500 sweater or a $25 sweater and make either of them look like a million bucks.

The dressing room door was wide open as Ginny handed Mom the blouse, and before we knew it, Mom was lifting up her shirt.

"*Mom!* Close the door! You never change in front of people. I don't think I've even seen you in your bra more than a few times my entire life."

Breathing loudly as she pulled the shirt over her head, Mom said, "Huh? I don't care. It's just you and Ginny. I don't care if y'all see me in my bra."

I was shocked. *Since when did you not care that someone saw you in your bra? That's weird. You're the most modest person I know.*

"Here, Sarah, help me zip this. I think it has a zipper in the back."

Mom put on the shirt and sure enough, it was fabulous. Ginny yelled and whistled, "Woo-hoo! I told you it would be striking on you."

Mom laughed. "Oh, Ginny. You're just staying that. Here, help me take this thing off."

And again, Mom pulled the shirt over her head with the door wide open for all to see. *Oh my gosh, Mom! Stop changing in front of us. What is up?*

I bought a few fun tops that day, but the main thing I left the store with was the thought of repeatedly seeing my mom in her bra. That was ten times more than I had ever seen her breasts, bra, and stomach in my life, and though Beauty did look pretty darn good for her age, it was still odd.

DAD AND THE KIDS RETURNED from fishing, bringing fresh catfish to grill for dinner.

I said to the girls, "All right—y'all go shower, and scrub hard to get that nasty fish smell off. I want you all cleaned up for dinner. I'll help Pop."

Mom and Ginny were drinking coffee in the living room while Dad and I went outside to cook.

Casually, I said, "Hey, Dad, has Mom been acting a little strange to you or messing up her numbers?"

He flipped the fish on the grill. "Well, yes. Strange not so much, but numbers, yes. I've noticed it lately. Why?"

"Remember that time she went makeup shopping with Kelly? She thought $1,500 was $150. I didn't think too much of it then. But Ginny told me today she's concerned that Mom doesn't seem right. She says Mom forgot the gate code to the Houstonian."

Dad immediately turned to me. "She forgot the gate code?"

"Yes, Dad. She completely forgot. And not just for a moment. It never came to her, and they had to get the security guard to let them in."

He didn't move. I could tell he was deep in thought as the catfish sizzled on the grill. "We go there all the time, Sarah. The gate code hasn't changed in more than a year."

"Well, you may want to talk to Ginny about it because she seems very bothered by some of Mom's behavior. Ginny said she was 'different.'"

We both grew quiet, staring at the catfish.

"Daddy, do you think Mom has a brain tumor?"

"I don't know. One thing I do know is that I don't know how I will get her to a doctor," he said.

"I'm so worried now. Her arm tingles, she can't tie bows on Christmas gifts, she gets her numbers jumbled, and have you seen her try to write her name lately?"

Dad nodded his head. "Yeah, sweetie. I have. Her penmanship used to be so pretty, and now she can barely write in cursive. It takes her so long to write that it's just quicker if I write it for her. I think she knows something is wrong. But I don't know what to do."

I put my arm around his back. "I really want you to try to get her to a doctor. If it's a tumor, perhaps she can have it removed. If she waits and it grows, it can kill her. We need to convince her to see a neurologist. We need to know what we are dealing with."

He smiled and tried to cover up his worry. "Don't worry about Mom. You have enough on your plate with those three children. I'll take care of her. Try not to think about it and just focus on your family."

No, I can't. That's impossible.

"Dad, you and Mom *are* my family. I will take care of Thad and the kids, but I also want to help take care of Pop and Beauty. That's life, isn't it? You raise us, then the seasons change, and we help you. It's the cycle of life."

THREE

THE DIAGNOSIS

November 2012

-•→✕←•-

A FEW YEARS WENT BY, AND Mom still refused to see a doctor. My dad, my brothers, and I watched Mom slowly worsen. Things were not right. I couldn't pinpoint it, but she was different somehow.

We took a trip to Mexico that summer for her birthday, and although it was one of the best trips I'd taken, there were times when Mom was delayed with her speech or didn't laugh when something was obviously funny. Her reactions slowed, as if she were in her own world.

She also couldn't sign the guest book in the home where we were staying. As she held the pen, Mom signaled Dad over.

"David, come here. Can you sign this for us? I don't know what to write."

Without hesitation, Dad took the pen and signed.

Mom always knew exactly what to write. She was the queen of long emails, and she could be quite the talker—she never seemed to run out of words.

Mom not knowing what to write was a signal to me of just how drastically things were changing. I knew in my heart something was wrong, so I scrutinized every little thing she said or did during the entire trip.

When we returned to Houston, my parents' friends Jan and Nyal hosted all of us at a dinner as a token of appreciation of our including them on the trip and to recap all of the fun.

When we were leaving, Jan pulled me aside.

She looked me in the eyes with love and concern. "I am worried about your mom. Have y'all noticed anything or seen a doctor? Her mind just doesn't seem right to me."

My heart skipped a few beats and my stomach turned. "Dad and I both think something is wrong, but he can't convince her to see a doctor. I think Mom has a brain tumor. She's had tingling in her arm for several years, and she says and does things that are out of character. She confuses her numbers, so I think there is something going on in her brain. I'm really scared."

Jan squeezed my arm. "Honey, I know you are. Is there anything I can say or do to convince her to see someone? I know your mom. She is stubborn, and I don't know if it's out of line for me to express concerns for her health. I don't want her to get mad at me."

I smiled and rolled my eyes in agreement. "She's one tough cookie, that's for sure. I don't know how to answer that, but I know she won't listen to Dad or me. Maybe it will take a good friend to let her know it's more obvious than she realizes. She thinks she is covering it up, but it's showing more and more every day. Please say something. And if you do, please let me know what she says. Call me in Dallas anytime."

She hugged me. "Of course I will, sweetie. You know how much we love your mom and dad. Nyal's mom had a brain disease, so we are more sensitive when we see things like this, and that's why we're concerned."

The car ride back to my parents' house was long and despairing for me. Mom and Dad were laughing about how funny Nyal was and already planning their next Cabo trip. I, on the other hand, felt nauseated.

Mom turned around in the front seat. "Wasn't that great, Sarah? I'm so happy you've gotten to know our 'newer' close friends! We have so much fun with them."

"I had a great time, Mom. I can tell they love being with you and Dad," I replied with a fake smile.

At the same time, I was thinking, *You should listen to Jan when she expresses her concern for your health.*

I prayed silently. *Lord, please help Jan get Mom to a doctor. What will it take, God? We need answers. I can't live in fear for my mom's health anymore. I need You to reveal the unknown, please. I'm begging You, God. You know what is really going on, so please bring it to light.*

When I prayed that prayer, I didn't realize the answer I was seeking would turn my world upside down.

A LITTLE MORE THAN A month later, Dad called shortly after I tucked the kids in bed.

"I have good news. Mom has an appointment with a neurologist next Monday. Whether or not she'll actually go, I'm not sure. But she has an appointment."

I let out a huge sigh. "I am *so* relieved, Daddy. Can I go? I would love to be there."

"You would need to ask your mom. She is hesitant as it is, so I'm not sure if she will want you there. I can call you with the results or any news."

That wasn't what I wanted to hear, nor could I settle for that.

"No, Dad. I want to come. If Mom will let me, I am there. No questions asked."

"Well, if you think it's okay with Thad, and if the kids will be fine without you, then of course I would love for you to be here. But it's ultimately not up to me."

"Can I call Mom and tell her you told me about her appointment and see how she reacts before I ask if I can come?"

He hesitated. "Sure. That's fine. I don't care anymore. She knows we are concerned for her and that we have asked her for a long time to see somebody."

"I'll be praying that she makes it to her appointment and that you have the strength to encourage her and give her the words she needs to hear. I'm proud of you, Dad—we need to know what's going on."

I immediately dialed Mom.

"Hey, Beauty! How about them 'Horns? Did you and Pop watch the game?"

She was in a great mood after the University of Texas football win, which was to my advantage. "Oh yes," she said. "Amazing game! Do you miss cheering?"

"I do, Mom. Those were some of the best years of my life." I smiled as we reminisced over the phone but I knew I had to push Mom out of her comfort zone with this conversation—just as she'd pushed me out of mine when she encouraged me to try out for college cheerleading all those years before.

"Mom, I'm calling because Dad told me you finally scheduled a doctor's appointment. Way to go!"

I made it light and slightly sarcastic so she wouldn't get defensive. She grew quiet. "I don't think I really need to, and I am going *only* for your father."

I didn't care who, what, where, when, or how she got there, even if she let me know it was only to satisfy Dad.

"Okay, Mom. I wanted to see if I can come. I would love to come in for the weekend and go to the appointment Monday morning with you two."

"I don't think so, honey. You don't need to be there. I can tell you right now they are going to say there is something wrong with me so they can put me on medication. So there is your diagnosis!"

I took a deep breath and decided not to take the bait, as my husband would say.

"Maybe that medication can help you, Mom. Just be open-minded, okay? And please, *please* let me come. Besides, I will be without the kids, so it would give us a lot of mother-daughter time."

I knew Mom craved that time as much as I did. It was rare for us to have that anymore with toddlers running around.

"Okay, love," she said at last. "But you can't come into the doctor's room. You will need to wait outside, so I don't see the point in you coming. But you can come if you really want to."

I sighed with relief as I hung up the phone and replayed the conversation in my mind. I thought to myself, *She doesn't want me in the doctor's office because if she gets a bad diagnosis, she won't tell me. She'll keep it a secret and pretend she's okay. I'll stay in the waiting room. I'll know by the look on her face when she walks out if there's something serious.*

ON MONDAY MORNING, MOM WOKE me up earlier than I expected. The sun was shining through the window, and I could feel the heat and the dreaded Houston humidity.

"Honey, wake up. I want to talk to you."

I stretched my arms, "What is it?" I asked.

She played gently with my hair.

"Well, you won't like this and you'll probably be upset with me, but I don't want you coming with us today to the doctor. I just want to be with Daddy and for us to be alone."

I couldn't move. I lay there dumbfounded that she would actually tell me I couldn't go to the doctor. *Why does she always have to hide things? She's so frustrating!*

"Mom, please. I understand you want to be with Dad, and you will be, in the doctor's office. Remember, I'm sitting in the waiting room. I won't be with y'all when you see the doctor. I just want to know what he says and be there for you to tell me in person. You are so dang stubborn."

She kept playing with my hair, staring at me as if she might change her mind, but she didn't.

"I know. I am a pain, aren't I? And it means the world to me that you want to be there. I just need to be with your father, though. I promise to call you after the appointment and let you know what the doctor says, although I know I'm fine. Really. I'm going to be fine."

I turned my back to her, rolling into a fetal position. She walked out and shut the door. Tears rolled down my face.

Why doesn't she trust me? Why is everything a secret? Why can't I help?

I want to be there for Dad, too. I can't stand Mom sometimes. Thanks, Grandma and Grandpa, for raising a stubborn pain in the butt.

DRIVING BACK THE 250 MILES to Dallas, all I could do was pray and beg God for answers. It seemed like such a long drive, and when I stopped for gas and called Thad, I started crying. I told him I was halfway home, but all I wanted was to be with my parents and hug them both.

Thad reminded me there was a reason for everything.

"Honey, I'm sorry you are disappointed. At least you got time with them over the weekend. Quite frankly, I am not surprised. I love Beauty, but she can be difficult, and you need to not take it so personally."

I couldn't speak on my end of the phone. I had a knot in my throat and tears were rolling down my face.

"Honey," Thad said, "are you there?"

My voice quivered. "Yes, I'm here. I'm just sad and worried for Mom. I'm scared for her and miss my parents so much. I've begged them to move to Dallas and prayed they would for years, and all they do is drive around and look at houses and get my hopes up, and then they don't move!"

I cried even harder as my emotions collided: fear, anxiety, love for my parents, worry for Mom's health, the realization she was too young to be sick. I thought of her jumping up and down with our kids, dancing with Dad, and the way she loved to entertain and bring people together. The thought of her dying was awful.

"Thad, what if she has cancer? Or a brain tumor? What if she dies? I can't even imagine—"

Thad cut me off.

"Honey, please. You are jumping to conclusions and listening to the lies of the enemy. He wants you to think and believe all of those things, especially in a state of sadness. Focus on the good, Sarah. God loves your mom so much. He loves her more than you do! She's His child, after all. You need to focus on His promises and remember that, even through the bad times, He still loves her and us."

Thad went on, "He never said there would not be pain and suffering, and the enemy would love nothing more than to bring you into a state of despair right now."

I sat there with my mascara smeared underneath my eyes.

"Let me ask you this," Thad said. "What would your mom say right now? Her faith is *so* strong. Don't you think she would agree with everything I have just said?"

My racing heart slowed, and the tears began to dry up. I could breathe again. I knew Thad was right.

I longed to be a part of Mom's receiving the diagnosis. But that didn't mean it was my place to be there. Not only was my dad with her, but God was with her.

At times, I felt like she trusted Him so much that she was naïve or impractical in her thinking, but I realized she simply had childlike faith. She trusted in God, and she believed He would carry her through the good and the bad, that He would shepherd her and take care of her. She knew He would never forsake her or leave her—just as young children trust in and depend on their parents wholeheartedly, unconditionally.

Thad was right. All I needed was someone to love me and speak truth to me, and God did both through my husband that day.

UNABLE TO TOLERATE THE SUSPENSE, I texted Dad. "Hey, are y'all still at the doctor? It's been six hours, and I haven't heard from you."

He texted back, "We are home. Long day. Just tired. I will need to call you later."

Wait, what? Later? I need to know now. *I can't wait any longer.*

"Can you at least tell me if it's good or bad, Dad?"

"I can't really talk about it. She doesn't want anyone to know."

I knew it. It's bad. No doubt she has sworn him to secrecy.

"Dad, that's not fair. Don't do this to me. Please tell me what he said."

"I will later, but now is not the right time. I will call you tonight or tomorrow sometime when I am not around Mom. Don't worry though; it's not a brain tumor."

It's not a brain tumor. Thank You, Lord. It can't be worse than that. Thank You, thank You, thank You!

Since I knew Mom didn't have a brain tumor, I was more willing to be patient and wait for her to tell me. I didn't push. Whatever it was, she needed her time and eventually she would tell me.

Several days later, my phone rang. "Hey, Sarah, it's Dad. You have a minute?"

"Of course, Dad. How are you? How's Mom? Is she ready to talk to me about her doctor's appointment?"

He hesitated. "Well, no. Not really. I thought she would be. We talked about her telling you kids in a few weeks over Thanksgiving, but I don't think she will be ready. I just can't say anything, Sarah. I promised her I wouldn't, and I just can't. I can't break her trust."

I stayed quiet and listened.

"It's just that, I think Mom needs to be the one to tell you kids, and she wants to tell you when you are all together."

Well, gosh, if it's not a brain tumor, then what is it? We all have to be together? What does that mean? Maybe it is cancer. Maybe she has breast cancer. Mom's sister, Aunt Cherry, had died in her early fifties of breast cancer.

I asked Dad directly, "Is it cancer? Can you just tell me that? You don't have to tell me what kind, but can you at least tell me that?"

"No. Look, I can't. I should hang up. I love you. I'm sorry. Don't worry about her or us. She will tell you when she is ready, but don't worry. All will be okay."

Not knowing the diagnosis was weighing heavily on my brothers and me. Our parents were trying to protect us, but I wanted more than anything to know. Thanksgiving and Christmas came and went, and Mom never shared her diagnosis. I continued to see her struggle, but I could not figure out the cause.

Then Mom's brother, Larry, passed away suddenly from a car accident in Houston on March 23, 2013, and she buckled emotionally. He was the last of her siblings to die, and they all had died young. Her parents were both deceased, and she was now the only one left in her immediate family. Mom was traumatized. Dad said that when she received the phone call, she fell to the ground screaming and wailing—she was inconsolable for hours. Now, he believes that phone call marked the day Mom's sickness took a turn for the worse.

"Sarah, the funeral is Friday. Come when you can," Dad's text read.

I immediately packed my bag and prepared to drive to Houston. Thad and I agreed I would stay with Mom and Dad for the week. Dad didn't ask when I could come or try to tell me it wasn't necessary. All he said was, "Come when you can."

I knew he needed me and he couldn't do this alone.

I asked him one last time before I left town, "Dad. What is wrong with Mom? I promise you with all of my heart I will not tell a soul, not even David and Gabriel, but I think we all have the right to know. You be the one to tell them if you choose, but *please*. I need to know what I am dealing with before I come for the week."

He knew it was time. He held nothing back.

"She has early-onset Alzheimer's disease, Sarah. They believe she's had it for a while now, but because it took her so long to see a doctor, it's hard to say how long she's had it. She will lose her memory and may need full-time care in the next five to seven years."

Did he just say early-onset Alzheimer's disease?

I maintained my composure and responded calmly, "Okay, Daddy. Thank you. Wow. I never even . . . I never would have thought of Alzheimer's. I don't even know anyone who has had Alzheimer's. Does that mean she won't know who we are?"

"Most likely, yes. And because it's early-onset, she will progress much quicker than if she had gotten it later in life. The younger you are, the faster the disease progresses."

"We will get through this. We are a family, and we have God. I'll be there this evening, and I promise not to say anything. I am so thankful you told me. I love you, Daddy."

He choked up. "It's been so hard, Sarah. It's so nice to be able to tell you. I've wanted to tell you since that awful day in November, but I just can't keep this a secret anymore."

The doctor had done a neurological examination of Mom, checking her reflexes, coordination, and sensory and fine motor skills. He had also assessed her mental status, which included memory recall, calculation, drawing, writing, and orientation, and he had taken a series of neuro-psychological tests and brain images by CT and MRI scans. The scan would reveal any brain atrophy and plaques and tangles. A true diagnosis couldn't be confirmed without an examination of Mom's brain tissue, which is typically done only during an autopsy.

I typed "early-onset Alzheimer's" into the Google search box. Wikipedia read, "A disease diagnosed before the age of 65. It is an uncommon form of Alzheimer's, accounting for only 5 to 10 percent of all Alzheimer's cases."

When I finished reading the definition, I sat in silence as the words penetrated my heart, soul, and mind. I felt empty, lost, and confused as I stared at the computer screen. I couldn't process the definition, much less the information about symptoms and different stages.

How did we not know? Dad did say her numbers seemed jumbled over-night. And her arm did start tingling one day and has never stopped. What does her tingling have to do with her memory? Her memory seems fine. I didn't understand. It didn't make sense.

THE MOVE TO BIG D

August 2014

⚬⟡⚬

I N AUGUST 2014, MOM FINALLY agreed to move to Dallas. Having lost her mother, sister, and brother within eighteen months, she had no immediate family left in Houston. Mom sank into despair, especially knowing an incurable disease would strip away her memories of the loved ones she'd just lost and of those still alive.

The doctors predicted Mom would require twenty-four-hour care within five to seven years. This woman of such strong faith was pierced to the core. She cried out to God, "Why? Why me?"

For a long time, Dad and I had been working on Mom to move to Dallas. I had prayed for them to move for years. They'd been looking at houses, but Dad knew she couldn't make a decision. Her disease was progressing, and too many choices made her anxious and confused. Mom would ask the real estate agent over and over how much something cost, and then she would repeat the number back incorrectly, taking away zeros. It was exhausting. She and Dad could never agree on a home; he had to make the decision for both of them.

Dad purchased a cute house on a corner within walking distance of a shopping center he knew Mom would love. He lied to her about the price of the house, letting her think it was the amount she believed was right. The tricky part was not having Mom in the room when it was time to sign the papers and get their new house keys. Her confusion with numbers and her inability to sign her name were problems, so

I redirected and distracted her so Dad could complete everything. It was a painful reality that he had power of attorney for her—but one we were thankful for.

Finally, the moving truck was booked to move my parents' things out of their old house. Or so we thought.

While I was getting my hair done by my close friend Martin, I got a call from Dad about Mom. My hair appointment always lasted about three hours, so I usually called Mom from the salon chair. It was our time to catch up without the kids hovering over me, and she would also talk to Martin and love on him from afar. They had a beautiful connection.

The moment Dad called, Martin said, "Go ahead. I know you need to talk to your daddy."

I smiled and picked up. "Hey, Daddy! What's up? I'm getting my hair done so I've got as long as you need." I looked at Martin in the mirror with a smile and a wink.

"Oh, Sarah. I don't know where to start." My dad took a breath. "I can't even begin to tell you what a nightmare this has been. I called a moving truck, had it all set up, and was even paying the movers extra to come and box everything up for us, but Mom can't handle it. It takes her thirty minutes to box up two bathroom shelves of things, and on top of that, she won't throw anything away. *Anything*. She is throwing shampoo bottles she's collected from hotels over the last fifteen years into a box! I don't know what to do. I am going crazy over here. The movers are supposed to come in two days, and she is telling me absolutely no movers and that we will do it all ourselves. She seriously thinks we are going to take all of the furniture and boxes and truck it all to Dallas, no matter how many trips it takes. She is fighting me tooth and nail, and I am about to explode!"

I could picture Mom's shampoo, conditioner, and lotion collection from the Marriott, Four Seasons, and Hilton hotels. We always laughed at her because whenever we returned from a vacation, she would pull out her new collection from her suitcase. When we teased her, she'd say, "Well, they left it out for us. I'm not going to just leave it there. That'd be wasting great products." The funny thing was that she never used them when she got home.

I tried to reason with my dad. "Can't you just tell her the movers are coming and be done with it? I don't really understand why she would want to do it all. Does she understand they will box it, label it, load it all up and literally unbox all of it for her in Dallas?"

I was confused as to why Mom was pushing back. In her right mind, she would have said yes in a heartbeat to the movers. She had delegated tasks before, and she certainly had housekeepers, caterers, and different people over the years come along to help her. Why would she not accept the help now with a task as large as moving to another city?

"Do you want me to talk to her, Dad? Maybe I can talk some sense into her."

I could practically hear him roll his eyes. "Good luck with that. You can try, but you know your mother. Her mind is set. She isn't budging."

Ugh, I thought. *Not again. Not now.*

Dad sighed. "I think I'm going to have to cancel the movers. I can't handle her getting uptight and anxious and going crazy. It's not worth it. I guess we'll take our time moving up there. Maybe we can bring some boxes and get a truck for some things and just move up there slowly. We don't have to be out of our house for a month, so I guess I could do a few trips. Do you have anyone who can help unload some furniture once we get there?"

"Dad! Are you being serious? This is crazy. Of course, yes, I can have someone help us unload furniture here, but this is nuts."

Is there another option?

"Okay, how about this: What if I call my upholsterer? He has a fairly large truck. Maybe he could drive to Houston and load some of the larger stuff and bring it here. This way, you and Mom don't have to drive back and forth, and I can meet him here and show him where to put things. It certainly would hold more than a moving van, but at least it's not as drastic as a massive eighteen-wheeler showing up and taking everything in one clean sweep. Maybe that's what Mom is afraid of?

Maybe she needs to take her time and warm up to the move a bit. I can ask him if you want."

Dad was quiet on the other end.

"Dad, you there?"

"Yes, yes, I'm here. I'm thinking about it. That may be a good idea. Maybe I could pay him to come here a few times. That way it won't be so overwhelming for Mom. In the meantime, we could also drive up with some boxes here and there so she feels like she is moving stuff herself. Go ahead and ask him and see if it's even an option. I wish I could just do this in one move, but she is flipping out. It's just not worth it."

I was heavyhearted for him. *This stinks. It flat-out stinks.*

As demoralized as Dad and I were, it got worse and worse. The mover, Jessie, made about six trips down to Houston and back over a four-week period. It ended up costing more money for Jessie to do those trips than the movers Dad had originally planned to use. He also rented a cargo trailer many times and transported it to Dallas with Mom, because she refused to let Jessie take some of her things in his truck—she didn't fully trust him. To make matters worse, Mom wouldn't get rid of furniture or anything else, even though they were downsizing their house. She was convinced everything would fit in her new home, having lost all concept of scale and design and space.

What were we to do? In the end, we got a storage unit in Dallas without Mom knowing. Each time Jessie would come to Dallas, he would meet me at the unit, and we would store half of what was in his truck— things we hoped Mom would not remember or realize were missing. Things that were in her attic that she didn't even know she had, boxes and boxes of Christmas decorations, chairs, consoles, and mirrors that she had hidden away in a large "storage" room in their Houston home— everything went into the storage unit.

Daddy and I felt like liars and manipulators. I was hiding my own mom's stuff from her. I was so afraid of Mom asking me, "Where is that mirror? Where is that black chair? I'm missing my console table, the dark mahogany one."

After working at the storage unit, I would meet Jessie again at my parents' house, and he would unload the boxes into their garage. My friend Jennifer, also a professional organizer, worked with me. She knew what I was dealing with because her father also had Alzheimer's disease. We unpacked every single box that arrived in that garage, and there were hundreds over the four-week period. The goal was twofold: first, to unpack everything before Mom arrived so she would not be overwhelmed; and second, to make her Dallas home look a lot like her Houston home. We wanted the transition to be as smooth as possible.

I labeled every cabinet and drawer, and Jennifer placed things on the bookshelves and in the china cabinets. We did not mess around and worked quickly and purposefully. Not only did I want to do this for Mom, but I also wanted to do it for Dad. He had dealt with enough in Houston. If he could just show up, with all of those boxes and pieces of furniture already unpacked and placed, I knew he would get much more rest—which wasn't much rest, anyway.

Because Mom hated the colors in the new kitchen, we discussed changing them one weekend while they were in Dallas.

"Beauty, what are you thinking for the cabinets? Do you have any colors in mind?"

She squinted her eyes at them and pursed her lips. "Hmmm. I think I actually want them to be like yours. Can I copy you?"

Perfect, I thought. *That's easy.*

"Of course you can copy me. I'll get the colors and call the painter."

She smiled. "That would be great. These colors are just way too dark. I know I would love them lighter, like yours. Let's do it."

Check! At least one thing will be easy with this move.

Mom and Dad went back to Houston, and I got busy. I had the entry and living room walls painted the same green as in Houston, and the kitchen, den, and cabinets painted like mine. I was slightly worried that she wouldn't like it and that she might change her mind. Mom tended to change her mind a lot during this time, so my dad and I kept our fingers crossed that she would love it.

As I eagerly waited for them to arrive one evening, I got a call from Dad.

"Sarah, we will be there late morning. We are staying in Corsicana tonight."

What? Corsicana? That's only an hour away.

As I began to question him, he interrupted me, "Can't talk. Awful drive. She lost it. Talk tomorrow. Love you."

Dad told me later that during the trip, Mom had wanted to drive the car. She got so angry with Dad that she tried to grab the steering wheel on the highway because he wouldn't let her drive. She was screaming things like, "You never let me drive!" and, "What's wrong with *you?* There's nothing wrong with *me!*" and, "Everyone treats me like a child!" She then hit him on the arm and climbed into the back of the SUV, which was packed with bags, boxes, and a large oil painting. She began ripping out the painting from its frame.

Corsicana was the next exit, so Dad pulled over in front of a Motel 6 and simply said, "That's it. We're staying here tonight. We will get to Dallas in the morning."

The next morning, Mom was happy and acted like nothing had happened. She walked into their new home, looked around, and said, "Do you like it, Sarah? Look at what I did. I had the cabinets painted, and I am not sure about these chairs in this room, but I can always move them around!"

Wait, what? You had them painted? You put those chairs there? Maybe she meant to say it differently. But it didn't matter. She was pleased.

"I love it, Mom! It looks great. Do you like your house better now?"

I knew she didn't love the house. And she didn't want to fully surrender to the fact that she liked even some of it, so she responded, "It's okay. You know, your daddy picked this house. I actually don't like it at all. I told him he made a big mistake. We won't be here long. I'm going to get a different one in a few months."

Ha! Now that is funny—I can guarantee Daddy is not letting you move again after this move. You aren't going anywhere!

. . .

SIX MONTHS LATER, DAD AND I were still listening to Mom complain about how awful her house was, how they were moving back to Houston, how Dad took her away from her friends and her life, how they were going back home.

It was heartbreaking to hear. She would say it day after day, hour after hour. After all of those years of praying that Beauty and Pop would move to Dallas, now they finally had—and I listened to her complain on a daily basis. What had we done? Did we take her away from her friends? Did we make the right decision?

Dad can't do this alone, I thought. *Their friends love them, but let's get real. Friends aren't like bloodline family.* I was in Dallas, and my younger brother, Gabriel, and his family were now in Rockwall, about forty-five minutes away. That meant five of their grandchildren were close to them. Mom and Dad loved being with my Dallas in-laws, Joan and Steve, and knew several of their friends who had always welcomed them. Dad knew deep in his heart they needed to be as close to family as possible, and that meant Dallas.

The first year after their move was difficult. Mom's disease was progressing, and her short-term memory was failing. We were learning as we went, so it was a tough year. Some days, after I'd spent several hours with her, she would come by our house with Dad and say, "We are moving back to Houston. We never get to see you anyway. You never spend any time with me. I don't know why we are even here!"

Her words crushed me. It broke my heart that she didn't remember being with me. My time with her was meaningful, yet her words made me believe our time was wasted or nonexistent. How could she not remember that I had spent hours with her that day, and that we'd enjoyed our time together? Other times, she would call me and say I never came to see her, never called her. Or she would leave me occasional messages saying I was not a good daughter. It was painful; we had always been so close.

Mom became more anxious and irritable and could never sit still. She would move furniture around nearly every day. She scratched the new hardwood floors by dragging tables and china cabinets. She even carried a chair upstairs to a bedroom by herself. She and Dad would go for a walk, and they would be back for not even an hour when she would say to him, "Do you want to go for a walk? I'm bored. Let's go somewhere. I can't sit in this house."

Dad would take her out, maybe on another walk, maybe for a burger, or maybe just to drive around. They would be home for about an hour when she would say, "Can we go somewhere? All we do is sit at home and do nothing!" This routine exhausted my dad.

One day I received a text from Dad. "Sarah, I hate to bother you, but do you think you can take Mom to carpool with you today?"

I couldn't text back fast enough. "Yes, of course! I would love that. Are you okay? Is she still going nuts over there?"

He texted back several minutes later. "Yes. I'm sorry to ask you to take her. You have helped me so much already. But yes, I need a break. She is wearing me out. She doesn't stop. I don't know how I can do this. I may need to figure out how I can get some help around here or a house-keeper who can watch her."

As I held my phone, thumbs poised, I thought about my response. Thankfully, a possible solution struck me.

"Dad, I'll take her with me several days a week for carpool. Those can be my days with her! Some of those days I'll grab her earlier—we can go eat lunch or get Starbucks—and it will easily be a three-hour window for you. You could even go hit golf balls."

I saw three dots pop up on my screen, indicating that Dad was writing his reply. The message read, "Wow. That would be great, if you think you have time to do all of that with her. I don't want to burden you. Golf balls! That sure sounds nice right about now."

Done! Dad golfs, Mom and I shop and do lunch, and she gets to see her grandkids all in one day. Perfection.

FIVE

THE HONEYMOON PHASE

August 2015 to January 2016

A FTER MOM AND DAD MOVED to Dallas, I felt like I was in a honeymoon phase with my mom in which we finally had unlimited time together. We moved things around her house, decorated, and grew even closer. Being together in the same city at last was a nurturing experience for us both.

Our time was special. Daddy would turn on the gas fireplace every morning for Mom. She would wake up, walk into the kitchen in her white terry cloth robe and slippers, make herself a fresh cup of coffee, walk straight to her chair in the living room, and just be. Dad would give her turkey bacon and two pieces of toast on her favorite Texas-themed paper plate, which she'd wash off and put right back in the pantry.

Mom and I had tender moments, eating bacon and having coffee by the fire. I savored those times when she first moved to Dallas. It brought us closer; sometimes we would even sit in the same chair and snuggle. We went everywhere together. For a while, I felt like she was okay, and at times, I thought she was actually improving.

One day, we were sitting in the carpool line and I popped a bubble with my chewing gum. "How did you do that?" she asked. "That was so cool!"

A bubble? Pop a bubble?

"What do you mean, Mom? How'd I pop my gum?"

"Yes!" she cried, with no shame and much enthusiasm. "That! Teach me! I want to learn."

I thought you were better, but clearly not if you can't remember how to pop your gum.

"Of course, Beauty. I'll teach you. Here, take a piece of gum first."

"Yum!" she exclaimed, putting the stick of gum into her mouth.

I was stunned. It was as if she were chewing gum for the very first time.

"This is weird," she said. "Do I swallow it? Or just keep chewing?"

Oh my gosh.

"No, don't swallow your gum. That's a big no-no. Just keep chewing it for a bit and get all of that yummy juice out."

Her eyes were huge for the first minute or two. She looked over at me, blinked, smiled, and nodded her head, as if to say, "Oh yes. I remember this now."

For the next twenty minutes, we laughed and laughed as we practiced blowing and popping the biggest bubbles possible. My heart ached that she failed to remember something so simple, yet I loved teaching her something.

But that day in the carpool line, I realized Mom's disease had progressed much more than I had thought. I wanted to hold her hand, put my head on her shoulder, and cry.

As I watched her attempting to blow bubbles, I prayed. *Oh God, please help me to cherish these moments with Beauty. I love her so much. Look at her. She's beautiful. She's fun. Her personality hasn't changed. God, give me more moments like these to laugh with her and enjoy her, rather than let the disease steal the joy of who she really is and always has been. Please, Lord. Don't let it steal our time together.*

ONE OF THE BIGGEST BLESSINGS resulting from my parents moving to Dallas was Mom being able to spend time with a favorite college roommate, Ginny Bond. Ginny and Mom were Kilgore Rangerettes together at Kilgore College in East Texas; Ginny was the captain and

Mom a lieutenant. Through their love of dancing, and rooming together for two years, they became friends for life.

After college, they each married and went their separate ways.

As Mom and Dad raised children in Houston, the Lord began to change Mom's heart and life through Bible studies, new friends, and church. Ginny, now divorced and in New York City, was living the fast-paced life of a single mom doing all she could to get by.

They stayed friends and traveled back and forth over the years, but their relationship changed. Mom ached for Ginny because Mom knew Ginny was finding "happiness" in material possessions, career advancements, and social standing and not in the worth and identity God gives. Mom prayed for Ginny continually through the years, expressing her concern to Daddy and eventually to me.

One weekend when I was home from college, we were sitting around the dinner table. Mom had just returned from a trip to New York City.

"All Ginny wants to do is shop, go out and party, or hang out with her daughter and her daughter's friends," she told Dad and me. "Her voice gets loud, and I would prefer to have more quality time with just her and talk about life. It's like she hasn't grown up since college." We all laughed. "Don't get me wrong, she is fun and we had a blast—I'm in a different season of life, I guess."

Dad and I listened patiently. "Just keep praying for her, Beck," he said. "God will change her. I know you worry about her, but she's doing the best she knows how to do. Being left by an adulterous husband with a new baby in your arms is crushing and taxing. She went from getting all the attention in the world, any material thing she could ask for, and knowing every wealthy person there was to know in Dallas, to being, in her mind, a nobody. She just doesn't know any different."

Mom understood what he was saying and was sad because she wanted Ginny to have all that she had. Mom and Dad had a great marriage and were financially comfortable, but more important, they had Jesus.

I also knew Ginny's daughter, also named Ginny—or Little Ginny, as I called her. We didn't know each other well because we were three and a half years apart in age and lived in different cities. However, our moms wanted nothing more than for our friendship to be like theirs, like sisters.

"Sarah, why don't you call Ginny and Little Ginny when you go to New York for New Year's Eve?" my mom asked. "Maybe see if you can stay with Little Ginny for a night. She's such a sweetheart, and I know y'all would get along so well."

I nodded in agreement. "I was actually thinking about going up a few days early to see another friend, so maybe the three of us can grab lunch and shop or whatever. I'll call her."

Mom smiled with delight. "Thank you. You and Little Ginny will be dear friends, also. I feel it."

I took a bite of Mom's crispy okra. "I know you do. You are a great friend and very patient with her. Just keep doing what you are doing, like Dad said. You never know how God will use you one day."

I didn't know at the time how powerful those words would be: "How God will use you one day."

IT WAS A SUNNY FALL day in Dallas. Mom, Dad, and I were enjoying the warmth of the fire Dad had made and the crackling sound of the burning wood. In their living room, I was snuggled up in my warm-up pants in my favorite big round chair, my hands cupping my coffee mug. The mug had a picture of our girls with Pop holding a big bass from their first fishing trip together. As I sipped my steaming coffee with a splash of French vanilla, the phone rang in their kitchen.

Dad answered then gave a big smile. "Hey there, Ginny! Well, she is sitting right here."

Mom's face lit up. She jumped out of her chair and met Dad halfway, grabbing the cordless phone out of his hands. "Give me that!"

She crowed into the phone, "Hey, hey! What're you doing today? Tell me we are going somewhere together. I'm bored."

Bored? I thought we were enjoying our peaceful morning together.

Dad sat by me while Mom chatted. We could hear her laughing and giggling, saying things like "Oh, Ginny, you are crazy. I'm not going there," and "You *what*? Oh my gosh!"

Dad and I were thinking the same thing.

"What a blessing," I said. "Can you believe she and Ginny are finally in the same city? This is God's gift to both of them."

He nodded his head in agreement. "It sure is. Did you know your mom still prays for her, Sarah? I hear her pray for Ginny almost every night. She loves her so much."

My heart melted. "That's a true friendship right there. Some people might have walked away in that kind of situation—being in different cities, with different upbringings, living different lifestyles, but Mom has loved her well, Daddy. It's wonderful that Ginny still wants to be around her, too. It's like they were never separated. I think God is still at work."

"I do, too. Ginny is seeking. I can tell. She's drawn to Mom."

I smiled. "She's drawn to the Holy Spirit, you mean."

"That's exactly right. She doesn't realize it, but she's being drawn to Him through Mom, and I can't wait to see what comes of it. I'm so happy Mom has a close friend out here."

"Me, too. Their friendship is beyond special."

THE HONEYMOON STAGE CONTINUED TO be glorious. Mom and I had time together, Ginny and Mom had time together, and Dad had more freedom in knowing he was close to family—he had help and support surrounding him. He could go hit golf balls without worrying about leaving Mom alone, and he could even take a short weekend trip knowing she could stay with me. They were surrounded by most of their grandkids, and they could attend soccer, flag football, basketball games, and a few track meets.

Some part of Mom seemed to like living in Dallas. The city's restaurants amazed her. She loved walking to a nearby shopping center; she would walk to the local CVS Pharmacy or Tom Thumb, grab a Starbucks, and walk back home. The two of us would stroll through the beautiful Southern Methodist University campus and talk about the churches she wanted to visit.

But soon an adjustment phase began. Mom began to get irritable and anxious, seeing the "big picture" of her permanent home no longer being in Houston. Being in a smaller home in a somewhat unfamiliar place, she hardly had any friends, with the exception of Ginny.

One morning, Mom pleaded with Dad to drive her to Houston. Because she persisted for several straight hours, he finally caved and packed an overnight bag and left town with Mom. He called some friends, and he and Mom met them for dinner. After dinner, my parents went back to their friends' house to stay the night. A quick overnight trip, or so he thought.

Around 8:00 that evening, Mom discreetly began nudging Dad's arm, expressing her desire to leave. After several under-the-table kicks and a few elbow taps to his arm, he told their friends they would get a hotel room instead of staying in their home. He knew she was getting anxious, so he chose to prevent a possibly embarrassing situation.

Dad pulled up to a Hampton Inn, and as he parked, Mom said, "I'm not staying here."

Dad questioned her. "Why not? It's fine for a night."

She shot back, "I'm *not* staying here."

Dad thought perhaps it wasn't nice enough, so he drove to a brand-new Embassy Suites. As he pulled up to the valet and began to get out of the car, Mom gave him a look of "absolutely not" and nodded her head left to right.

"What's the problem, Beck?" Dad asked.

"I don't want to stay at this hotel, either. I don't like it."

"You *what*? And where is it, exactly, that you want me to take you, Beck?" Dad asked sarcastically.

"I don't know," she responded, "but it isn't this place."

Dad got back in the car, turned to her with a no-nonsense expression and said, "Then I'm heading back to Dallas. I'm not doing this all night. We are going home."

They drove two hours and came upon Huntsville, Texas. Mom turned to Dad and said, "Huntsville? Why are we in Huntsville? I thought we were going to Houston."

MOM BEGAN MOVING FURNITURE AROUND the house again and scratching up the floors. Dad would find that the glass coffee table from the upstairs playroom had been dragged down the stairs to the living room. A leather couch had been moved to the den.

One morning, I walked in with my coffee, expecting to sit by the fireplace for bacon and toast, and heard the words, "Becky! What in the world are you doing? You're going to hurt yourself!"

I saw Mom, but she hadn't yet spotted me.

"Leave me alone!" she shouted at my dad. "I'm not scratching anything! Just go back to what you were doing. If I need you, I'll call for you."

"Becky!" he cried. "You can't just move furniture around by yourself. Are you nuts? You can't bring a coffee table down the stairs by yourself!"

She looked him right in the eye, and with a calm yet stern voice said, "I just did, didn't I? Now go on. I don't need you."

I was frozen. I looked at Dad, pointed to the door, and mouthed the words, "Should I leave?"

He shook his head no and waved me back in. I threw my keys on the table to announce myself. "Hey, Mom! What are you doing? Need some help?"

She turned around with her white terry cloth robe on, hair pointing in every direction and no makeup on her red, sweaty face. "Hey, honey. No, I think I got it now. Actually, yes, will you help me slide this thing over just a few inches this way?"

A few inches this way? If we do that, it will be totally off center.

"Do you mean a few inches *that* way, Mom?" I pointed in the opposite direction.

"No, Sarah. This way. It needs to be moved this way."

You can't see that this is way off?

I calmed myself down. *Okay. Whatever you say. Just keep the peace, Sarah. Just keep the peace.*

"You sure are busy this morning, Mom. It's early to be breaking a sweat. If you're going to break a sweat, at least go put your workout clothes on, and we'll go for a walk."

She stared at me as if playing those words back in her head, then softly smiled. "Hang on. I'll be right back."

I looked over at Dad as he was standing behind her. He nodded his head up and down, mouthing a big, "Thank you."

Dad and I knew we had ten to fifteen minutes alone, as it took Mom longer to get dressed these days.

"She is exhausting me," he confided. "She can't sit still. It's like all of a sudden she has to go, go, go. I don't know what's going on."

"When you say 'go, go, go,' what do you mean exactly?"

He massaged the bridge of his nose. "I take her on a walk, then we come home and she asks where she is going next. I take her somewhere else, and we get home, and she asks where we are going next. Then she tells me I'm boring and that I never do anything with her. She says things like, 'I don't know why I married you.'"

My heart ached. "Oh, Daddy. I'm so sorry. You know it's the disease talking, right?"

"Yes, I know that. But it doesn't make it any easier sometimes. You still hear the words. I haven't told you yet what happened the other day."

My heart skipped a beat because I knew I was about to hear something I didn't want to hear.

"She went for her usual walk. She knows her way around here, Sarah. You know she goes on the same route every day. And she doesn't go very far. She is usually home in twenty-five minutes or so. Anyway, the doorbell rang, and the SMU police had her. The officer said she was wandering around campus. She asked him which way to go to get back to her house, but she couldn't tell him the address and didn't know her own home number or my cell number. So he put her in his golf cart and drove her around until she recognized a street and found her way here."

My mouth fell open in disbelief. "*What?* Dad, this is a big deal. She's disoriented. Maybe she is in a new stage. We need to find an ID tag she'll be willing to wear and not remove, a pretty necklace or bracelet perhaps. She doesn't know any phone numbers to call for help. You can't let her go on walks without you anymore."

"I know, and that's the problem. She can't sit still for even twenty minutes. And if I don't take her walking, then she's dragging furniture around!"

I looked at my watch, tracking the time to talk before Mom walked in. "Do you think she needs her dosage changed or a different med? You can't live like this. It may help her be more at peace like she was when she first got here."

I could tell by the look on his face he didn't want to talk about medication. "I hate medicating her. You know that. I am afraid if they give her more it will take away her personality, the Becky I know. I don't want it to bring her down. But I certainly know what's going on now is not my Becky, so I don't know what to do."

I could hear Mom's footsteps. "Let's talk about this later. But I think you must make an appointment with her doctor. It could get a lot worse, Dad."

It did get worse. There were more scratches on the floor, more dents and marks on the walls, and much more stress for Dad.

THE GIRLS AND I WERE headed to a soccer practice when I remembered I had to grab something from a store before it closed. We bought the item, rushed back to the house to put it in the fridge, then were off to practice.

I think that delay was divine intervention, because when we left the house and turned the corner, we saw Mom walking down a street in the opposite direction from our house—and hers.

We followed her for a bit to see where she would go. I was curious about whether she was just taking a different route, or if she had gone down the wrong street. My gut told me she was lost, but I didn't want to "rescue" her just yet.

I called my dad. "Did you know Mom isn't home?"

He paused on the other end of the phone. "Well, no. I dozed off, I guess."

"She is on a walk, by my house, but not close to my house. She is heading toward the children's park near Boedeker and Purdue. She's not even on my street."

"She's lost, then. She knows how to get to your house, but she took a wrong turn. Can you see her?"

I kept trailing her. "Yes, I'm following her, but she doesn't know it. Do you want me to pick her up, or do you want to come and get her?"

"I'm getting in the car now. Stay with her. I'll be right there. I think it's best I tell her I've been driving around looking for her. Maybe that will scare her enough to stop wandering off."

Hanging up the phone, I stared through the windshield, thinking about what Dad had said. *If she doesn't realize she's wandering off, how can this be teaching her a lesson? And how do you teach someone a lesson if they are losing their short-term memory and can't remember what they were taught?*

Suddenly, I heard sniffling from the back seat. "Mommy, I'm scared for Beauty. Is she going to be okay? She's lost!"

I was so caught up in following Mom and calling Dad, I'd forgotten my girls were in the car with me.

I turned around. Emery had two tears rolling down her cheeks. "Oh, Emery, honey. I'm so sorry. I didn't mean to scare you. Beauty is going to be okay. I would pick her up, but I think it's best if Pop gets her so he can explain to her what happened. Also, I need to get Frensley to soccer practice. Beauty is going to be okay, sweetie."

Emery's two tears were followed by more. "No, Mom. She's not. She's dying! Beauty is dying, Mommy!"

And with those words from a young child, I fell into a deep sadness for weeks afterward. No longer in the honeymoon phase, we were passing through the adjustment phase, and the reality of watching this disease take my mom's brain day by day began to sink in. There was no "great escape" phase. The unforeseen struggles had erupted, and before long, it would be time for us to decide if the disease would win—or if our love for Beauty would triumph.

SIX

BRING MY MOM BACK

January 2016

-•❊•-

M OM AND I WENT TO lunch at the country club. The staff knew us and about her disease. Their patience and understanding freed me from any anxiety of what she might say or do in front of them.

"Sarah, what are you going to have to drink?"

"Oh, just my usual. Water with no ice."

Then Mom said, "I was kind of wanting that other drink we like."

Other drink? She wants a glass of wine? She never orders wine at lunch. She can't have alcohol this early . . . or can she? Lord, help me! What do I say?

"Oh, Mom, you don't need a glass of wine right now! It's only 11:30. Wine's for happy hour or dinnertime."

She quickly responded, "Who cares what time it is? You don't want one?"

"No, thank you. I'm trying to stay healthy. Besides, I have kids to carpool."

"So? You can still carpool, can't you?"

What is she thinking?

"Mom, if I have a glass of wine, I still have to drive—and I don't want to be driving under the influence with my children in the car."

She shrugged her shoulders. "I guess I won't have one if you're not."

Phew. Thank You, Lord.

• • •

DRINKING WAS A NEW THING. Mom and Dad never drank when I was a girl. They occasionally had wine when my older brother was young, but that changed the day David Jr. came to them and said, "You're drinking wine? Doesn't that have alcohol in it?" They never had a sip of wine again until my wedding.

Alcoholism and addictions run in Thad's and my families. It was a sensitive subject, and one we did not realize would deeply affect our marriage. When Thad and I got married, we both drank. We had nights when we would go out with friends and drink socially, but there were also nights that Thad's friend Jack Daniel would join in the fun and ruin everything. We did not know the first year of our marriage that years later, alcohol would nearly tear us apart.

Thad and I thought alcoholism meant someone needed a drink every day or got drunk every time he or she drank. Not in Thad's case. Once every two months, he would drink, black out completely, and remember nothing from the night before. He was making choices and decisions that were dangerous to him, others around him, and our growing family.

After we underwent several years of counseling, God redeemed our marriage by tearing the layers off and breaking the barriers down. He completely took away Thad's desire for alcohol. Thad gave up drinking on January 4, 2008, and I can honestly say that our love for each another, our ability to communicate, and our level of trust grew stronger every day after. The hidden benefit of his alcoholism and our counseling was that they prepared me for the even-more-difficult circumstances that came with Mom's disease.

ONE DAY, MOM AND GINNY went out for lunch and a manicure. Whenever Mom left the house, Dad would call me to share the latest update. We couldn't talk in detail with Mom around since she would know we were talking about her. We avoided conversations about her in her presence because she wouldn't believe that what we were saying was true.

Dad called the moment Mom and Ginny drove away.

"Sarah, I don't know what to do. Your mom wants a glass of wine at 10:00 in the morning sometimes. She doesn't even know or care what time it is."

I thought for a moment then said, "Dad, can't you hide the wine or not keep it in the house?"

"Easier said than done. She will find her purse or some money and go to CVS and try to buy her own. If I push back, you know how she is. She throws a fit and gets mad, and it makes everything worse. I don't know what to do."

"Let me think," I said. "There's got to be some nonalcoholic wine, right? Let me Google it."

Sure enough. I found nonalcoholic wine around the corner at a large liquor store and bought two bottles of white and two bottles of red. I just knew this would end Mom's craving for alcohol.

Wrong.

A few weeks later, Dad sent a text that read, "Sarah, I need to talk to you. Are you busy?"

I texted back immediately. "I can talk. You okay?"

Within seconds, my cell phone rang. Dad sounded upset. I could tell he was down, and I was concerned for his health and Mom's. Something had gone terribly wrong.

"It's Mom," he said. "She's drinking all the time now, and she can become violent if I try to take it away, and I just don't know what to do."

"You have nonalcoholic wine at home, so I'm not sure I understand."

"Well, that works at home, but it's when we go out to lunch or dinner at a restaurant. She ordered a glass of wine today at Francisco's. The waiter brought it out, and she drank half the glass, then flagged him over to fill it back up. She hadn't even finished the first one. She's never asked a waiter to come refill a glass of wine that's half empty!"

"Oh my gosh, Daddy. What did you say?"

"Well, I tried to tell her she needed to finish the glass before she got another, and she said, 'Stay out! This is *my* drink, and this guy here didn't fill it all the way. It costs money. I want what I'm paying for!'"

"How embarrassing. She's ordered wine at restaurants and knows wine is never full to the rim. When did she start thinking a wine glass should be filled to the top?"

"I guess since today, although I have noticed at home when I pour her a glass, she will go back and fill it up before she drinks it. I didn't think it was because it didn't look full. I thought she just wanted more."

"So what did you do? What did the waiter say?"

"Well, thankfully, I think he knows something is wrong with Mom because we have been there before. He was very nice and winked at me as if to say, 'Don't worry,' and went and filled it up. But the problem is, Sarah, she asked him to refill it four times! There is no telling how much wine Mom had at lunch today. She's turning into a drunk. She starts slurring her words, she can barely walk, and then when I try to say something, she gets angry. She tells me to be quiet, and she won't let me help her get up from the table."

"Dad, I can't believe this. I think I need to call Francisco's and see if I can take the nonalcoholic wine up there and leave it. Since you and Mom are regulars, let's see if they will keep some of it on reserve for her. When she asks for a glass, they can just pour the nonalcoholic wine."

"I guess. I don't know. I just don't know how long I can do this. I didn't marry an alcoholic, and she wants to drink all of the time now. It's not her. And now I don't want to leave her with Ginny because Ginny drinks too, so the two of them together may make it worse."

Ginny and Mom could be trouble if they started drinking together. Ginny was tall with red hair and the bluest eyes. When she walked into a room, every head turned. She had a voice that could boom for miles and an infectious laugh that could make Mom laugh just by hearing it. The two of them together were double trouble and so fun to observe.

The truth was, we all wanted Mom to be happy, so why would a little wine hurt when she was losing her memory anyway with this incurable disease? Dad, Ginny, and I had always agreed, "Well, why not? If it makes her happy!"

Only later did we realize "why not." It was because she couldn't remember what time it was, how much she'd had, or even if she had it the day before. We also knew it couldn't be good for her brain with the medications she was on.

SOON AFTER MY FATHER TOLD me about the first incident at Francisco's, he told me about something even more embarrassing that had happened after that, again at Francisco's.

After my parents had finished eating, Dad said, "Beck, come on, let's go," his voice low. "I've already paid."

"I'm not finished with this yet! What's the rush?"

"Well, we are taking up a table, there are people waiting, and this is your fourth glass. Let's just leave it and go."

"Fourth glass? What are you talking about? This is my only glass!"

"Beck, it's your fourth glass. You've had three already."

"I have *not* had three. Stop trying to tell me what I can and can't do. I am a *grown* woman!"

Mom was beginning to slur her words, and Dad was desperate to keep her from finishing this fourth glass. He didn't want to be embarrassed at Francisco's again. He'd also promised to preserve her dignity and not let her humiliate herself.

"Come on. Let's go. There is someone waiting on our table. I'll give you more wine at home." In his mind, Dad finished his thought: *the nonalcoholic wine. You're drunk, and I've got to stop this now.*

Mom gulped her glass like she was taking a shot of whiskey. She slammed the wine glass down so hard it fell over. Mom then turned to her right, looked down at the carpet, and spit. Mom *spit* on the floor in the restaurant.

Dad put his head in his hands, feeling the heat from the blood flowing to his head. Then he stood up and walked around to Mom's chair.

"Come on, Beck. Let's go."

As Dad helped her pull her chair out, she immediately slapped his hand away.

"Leave me alone. I don't need help."

Suddenly, when she set her hands on the table and began to stand up, she gripped the tablecloth so hard, the silverware and glasses hit the floor. Barely able to stand, she was *not* going to let Dad touch her. I'm not even sure Mom noticed the things she'd knocked to the floor, the white ball of her spit, or the tablecloth hanging halfway over the table. Putting one foot in front of the other, she walked right out the front door. No shame. Nothing. She was utterly clueless.

Dad, on the other hand, walked out with his head down, apologizing to the staff, and swearing to himself he would never again step foot in Francisco's with Mom.

Exiting the door and approaching some steps, Dad grabbed her arm. "Beck! Watch your step—you have some steps right there."

"I see them! Leave me alone," she snapped, pushing his hand away.

Mom stumbled and missed two steps but didn't fall. She pretended like she was totally fine.

Dad couldn't get her in the car soon enough.

ALCOHOL WAS NOW A HUGE problem. How could we keep Mom from drinking at a restaurant, especially if we couldn't always plan ahead? If Mom had known what she looked like and that she was drinking this much, she would have flipped. But if you told her the next morning why she had a bruise on her leg, she wouldn't believe you. Why? Because she couldn't remember.

"Mom, that bruise is awful. I really wish you wouldn't drink wine anymore."

That was dumb of you to say, Sarah. She can't remember or rationalize with you.

"What? I don't drink wine. Maybe sometimes, but your father and I don't really drink." She poked at her bruise. "This thing doesn't hurt, but it sure is ugly. Wonder how I got it?"

I want to see if she remembers anything at all. I hope I'm not making a mistake, but just this once I have to tell her what happened.

"Mom, you fell down last night. Hard. You were drinking wine with Ginny yesterday, and when you got home, you fell."

"*What?* I didn't even see Ginny! She never even calls me. I'm mad at her."

"You spent several hours with Ginny yesterday. Y'all went to the mall and shopped, and then you had a long lunch at P.F. Chang's."

"We did?" For a moment she looked confused, then shook her head. "No, you're wrong, Sarah. I haven't seen her in weeks. I'm mad at her because I have called and called, and she won't call me back."

"Look, Beauty. Here is a picture from yesterday. She sent me a picture of y'all eating lunch. See, you are drinking a glass of wine."

She squinted at the picture and then shook her head again. "Oh, yeah. That's from another time—I'm telling you, Sarah, I have not seen Ginny in a *long* time."

My stomach hurt. I got up, went to the restroom, and put my head in my hands to take a few breaths.

Oh, Lord. Help me. I just want Mom to remember. Thad used to black out, and now my mom blacks out. Why do I have to live with this all over again? If Mom knew the damage it was doing to her and the pain it was causing, she wouldn't do this. Lord, please take this desire away from her just as You took it away from Thad. I don't know if I can handle this. I know Alzheimer's is an incurable disease, but I also know You can do anything. Mom taught me that. I trust You, God, and I trust that You can help us get through this stage. Please Lord, do something. Please tell us what to do and how to handle this. I want this all to go away. Bring my mom back, God! Why Mom? Why did You choose her? I just want her back!

"Sarah? Sarah?" Her voice was strained. "Where are you?"

"I'm in the restroom, Beauty. Are you okay?"

"Yes, I just didn't know where you were."

"I'm here. I'm still here. I'll be right there."

I'll be right there, I thought, *so I can sit and answer the same questions over and over again and tell you over and over again that Ginny does call you and that she does spend time with you. I'll sit there and listen to how much you want to move back to Houston so you can be with your friends. And I'll remind you over and over again that we just bought you new shoes, and then we'll walk to your closet every ten minutes over the next hour when you say you need new shoes, and I'll show you the new shoes you just purchased. I'm literally going crazy. Maybe I'm the one who needs a glass of wine. Lord, help. I need You to take this for me, and I need You to give me strength for today. Please God, take over today.*

A few breaths later, after glancing in the mirror and washing my hands, I opened the restroom door.

"Hey, Mom. I'm back. What do you want to do? You want to go get a Starbucks?"

"I've never had that before!"

"But the iced soy chai is your favorite! Come on, I'll take you. You'll recognize the taste. And Mom, have I told you lately how much I love you?"

"Oh, Sarah, I love you, too. More than you know. Thank you for being with me."

"I love being with you, Mom, and I love you more! Time is short and life goes by fast. Let's go get our Starbucks."

She hesitated. "Starbucks? What's that?"

SEVEN

GOD, PLEASE RENEW MY MIND

February to April 2016

-••◦✕◦••-

TYPICALLY, FEBRUARY IS ONE OF my favorite months of the year. It's my birthday month, and I'm a firm believer in celebrating birthdays. In 2016, I spent it with Mom and my children while Dad and Thad were away. My heart was filled with joy and peace knowing my dad was doing one of his favorite things: golfing. He would be gone for six days, and I was prepared to take on anything and everything that came my way.

Beauty stayed with the kids and me at our house, in her in-law suite on the third floor, and for six days I gave up any me time. There were no workouts, and "flexibility" became my new favorite word.

It was Wednesday evening, Beauty's first night to stay with us, and I had gotten her all settled in upstairs. She had her room-temperature bottled water and a bowl of salty chips. I drew a picture of her remote control on a sticky note, including the arrows to change the channel up or down, as well as the volume symbol to adjust the sound. I wrote down steps numbered 1 to 5 so she would be able to turn the television on and off and find Fox News, CNN, and *Family Feud*. I also placed a sticky note on her bathroom mirror so that when she woke up the next morning, she would be reminded I had to take the kids to school. Since her short-term memory was shot, she asked the same questions over and over and constantly needed reminders of the plan for the day.

I tucked myself into bed that night, feeling happy and grateful that Mom was safe and settled. A few minutes later, I heard footsteps coming down the stairs. She knocked tentatively on my door.

"Sarah? Can I come in?"

"Yes, of course."

She opened the door and wandered to the foot of my bed.

"Do you have any chips?"

More? I thought. "Yes, I do. Did you finish the ones I already gave you?"

She tilted her head with a puzzled look. "I haven't had any chips."

Yes, you did. I saw you eating them. Deep breath. It's all about the response, Sarah.

"Sure, Beauty. I'll take you down there and show you where they are." She had a soft smile on her face like a child about to receive a treat. I knew she felt bad I was getting out of bed, but we both knew she didn't know where to look for the chips.

In the kitchen downstairs, I pulled out some baked potato chips and poured them into another bowl.

"Here you go! Is that enough?"

"That's plenty. Thanks, honey."

We both walked back upstairs, Mom padding along in her furry white slippers as I led her back to the third floor. She sat down in her white barrel chair with the pale-blue painted legs and started crunching away.

As I left the room, she pretended to watch the news, but sadly, I knew she couldn't follow anything they were saying.

I climbed back into bed and glanced over at the clock. It was 10:30 p.m.

I'm beat. Lord, please help Mom and the kids sleep well tonight. Thank You for a great day. I sank into my silk pillow, face mask over my eyes, the calming smell of lavender wafting into my nose as I dozed off.

Suddenly, I heard a knock. I thought maybe I was dreaming but wasn't sure. Then I heard her voice again.

"Sarah? Can I come in?"

Are you kidding me? All I want to do is sleep! Be patient, Sarah, deep breath.

"Sure, Mom. What is it?"

She spoke softly through the cracked bedroom door. "I'm hungry. Do you have any chips or anything?"

My eyes rolled in my dark room. *What? I just gave you a bowl of chips, and that was your second one! Is this really happening?*

"I do, Mom, but we just went down and got a bowl about thirty minutes ago. What about a piece of turkey? Turkey supposedly can help you sleep."

She hesitated and then firmly responded, "No, that doesn't sound very good. Do you have some chips or anything?"

I rolled my eyes again under my face mask, pulled it on top of my head, reached over to turn on my lamp, and stepped into my slippers. *You have got to be patient, Sarah. Just breathe.*

"Sure, Mom. I have some chips." She smiled with gratitude, once again, and I could see in her eyes a "Thank you, darling."

We went downstairs, filled another bowl with chips, and went right back up to the third floor. As we walked through the door, I noticed two empty white bowls sitting on the dresser. *Maybe if I show her the bowls, she will remember.*

I pointed to them. "See, Mom, you've had chips already!"

She looked over at the bowls, thought for a minute, and confidently replied, "Well, I don't know whose those are. They were there, you know, when I came."

She's tired. She can barely speak. She doesn't remember.

I did not officially go to bed until 11:45 that night. I made three separate trips downstairs with Mom for chips. She was so unpredictable, and I knew she needed to be watched. I even told her she could sleep with me, but she preferred her in-law suite.

My alarm went off at 5:30 a.m., and as much as I wanted to stay in bed and hit snooze, I knew I could not get through my day without starting it with God. The early morning was my time to be alone, pray, and meditate and ask for His guidance and strength. I needed Him more than ever during this time, and I knew in the deepest part of my soul that I could not get through any of this without Him.

That morning, my *Streams in the Desert* (written by L .B. E. Cowman) devotional read:

> We must learn to take God at His word and walk straight ahead in obedience, even when we can see no way to go forward. The reason we are so often sidetracked by difficulties is that we expect to see barriers removed before we even try to pass through them.
>
> If we would only move straight ahead in faith, the path would be opened for us. But we stand still, waiting for the obstacle to be removed, when we ought to go forward as if there were no obstacles at all.

A few sentences later, it closed with these words:

> Faith that goes forward triumphs.

Those words were exactly what I needed, not only because of the night before with Mom but also because of what was to come. I was feeling led to serve Mom and help Dad so that he could take some breaks, but I found myself either wanting to remove the obstacles myself or waiting around on God to move them before I stepped forward.

Mom's disease was moment to moment, so I was learning how to walk by faith and not by sight. I felt blindfolded and in the dark, yet I knew I needed to trust Him to pave the way.

THURSDAY WAS A NEW DAY, and I had renewed my mind. Romans 12:2 says, "Do not be conformed to this world, but be transformed by the renewal of your mind, that by testing you may discern what is the will of God, what is good and acceptable and perfect" (ESV). I never knew how much this verse would play a role in my life throughout the next year.

The mind is a battlefield, and the power of early-onset Alzheimer's disease and its horrific side effects consistently challenged my mind and heart. No matter how hard I tried, there was always some point in the day when I felt like I had failed. I lost my temper, felt discouraged, and felt my confidence being destroyed. The constant battle in my mind began to eat away my heart's desire to be around Mom. My attitude became "I have to" instead of "I get to" on some days. On one day in particular, I struggled to renew my mind.

"Mom, Emery, and Elijah!" I called out from the kitchen. "We need to leave in five minutes to get to Frensley's game. There will be a lot of traffic, so we can't leave late."

Mom was sitting in our breakfast nook around the corner in one of the plush chairs, with her feet propped up on the round flax linen ottoman. "Sarah, I don't think I'm going to go to the game. I'd like for you to take me home."

Oh, shoot. Not now, please!

"Well, Mom, Frensley is really looking forward to you watching her championship game today. She's expecting you to be there."

Mom shook her head. "I'm sorry, but I want to be in my own house. I don't feel like a game."

Crap. This can't be happening. Not right now.

"*Mooommm!*" Elijah called from the playroom upstairs. "I need you!"

"Okay, honey!" I yelled back. "Just one second!"

He yelled again, "No, Mom, I need you *right now*!"

I smiled. "Mom, hang on a minute. Let me see what he needs."

I ran up the stairs, my heart pounding. *She can't go home! I can't leave her at home for three hours by herself. She* has *to come with us.*

"Elijah, where are you? What is it, honey? We really need to go."

I was suddenly struck by the worst smell I'd smelled in a long time. It was like the smell of a child's dirty diaper—one that you can't bear to handle unless it's your own child.

"Ummm, I'm in the bathroom, Mommy."

Elijah was standing there with his pants to his ankles, poop on the toilet seat, and the toilet so full of toilet paper I couldn't see the water.

"Can you help me?" he asked. "I can't flush the toilet. It won't go down, and now I have poop on the back of my leg."

He started crying out of embarrassment and shame.

"Oh, honey. Don't cry, buddy. It's okay. Stay right there. Let me go see if I can find some wipes."

I ran downstairs toward the pantry, right past my mom. "Hang on, Mom. I'm sorry, Elijah's had an accident."

I was in the pantry, shuffling through emergency kits, a shelf of vitamins, and thermometers, when I heard, "No worries, honey! I can just walk home. No big deal."

Wait, what?

"Excuse me, Mom, what did you say?"

She repeated herself, clear as day. "I can just walk home. No big deal."

Please, no. Not now, please. Lord, please help me.

"Mom, please don't walk home. Stay right there. Let me just help Elijah, and I want to talk about it some more with you."

I blew past her again and ran up the stairs. As I did, I noticed a piece of the stair runner was worn down and found myself thinking we might need to replace it soon. *As if you don't have enough going on right now, Sarah. Forget about the dang runner!*

I got Elijah cleaned up, and as I was shoving the plunger into the stuffed toilet, I heard Emery yell from her bedroom, "*Mooommm*! I can't find my white Converse shoes. Where did you put them? I need them."

I'm going to explode.

"Emery, I'm busy right now. Find a different pair of shoes, please. We need to go. I will *not* let you make us late because you can't find one pair of shoes when you have five more to choose from!"

"But I want my *Converse* shoes!" she yelled back.

I'm going to take this plunger and throw it down the hallway if one more child yells at me. Breathe, Sarah. Breathe. Renew your mind. Renewal of the mind.

Back downstairs, I tried again with my mom. "Mom, I understand you want to go home. But please, for Frensley, please come with us to the game. This is her last game of the season. If they win this game, they win the big championship. Since Pop can't be here, she was really looking forward to you coming to her game. *Please* do this for her?"

Please, Lord. Please, Lord.

"Okay, fine. I'll go. But I want you to take me home after the game. I miss my home."

Not happening, but just agree and I'll figure it out later.

"Sounds good!"

We left ten minutes later than planned. We hopped on the Dallas North Tollway and headed north toward Carrollton. *Traffic. So much traffic already.* I unplugged my phone from the charger and stretched my arm to the back seat, handing it to Emery.

"Can you pull up my Google Maps and type in this address?" I gave her the address. "Is it red all the way down the tollway?"

As I waited for Emery's reply, Mom chimed in. "Sarah, where are we going? This is *so* far away."

We've been in the car for seven minutes.

"Well, the game is a little far, but it won't take too long because I'll take some shortcuts here in a minute. It's only about fifteen miles away." She gave me a look that said, "Fifteen miles? More like two hundred!"

"Oh, Mom, you used to drive me to gymnastics over an hour each way, morning and evening, Monday through Friday. That's almost five hours of drive time a day. This is nothing."

Again, her look said it all: "What the heck are you talking about? I would never do this."

I had a flashback and spaced out as I thought about the special times Mom and I had in the car to and from gymnastics practice. We called into the radio station at least three days a week trying to win prizes as Mom drove me back to school from early morning practice. She reviewed me for tests as she drove the car with one knee on the steering wheel, one hand holding her Burger King coffee, and the other hand holding my review sheet. We drove through Burger King several mornings a week for my favorite sausage, egg, and cheese croissant sandwich. *My breakfast of champions*, I thought and smiled to myself. *Wait—maybe it was my 9:30 p.m. dinners when we drove through Grandy's for chicken nuggets with sweet and sour sauce on the side and an extra dinner roll.*

"Uh, Mom?" Emery said from the back seat, causing me to snap out of my daydream. "It's kind of red all over on Google Maps."

She did not sound confident that there were any shortcuts to make our drive any shorter.

"Let me see that for a second. Oh here, right here. We're going to exit here and take this road all the way to the school."

So I exited, thinking all would be fine.

Mom pointed from the front passenger seat. "Sarah, I think you need to turn right here. I've been there before. You are going the wrong way."

Huh? I've never even been to Prince of Peace School, so I know she hasn't.

"Mom, it's this way. I think you're thinking of another school."

"No, I'm not. I'm telling you. I've been there before, and it's this way. Over here."

Mom kept tapping my tinted window with her knuckle, and the more frustrated she became, the louder she tapped. She bent her finger and started hitting my window with her knuckle. "Over *here*, Sarah, turn *here!*"

My mind was racing. I gripped the steering wheel tighter with my sweaty palms. My heart pounded and my chest tightened. *Stay calm. She thinks she's been there before so play along. Tell her they moved it.*

"Oh, Mom. You know what? I think you are right and are thinking of the *other* location. She plays at the location off of Midway."

She looked at me like I was stupid. She was irritated, and I could see in her eyes that her anxiety level was rising and frustration was setting in. Her eyes locked onto mine with laser-like focus, convincing me to do exactly what she said. She needed to be right, or all hell might break loose.

"*Sarah*. Listen to me. We are too far away! This is too far!"

I looked in my rearview mirror to check on Emery and Elijah, and Emery's brown eyes were huge. She was confused. She had never seen my mom get so indignant over something like this. Elijah just sat there in his car seat like nothing was going on.

"Beauty, I promise you I know where I am going. There's a lot of traffic, so it seems much farther than it is because it's taking longer to get there. Please calm down and trust me."

And with the words "trust me," all hell broke loose.

"*Trust you! You want me to trust you?* I'm sitting here driving two hours in the car with you, and you don't even know what you are doing! You don't know where you are going! If I had known it was this far away I would never have come. Take me home! I want to go home right now!"

As she was yelling, I heard my phone chirp in a funny British accent: "U-turn. U-turn." *Crap, I missed my freaking turn!*

"What was that?" Mom shouted.

"That's my directions talking. See, Mom, I even have the directions plugged into my phone, and it's telling me to go the way I'm going, but now I've missed my turn because you are raising your voice at me to go in another direction."

Mom turned bright red. "I *told* you that you missed your turn. You don't need that stupid thing. I know where I am going!"

Yeah, Mom, except that your turn was the opposite direction of where I'm supposed to be going. Just shut up, please!

My legs trembled with stress, my stomach rumbled, and my face was beginning to sweat. I forced myself to inhale and breathe deeply. *Breathe, Sarah. Breathe.*

I looked at Emery in the back seat. Tears rolled down her cheeks.

"Emery, it's okay, honey. All is good. We will be there soon."

She started panting. "Mommy, I don't feel good! I don't feel good, Mommy!"

I tilted my rearview mirror down so I could see her better, then pulled my sunglasses off so she could see my eyes. "Honey, I know. I understand. Please take some deep breaths. Lie down if you need to. Don't worry about Beauty and me. I will get us there soon."

Mom turned around, looked at Emery, rolled her eyes, and said to me, "What's wrong with her? Why is she crying?"

She turned around again. "Why are you crying? Quit that!"

She's so mean right now. I'm going to lose my mind. I'm about to lose my mind.

"Mom, she's crying because she's getting carsick, and she doesn't want to hear us griping at each other." Mom looked at Emery again, smirked, and gave her another eye roll as if to say, "Don't be such a wimp. Give me a break."

She turned back around and continued to side-seat drive. "Sarah, I am shocked that you would drive this far for a game. This is absurd. No kid is worth driving this far."

I looked back at Emery once again in the rearview mirror—I saw the tears in her eyes and her quivering lips, and I felt her broken heart.

Then it happened. No more nice daughter, no more playing the Just Agree With Everything She Says game, and no more telling me what I should or shouldn't do.

"Mom. *Enough.* You are making me crazy! We are already late to her soccer game, and I don't need *you* to tell *me* where to go. You haven't even lived in Dallas two years, and you are trying to give me directions to a place you have never even seen. Just be quiet, *please.* You are upsetting Emery, and all I want to do is concentrate on finding this stupid place and watch my daughter's game." *And you have freaking Alzheimer's, so shut the hell up!*

My hands were shaking, my heart was pounding, and my eyes started to tear up behind my sunglasses. We still weren't there, and I had taken several wrong turns because my GPS was taking me up and down the same street with no school in sight. Mom kept pounding the window for me to pull over and ask a bunch of kids on a soccer field, so I finally did.

"Excuse me, do you know where Prince of Peace School is?"

They looked at each other, dumbfounded. "No."

I rolled the window up and sped off. "See, Mom? They don't know where the dang school is."

Mom began to yell, continuing to tell me where to turn and who to ask, and complaining that my kids weren't worth the drive. She also kept turning around and rolling her eyes at Emery and shushing her. "Be quiet. Stop acting like a baby."

I called at least five of the other team moms on their cell phones. None of them answered—they were outside, in the cold, watching a soccer game.

Sweet Elijah was as calm as could be most of the ride. Finally he said, "Mom. Did we miss the game? Is the game, like, over? Are we ever going to be there?"

Hold it together, Sarah. He has done nothing wrong.

"Buddy, I don't know. It might be over. Thanks for being so patient. I know we are very close."

As I finished my sentence my cell phone rang. It was Kate Meyer, a friend and one of the other soccer moms.

Thank You, Jesus!

"Kate, I'm so lost. I need help. Is the game over?" I think she could tell by the sound of my voice that I was distraught. She knew I had Mom, and she felt bad she had missed my calls.

"I am so sorry. I just saw you called me. I got my phone out to call you because we all realized you weren't here yet, and then about four of us noticed we'd missed calls from you. Game is still going, we are playing great, but we only have about eight minutes left. Where are you?"

And with that miracle phone call, we made it to the stadium. I parked, mouth quivering, tears running uncontrollably down my face underneath my sunglasses. I had lost my composure, yelled at my mom, lost my patience, and basically missed my daughter's last game of the season. All I could think about was what a disappointment I would be to Frensley and also what a terrible caretaker I was for running out of patience with my mom. I couldn't hide my own heartache as I tried to console Emery, who jumped out of the car sobbing.

I hugged her, and before my mom came around from the other side of the car, I said, "Emery, we can do this. I know you are upset, and so am I. I am so sorry, baby. Beauty doesn't know what she's saying, and she doesn't mean anything she said to you. Please know that. It's the disease talking, not your grandmother. She loves you very much. Let's try to pull it together, okay? You and me. We can do this. Let's choose to renew our minds and keep our heads up high, okay?"

Her little body was shaking, tears flowing as she looked up at me. "Okay, Mommy. I'll try." We wiped our snotty noses, rubbed our red, swollen eyes, and walked hand in hand like nothing had happened.

Mom came around the corner, smiled brightly, and said, "We're here! Where do we go?" As if nothing had happened at all.

I held Elijah's hand with one hand and wrapped my other arm around Emery's tiny waist. Mom looked at Emery and back at me. With genuine concern, she asked, "What's wrong? Why is she crying?"

I looked down at Emery, pulled my sunglasses down, and gave her a big wink. "Oh, nothing, Beauty. She just got a little carsick, that's all."

We walked over to the bleachers, sat next to the other moms, and with two minutes to go, we watched Frensley and her team go into overtime and penalty kicks to win the championship game. I called it God's grace. We missed most of the game, but He allowed it to go into double overtime.

I will always believe the overtime was for us. It was God's reminder that He is always present and He hears our cries. He allows us to witness His mercy if only we take the time to watch, listen, and trust.

I thought of Romans 12:2 again. I may have lost the battle in my mind during that drive, but what I knew to be true was that He forgave. He quickly renewed my mind and reminded me that what I was doing for Mom and Dad was pleasing to Him. I was walking in His will by faith, not by sight. And He was teaching life lessons to our children along the way.

• • •

TWO DAYS LATER, SATURDAY MORNING, Mom and I were sipping our coffee in our pajamas and robes, our feet propped up on my round ottoman. It was a special day, yet it didn't feel so special. Thad was out of town, and my own mom sitting next to me didn't even know what day it was.

As Frensley and Emery peeked around the kitchen corner and into the breakfast nook, I heard their soft, scratchy, tired voices say, "Happy birthday, Mommy."

I could see my mom out of the corner of my eye, staring at me, slowly processing what they had just said. As I hugged the girls tightly and told them thank you, I heard the words, "I didn't know it was your birthday. Happy birthday! How old are you? What is today, anyway?"

My heart sank. *This is so depressing.*

Mom and I decided to get out of the house. I had arranged to have a sitter there for most of the day just in case my mom got anxious or irritable or needed a break from the kids. As we were driving around and running a few errands, I received several phone calls and messages from friends with birthday wishes. I must have answered, "Yes, Mom, it is my birthday today" at least twenty times. I never in my life imagined there would come a time when my mom didn't remember it was my birthday. It was a hard and painful day. It was a day filled with mental exhaustion, and I felt like the life had been sucked out of me by bedtime.

"Goodnight, Beauty," I said softly as I helped get her ready for bed. "I love you. Daddy will be back tomorrow."

And, with her childlike personality and grin, she responded, "Oh, goody! What day is tomorrow again?"

Happy birthday to me.

God, help me. I am feeling so low and bitter and sad. I can't even think anymore. Please renew my mind.

EIGHT

GOD, ARE YOU THERE?

April to May 2016

--◦❊◦--

OM'S DECLINE WAS SPEEDY. WE'D go days and weeks locked in the same patterns, and then suddenly a big plummet. Practically overnight she would enter a new phase, and it was always unexpected.

Dad and I had heard about Friends Place in Richardson, an Alzheimer's adult day-care center. Families could drop off their loved ones for a half or full day, knowing they would be well cared for and safe. Over the course of a day, they participated in activities such as exercise class, arts and crafts, musical games, outdoor planting, animal therapy, bingo, and more. The employees and caretakers were trained specifically for Alzheimer's and dementia care.

Ginny took Mom out for lunch one afternoon, so Daddy and I took advantage of our time together to go to lunch.

I could tell Dad was relieved to have a break from Mom, and I could also tell something was on his mind. As we drove down the street toward the restaurant, not two minutes went by before he came out with it.

"I met with someone at Friends Place."

"Really? What did they say? Are you going to try it? Do they think it would work?"

"I think I'm going to give it a try. They said it sounds like Mom would be a perfect fit. She's active, she could lead the others, and they said they can even delegate tasks for her to do—like setting the table, arranging flowers, and helping serve others food."

My brown eyes got big. "Wow, that sounds wonderful. That's exactly what she needs, Dad. She's always served others. That's who she is. If she can feel like she's helping people, and they are willing to let her take that on, then I don't see why it wouldn't work. The only thing is how you're going to get her there. You're going to have to have a good story."

He nodded and began telling me the story he'd been rehearsing for weeks.

"I've been telling your mom that I'm thinking about going back to work. I know she doesn't remember each time I tell her, but if I just keep saying the same thing I'm hoping that it will plant a seed in her mind and eventually stick. If I tell her I'm going back to work, maybe she'll be more open to getting out and doing what she used to do—volunteer work."

"Volunteer work. That's genius!"

Mom had volunteered at church, for the women's prison ministry, and in nurseries for years.

He gave me a confident nod. "I think so, too, Sarah. Now, here's the thing. The lady I met with, Susan, and I both agree it's best for you take her the first week. If I try to take her, she will want me to stay every time. But if you take her, you could stay with her the first few days and then gradually step away and say things like, 'Mom, I'll be back. I need to grab the kids at school,' or 'Mom, I've got to meet with Thad, and Dad will pick you up in a little while.' Eventually, our hope is that she will get used to both of us being away and not be so attached. What do you think about that? Do you think you could handle it and get her there?"

This could work.

"I definitely think I can get her there. I'll just tell her that I volunteer at this place and have some friends I want her to meet and that I'd love for her to do it with me. The only thing that concerns me is the reality of me leaving her there and her being okay with that. She is so attached to me. But I'm happy to try anything, and I think this would be very good for Mom. She'd be using her brain so much more than sitting at home, she would meet new people, *and* she'd be surrounded by others."

Dad sensed my hesitation and fear. "It may not be easy leaving her at first, but they do this all the time. Susan said one lady there thinks she's helping with their financial books because she used to be a financial consultant, and so they give her all of these made-up numbers and let her 'advise' them on their financial planning and investments. There's another guy who was a professor, so he thinks he's coming to teach a class each day. The lying kills me, but this is what they have to do all of the time, and they are professionals, so I feel like this could be our huge break."

"So, when do we start?"

Daddy put his hand on my shoulder and gave me a quick, loving squeeze.

"Sarah, thank you. I couldn't do this without you. You have done so much more than you will ever know. I don't know how I would survive Beck's disease without our precious daughter."

Those words penetrated and encouraged my heart. Spending time with Mom was emotionally exhausting, yet our time together was priceless. I loved her so much, but some days I felt conflicted when leaving her house after we'd spent hours together—I valued my time with her, yet I also wanted to complain to someone. I always held my head up high when Dad returned home, gave him a big hug and told him I loved him, but I would get in my car and start crying almost every time.

While thankful for my parents living in Dallas and our time together, I was still mentally exhausted every time we parted. I felt alone, like I was the only one of my friends losing her mother minute by minute and watching her slowly die. Sensing my self-pity, I would then tell myself to "suck it up" and move on to the next thing, which was put on the mom hat and take care of my kids.

Dad's encouragement reminded me of Ephesians 4:29: "Do not let any unwholesome talk come out of your mouths, but only what is helpful for building others up according to their needs, that it may benefit those who listen" (NIV). Dad and I constantly needed to be reminded of the good we were doing, and how much we were helping each other get through our most trying time. His words that day built me up, nourishing my heart, soul, and mind.

As we pulled up to Francisco's for tortilla soup, I thought of Ephesians 4:29 again, and I returned the encouragement to him.

"We are in this together, Daddy. We can do it. We just have to support each other, and God will do the rest. He knows your heart. I know lying to Mom is very painful and new for you, but I do believe with all my heart that this is different. This isn't 'lying' the way God sees it. He knows you pray to Him daily, meditate on His word, and that you want the very best for Mom."

I smiled and patted his arm.

"He will open the doors that need to be opened in His perfect time. We just have to trust and rely on Him and on each other."

THE FOLLOWING MONDAY MORNING, I called my mom.

"Good morning, Mom! I have something for you to do with me today. How would you like to go volunteer with me at one of my favorite places?"

She replied very slowly. "Well, what kind? I've done that already. I've done what you're talking about."

This isn't going the way I anticipated. And she can't speak very well today.

"Come on, Mom. It will be fun for us to be together. And besides, Dad has a meeting today, so you don't have anything better to do, do you?"

She laughed, and I could feel through the phone that she was looking over at Dad, rolling her eyes, convinced I had her up for something she didn't really want to do.

"Okay. I'll get dressed. When? What time will you . . . uh . . . here?"

"I'll be there at 9:00." *Yes!*

"Okay, 9:00. Dave, did you hear that? She will be here at 9:00."

I heard Dad reply loudly enough so I could hear him. "Yes, 9:00. I'll make sure she's ready, Sarah!"

As I pulled up to their house, I felt nervous. I felt like I was being deceitful and sneaky. I was taking her somewhere to "volunteer," yet I wasn't. *Lord, this is so hard. Please know we don't want to be lying to her. And God, please don't let her notice the sign that says "Alzheimer's Day-care." I'm trusting You, God. I can't plan or know what's ahead, but You are in control. Please be with me today.*

As we headed out the front door of their house, Mom started picking up pecans along her sidewalk, as always. Their pecan tree was so messy it drove her crazy. She would pick up leaves and pecans, and a few minutes later, she'd look up at the tree and gripe, "I hate this thing!" As she bent over and grabbed a handful of pecans, I looked at Daddy with one eyebrow arched, as if to say, "We will see how this goes."

He gave me a thumbs-up and mouthed, "Thank you."

Mom walked back and handed him some pecans and said, "I'll see you later, my love."

Poor Dad. I know he's weeping inside. To hear those words and know he's not telling her everything must kill him. God, please be with him today, give him Your peace and help him be patient with Your perfect plan for him and Mom.

They kissed goodbye as they always did. Mom and Dad were smitten with each other. They'd been married forty-nine years, but they acted like it was their one-year anniversary every time they were together. It was beautiful to see them hugging and kissing each another and expressing their love, no matter where they were or who was watching.

As Mom and I drove up the highway, I kept thinking of things to talk about to distract her from our destination and the time it took to get there. Since everything seemed so far away to her these days, I didn't want to repeat the soccer game scenario.

"Mom, tell me the story about you and Elvis again. I would love to hear it. It's one of my favorites."

At the mention of Elvis's name, she lit up. She stared straight ahead, her eyes half-closed in nostalgia. As she sat deeper into her seat, she giggled and looked at me with a relaxed smile.

"Well, I got to meet him!" That was all she said.

I'm going to need more than that to get to Richardson.

"I know that, silly. But tell me again what he was doing. Wasn't he sick or something? I can't remember the whole story. I just remember you and Dad pulled up in his driveway at Graceland, and the next thing you knew you were sitting there talking to him."

Mom laughed again. "Yep, I sure did. I talked to Elvis!"

She looked out the passenger window, then looked straight ahead as she told her story. I knew she wasn't really looking at the highway—she was looking at the front door of Graceland. She was picturing herself sitting in the leather passenger seat of their 1965 burgundy Chevy Impala with the black vinyl top. She went on to tell me how Dad started talking to a guy standing outside, perhaps a security guard or caretaker, while she walked right up the sidewalk and knocked on the front door.

As Mom told the story, I noticed how her speech was declining. She couldn't speak clearly or verbalize her thoughts well, and her words were jumbled and not making much sense. But I still knew what she was saying.

"I just knocked on the door," she said, "and it answered. She asked who I am and told me to wait, you know, out there a minute. She left, came back, and said, 'Come on in. He's waiting for you.'"

Mom said she just put one foot in front of the other and walked right in. She never even looked back at Dad. The woman told her that Elvis was sick in bed but that he wanted to see her. Mom knew he didn't know who she was, but he told the lady working for him to let her in anyway. So in Mom's mind, he *did* know who she was.

"Well, he was lying there in his bed, and he didn't look real, uhhh, look real good. But, you know, he's Elvis, and Elvis can't look bad!"

We both laughed.

"Actually, Mom, I don't know, but I'll take your word for it."

She laughed again and went on. "I came in there, sat down by him, and he said, 'Tell me your name again? Becky it was?' 'Yes,' I said, 'it's Becky. I'm sorry you aren't well. I didn't mean to come here when you were sick.' And so we talked for a time, I don't remember about what, and then that was it. He said, 'It was nice to meet you, Becky, and I'm glad you came by,' and I said, 'Thank you for having me come in here. Good luck to you.' And he grabbed my hand, and that was it."

This is the funniest story ever. I wonder how much of it is true. I swear it gets embellished every time.

"Oh, Mom. Only you would walk right in and meet Elvis! Meanwhile, Dad is outside chatting it up with some random guy, and you could have cared less where he was at that moment."

We pulled into the parking lot with no hiccups. It was a small one-story building with a porte cochere. The building was brick, painted pale pink with white columns out front. It looked a little run-down, so I was starting to second-guess this idea of Dad's.

The moment we walked in, the sweetest lady greeted us. She pretended like she knew me and even said, "Welcome back, Sarah! We've missed seeing you here." I was shocked. She was committed to playing the game.

"Thank you," I said, regaining my composure. This must be Susan, the woman my dad had spoken to. "It's great to be back. I have my mom with me today. She's going to volunteer with me, so please let us know any way we can help."

Mom chimed in almost immediately, "Yes, please let me know how I can help. I'm just here with her, my daughter. This was her idea, so I'm just doing what I am told."

Of course she had to give a disclaimer: "I'm here with my daughter. This was her idea." Because she's been there, done that.

Susan gave us a tour of the facility, and I acted as if I had been there before. I even said hi and patted a few of the adults on the shoulder to express my love and willingness to serve. I was hoping Mom would do the same. Then Susan took us to a small group where the other adults were sitting in chairs arranged in a horseshoe shape with an employee at the head, holding a binder with some laminated papers, leading the group. They were playing a game where they filled in the blanks to phrases or songs. As Mom and I joined the group, I watched her as she smiled at the other adults and mouthed "hello" to some of them and waved to a few. She was a natural.

Suddenly, the leader called out the beginning of a line of lyrics from "Blue Suede Shoes."

Mom, along with most of the group, belted out the rest of the line.

I couldn't believe it. It was like God specifically had the group leader throw in an Elvis song just for Mom. *Thank You, Lord. This is amazing.*

Mom's face brightened, and I knew what was coming. With a grin, she turned to the others in the circle then back at the leader. In a joyful, high-pitched voice she said, "I've met Elvis, you know!"

DAY ONE AT FRIENDS PLACE was great, and I felt like a doorway leading to respite had been opened. I had been praying for relief for Dad, and I felt sure this was God's plan for him. It might take a few weeks to get Mom settled into the new routine, but surely things were about to get so much easier on us all.

The next day, I called her in the morning. "Hey, Beauty! I'll be there at 9:00 again. Susan texted me and said she was so thankful for our help yesterday and couldn't wait to see us both again today."

Mom paused. "Who is Susan? Yesterday?"

Please tell me she remembers some of yesterday. It was too good. I don't want to start all over.

"Yesterday, when we volunteered at Friends Place. You know, when you helped set the table and arrange some flowers?"

"Oh, yeah. That. I'm not going today, but thank you. I'll go another time, just not today."

Ugh.

"Mom, *please*? We both told Susan we would be there, and I don't want to disappoint her. They really need us today. They are short-staffed."

There was silence on the other end of the phone. As much as I tried to be a cheerleader and persuade Mom to join me, I felt sick to my stomach. The day before was perfect, and I really believed it was God's plan, and now it was as if yesterday had never happened. How could I feel so great one day and within a matter of hours feel so low?

"Are you there? Come on, Mom. Please do this—for me. I'll be there at 9:00."

She was still silent, and then I heard her soft voice say, "Okay, sweetie. I will be ready."

Once again, I pulled up to her house at 9:00. On her way out the door, she chewed out the pecan tree, grabbed her handful of nuts, took them over to Dad, and gave him a kiss goodbye. I had the eerie déjà vu I often felt when I spent time with her lately: We had lived out this exact day before.

As we drove down the highway, I thought to myself, *Well, if she doesn't remember much about yesterday . . .*

"Mom, tell me about Elvis. I want to hear that Elvis story of yours."

Once again, she lit up. She turned to me and grinned.

"Well, I met Elvis!"

DAY TWO AT FRIENDS PLACE was okay. Not great, but okay. Mom seemed to enjoy some of the activities, hugged some of the people, and she offered to help set the table. But after a few hours, she was ready to go home. Once again, I found myself urging her to do something she didn't really want to do.

I quietly pulled her aside and whispered, "Mom, we can't leave just yet. We really need to stay at least through lunch and visit with some of the people here. We will go after lunch."

She rolled her eyes, but then nodded and said, "All right. But after lunch, we go."

Lunch was difficult for me. It was the first time I had been around Mom and others with dementia and seen firsthand their lack of communication with one another. Mom tried to talk with the sweet lady next to her but had a hard time with her words, and the lady wasn't totally sure what Mom was saying. When the lady replied, Mom, who had already lost her train of thought, would wonder what she was talking about.

It was surreal. I pictured Mom, had I not been with her, sitting there at the table, totally lost, not knowing how to talk or carry on a conversation without me filling in the blanks. I was reluctant to let her be anything other than normal. I felt like she needed me there to help her seem "normal" and to keep it fun, not boring. I was trying to protect her in every way; I wanted to compensate for her speech, preserve her dignity, and prevent the others thinking she was strange. I didn't want Mom to think or feel like she was "one of them." But she *was* a resident with Alzheimer's just like the others, only younger than most.

Day three was worse, and by day four, I was tired of trying to persuade her to go. Thinking about Dad trying every week to take her in the car and drop her off made me anxious. It would be impossible for him to do—he would throw in the towel for sure. He would rather take care of her himself, no matter the cost to his own health, than deal with the consequences of arguing with her or dragging her into a car and taking her somewhere she didn't want to go.

It was day five, a Friday. This was the day we'd been planning for: I would go with Mom in the morning, then step away for "a phone call from the school" and then go "pick up a child." I was scared to leave her and terrified of her reaction.

When it was time, I watched Mom walk outside and engage happily in helping others plant flowers. This was my moment, my open door. I ran for it.

Susan hid me in a room just in case there was an emergency and they couldn't contain Mom. And that's exactly what happened. As Susan talked to me in that room, trying to soothe my nerves and walk me through what Mom would do the rest of the day, I heard her yelling from the back room.

"Get me *out* of here!"

I started tearing up. "Susan, that's Mom. She's yelling."

Tears flowed down my cheeks, and my hands shook. Susan calmly said, "Sarah, be patient. I know this is hard, but please let us try. I know you and your father have said she can be difficult, and she's clearly a very strong woman. But this is our job. Let us try."

I shook my head in fear, but like a child, I put complete trust in Susan, knowing they had dealt with these things before.

But then I heard it again. "I want to leave! Get your hand off me! I want out of here!" My heart raced. I couldn't hear what the others were saying, but I knew they were trying to redirect her.

"Where's my daughter? Let me *leave*!"

I looked at Susan. "I don't think I can do this. I can't break her heart or make her feel this way. She feels abandoned. This isn't working. I can't do it!"

I sobbed, begging God to stop this. But He didn't. He let it happen. He didn't fix what I wanted fixed. And I couldn't understand why.

Susan quickly said, "Sarah, she's coming this way. Put the phone to your ear, and we are going to tell her the school called and you had to step away. It's up to you if you want to go with or without her. It's your choice. We can try to keep her longer, while you park around the corner, and I'll call you if we can't calm her down. Or you can take her with you now."

I didn't know what to do. *This isn't my decision. This should be Dad's decision, not mine.* How was I supposed to know what was best for Mom? How could I tell her I was leaving her there when she was screaming and wanting to go home?

Oh, God. Please, she's coming. Please speak. I need You. Help me. Oh God, she's coming.

My heart felt like it was going to explode through my chest. My knees were buckling. My hands were freezing. I felt nauseous.

Lord, she's here!

"*There* you are! Where were you? I've been . . . they won't let me . . . I . . . Sarah . . . take me home. They . . . these people . . . *mean*."

I calmly responded, "Mom, I'm really sorry, the school is on the phone. Just a minute."

I wanted to see if she would calm down. I let Susan talk to her while I pretended to be on the phone with the school nurse. I heard Susan say to Mom, "Becky, please calm down. Everything is okay. Sarah needed to take a call. But we would love it if you could stay even if she needs to leave. You are such a huge help for us here."

I looked at Mom, who was now red and shaken. She was not staying, and there was no way in hell anyone could persuade her to stay.

She turned to me while I had the phone to my ear. "Take me home. *Now*. I want to go. I tried, and they won't let . . . they wouldn't let me out, Sarah."

Mom's eyes started watering at those words: "They wouldn't let me out, Sarah." It crushed me. My stomach sank. I had allowed her to feel like a prisoner. I felt so helpless, yet saturated with guilt. It was my fault. I should have never left her and let her feel this way. I held up my finger, saying, "One minute," trying desperately to figure out what to do. My heart was pounding, and I was at a loss for words.

Mom looked at Susan and said, "I'm never coming here again. This place. These people. Never again. You hear me? Sarah, let's *go*."

At that moment, Susan turned to me and gave me my answer. "I think you should go and take your mom with you. We will talk another time."

And with that, I said into the phone, "Okay, Nurse Dunn. I will be there in about forty-five minutes. I'm not close to the school, but I will be there as soon as I drop off my mom." I put my phone back in my purse.

"Thank you, Susan. I'm sorry that you needed us today and that we can't stay. I hope to be back some other time."

She flashed us a delightful smile and gave me the softest rub on the back.

"Don't worry, Sarah. Everything will be just fine."

Susan was trying to speak to my heart, trying to tell me everything would be fine. I didn't believe her. As far as I was concerned, Dad and I would be starting all over. I had lost all hope. What started as pure bliss, gratitude, and rejoicing four days earlier had turned into a disaster.

As I thought of God's words in Jeremiah 29:11, "For I know the plans I have for you" (NIV), all I could say to myself was, *Really, God? Because I'm not understanding what your plans are one bit. This sucks.*

The drive home was miserable. Mom went on and on about how she hated those people, and she told me to never "drag" her there again. For someone whose speech was often muddled, her words were crystal-clear spikes to my heart. I had damaged my mother. She was so angry with me. I had done something terrible, and Mom was hurting.

I should never have done that. I only wanted the best for her. Daddy only wants the best for her. God, what is the best for Mom? Where are You? Why?

I pulled over to get gas and take a deep breath after Mom's venting, then texted my dad.

"Daddy, it didn't go well. We've left. Complete disaster. I don't think she will ever go back. At least not with me. I will tell you more, but will you be home in the next twenty-five minutes? It's best if I can drop her off and go home. I am on the verge of a breakdown. I freaking HATE this disease. Have I ever told you that? HATE IT. If you want, call Susan before Mom gets home so you have an idea of what went on. I love you, and I'm sorry."

Daddy responded almost immediately.

"I'm sorry, Sarah. I'm here. Just bring her home. I just hung up with Susan—she called me. I already know. I love you very much. We tried."

We tried. Yes, we did. So now what? What's next, God? Are You there?

NINE

IN SICKNESS AND IN HEALTH

May 2016

-•✕•-

"D AVE?" MOM YELLED FROM THE bottom of the staircase. "Dave?"

"I'm up here, Beck, on my computer." Dad was sitting at his small desk in the middle of the upstairs hallway. "What do you need?"

Mom grabbed the iron stair rail as she slowly walked up the carpeted staircase. Watching from the dining room below, I noticed her steps were becoming slower. She had to work a little harder to lift one foot in front of the other, and her eyes were focused on each step so she wouldn't trip. The decline in her motor skills and physical strength was noticeable, and all I could do was stand there, praying she wouldn't lose her balance and fall. If I tried to assist her, she would laugh at me or be offended that I thought she needed help.

"Dave? Where are you? I can't get the thing on."

Dad peered over his right shoulder, and as he began to say, "What thing?" he noticed she was holding a lighter.

"The thing down there. I can't get it to come on. How do you turn it on?"

Dad pulled off his reading glasses off and stood abruptly. "The fireplace? You want me to turn on the fireplace?"

Mom nodded. "Yes, that! I'm trying, and I can't get it to come on."

Dad's eyes widened in fear. "Beck! Are you trying to light the fireplace by yourself? You can't do that!" Grabbing the lighter out of her hands, he rushed downstairs.

I had gone into the kitchen to finish unloading the dishwasher when I heard Dad running. I smelled the gas, the odor suddenly strong, and I felt such guilt that I had not been watching Mom for the last ten minutes.

As I hurried into the living room, Dad was bent over, turning the metal fireplace key to turn off the gas. He stood up, his face red and sweat dripping down his cheeks.

"Oh my gosh," I said. "Daddy."

He shook his head in disbelief, and I could see he was fearful for Mom's safety.

Oblivious, she stepped down the last step and onto the hardwood floor. She had her hands on her hips as she walked into their cozy sitting room. "Did you get it? I want you to show me how, please."

"Beck, I'm sorry, but I can't have you using the gas fireplace. Let me do this for you. Please don't ever do that again. You could have blown up our home. You left the gas on."

Mom looked at me like *he* was crazy. "I'm not going to blow this up. Are you nuts?"

I knew Dad was probably thinking, *I'm not nuts, but* you *are.*

"Becky, if you want the fireplace on, just ask. It's dangerous for you to try to light it yourself. You can catch your hand on fire or blow up the house."

Mom looked at him with disgust and anger. "You don't tell me what I can or can't do in my own home! I'm a *grown woman.*"

I knew at that moment that all the interviews we had with potential caretakers, all the books and information we had read on how to love a family member with dementia and keep her safe at home—that was the "blowup" headed our way.

· · ·

DAD AND I HAD COME up with story after story we could tell Mom that might pave the way for us to bring in a caretaker to help Mom feel at peace. But Mom was a strong woman—mentally and physically. We had already tried several people, and after weeks of "volunteering" and delivering flowers "from a church" with a potential caretaker, Mom was ready to boot them. She even picked up one lady's purse and set it outside the front door to let her know it was time to leave.

Dad was tired. It was getting to the point where he couldn't even go upstairs for ten minutes to pay bills. He had to monitor Mom twenty-four hours a day, seven days a week. She was like a toddler in a new home, wanting to touch every button, stick a finger in every hole, and even eat food off the ground. The hardest part was Mom knowing she could do certain things, even if she had forgotten how to do them. And we couldn't teach her because minutes or hours later she would forget it all.

Dad was drained, and I could see him aging with each passing day. He would lie awake at night thinking about what he could do with Mom the next day. He was cooking for her, walking with her, running errands with her, and even taking her to the golf course and the gym with him. He had no alone time unless I was there to relieve him. She wouldn't accept other help, and he struggled to find a balance between protecting her and pleasing her; he didn't want to cause any extra anxiety by leaving her with someone she didn't know. Dad, occasionally Ginny, and I were her only choices.

Dad turned all the gas off in the house. No more gas stove and no more gas fireplace. He also hid all the cleaning supplies and anything else he could think of that might be dangerous. He did everything he could to make the house safe, but no matter how hard he tried to prevent accidents, they continued to surface.

The situation was spiraling out of control.

• • •

I FELT SORRY FOR MOM for all that she was losing, and I felt sorry for Dad thinking he could do this on his own.

Standing in his garage, I said to Dad, "She's getting worse, and we have to figure out how to get you more help. I try to help three days a week, but even that is not enough. Three or four hours a few days a week just isn't going to cut it. I'm worried about you—your health and your lack of sleep. And quite frankly, I'm worried about Mom's safety."

I could feel his heart breaking and saw his eyes water.

"Daddy," I said gently, "it will be okay. We will get through this. Please call Lee, my friend's dad who started the support group I told you about. I know you don't want to go, but it might be helpful, and it will certainly be informative. We've tried calling the caretakers they suggested, and we've looked into memory care, but maybe there is something we are missing. If anything, you need the support of other men going through the same thing."

"It's not that, Sarah—that's not why I don't like going to the group. The men are all very nice. It's just that I don't want to hear about what kind of Depends I may need to buy Mom, or what kind of clothes to purchase and whether the tops button or pull over, or what hospice service to call. It's so depressing. I leave there discouraged, not lifted up. I feel depressed and sad, and I dread what's ahead. I would rather try to stay positive and take it day by day than constantly think about what's to come."

He sighed. "I'm committed to your mom. In sickness and in health. When I said my vows, I meant every word."

I felt Daddy's pain and confusion. He wanted to live in the moment, and he wanted to take care of her. But he also did not want to worry about things that were likely ahead, such as incontinence, or her not being able to dress or pull her pants up and down to use the restroom. After all, she could still shower and, for the most part, get dressed by herself.

But he was also somewhat in denial about how much Mom had declined. He was living and breathing this disease with her every minute of every day, and in turn, he couldn't see clearly what was happening to her. He would say, "Well, she's okay for now. I'm keeping an eye on her." Or, "I'll let you know when I can't manage it anymore."

The truth was that he couldn't manage it anymore. But he didn't want to give up or admit he couldn't do it. "In sickness and in health" meant *he* would be the sole caretaker until the day she died—at least in his interpretation. And I was no longer sure that was the best thing for him or Mom.

I BECAME BUSIER AND BUSIER with the kids' schedules and activities. The last two weeks of school, I had class parties to attend and teacher gifts to purchase. The girls and I were also packing for two weeks of camp that would begin the first day of summer. Knowing I couldn't help Dad as much, I felt heavy with guilt, especially in light of Mom's worsening condition. Even though Dad was in denial, I couldn't deny the truth any longer: She was a danger to herself.

Stopping by the house one afternoon, I noticed Mom had an adhesive bandage just below her collarbone.

I gently touched her chest. "What happened here, Beauty?"

She waved me off. "Oh, that. Well, I don't know. I can't remember. David, why do I have this thing?"

Dad blushed, and I knew he was a little embarrassed to tell me the story. "Your mother decided she didn't like a mole on her chest, so she grabbed a pair of scissors and tried to cut it out."

He stared up at me to gauge my reaction. I think my jaw had dropped to the floor.

"*What?* You tried to cut a mole out of your chest? Oh, Mama!"

I hugged her so tight. She laughed as I hugged her, but tears filled my eyes. I tried to hide the tears from both of them, but my heart was so broken that my intelligent mom had put a pair of scissors to her chest—or anywhere near her body, for that matter.

"Dad, how did you know? Did you see it happen?"

He wouldn't look at me. I could tell he was ashamed, and I knew he felt like a failure.

"Yes. Thankfully, I walked in early enough to stop her from damaging her skin. I think she must have just picked up the scissors, because it wasn't bad—just the top of her skin was scraped off, and there was no hole or gash or anything major. I was in the kitchen cleaning up breakfast, and she was getting dressed."

I didn't ask any more questions. It wasn't his fault, but I knew he blamed himself. There was no doubt in my mind he wondered why he hadn't moved the knives, scissors, and other sharp items out of her sight. Mom just didn't understand the danger.

"I didn't like that dark spot right there," she said, pointing under her collarbone, "so I wanted it off."

I became fearful. I started to feel like I was not good enough or capable enough to take care of my own mother. What if something happened to her under my care? Would Dad be mad at me and never forgive me if something happened to her? Would I be able to forgive myself?

So many thoughts flooded my mind, I couldn't sleep for several weeks. The disease was progressing, and Dad was still her sole caretaker. What if something happened to him? Then what? Something needed to be done, but I couldn't make that decision for him.

I prayed every single morning for God to give Dad clarity. He knew she had gotten worse, but there were many moments when she would be present, lucid, and sharp. She would snuggle with him in the mornings and tell him how much she loved him. She would talk about their friends in Houston in vivid detail. Or she'd have Dad dial my number so she could talk to her grandchildren, and she would know each of them by name. Those moments overpowered the dangerous things that happened, such as the gas incident, getting lost on a walk, or nearly cutting off her finger with a knife while slicing an apple, and I could see he wanted to prove to himself and to her that he could be her one and only caretaker.

In sickness and in health. The vows he said to her on September 10, 1966, played over and over in his mind, and he did not want to fail his beloved.

TEN

I'M A GROWN WOMAN

June 10 to June 15, 2016

-•◦✕◦•-

THE WAVES WERE HUGE. RED flags billowed in the breeze, warning residents and tourists to stay out of the Pacific Ocean. The Sea of Cortez was much calmer, but we always stayed in Cabo San Lucas, on the Pacific side where swimming was limited. On this particular part of the beach, the water could be rough and the undertow strong.

For years, my family and I had stayed in the same vacation home, and it was a place to relax and spend quality time with family and friends. This time we were embarking on an adult vacation with my brothers, their wives, and a few of Mom and Dad's closest friends. It seemed like a miracle we were all there at the same time without our kids. This would be our last trip as a family with Mom—but we didn't know that yet.

June is beautiful in Cabo. The air is warm, and there is a brisk breeze in the evenings. The smell of the salty ocean water and the sounds of the waves crashing against the rocks brings serenity.

I relaxed immediately as we walked into the vacation house. Seeing the linen couches and armchairs with their blue and white pillows and the cheerful seashells and starfish lining the glass shelves on the wall generated an instant peace in me. The furniture provided the perfect ambience and spa-like feel, and the large floor-to-ceiling sliding glass windows were open to the endless view of the ocean. As I watched the white waves crash over the beautiful rocks, I was flooded with gratitude for God's creation.

We made it to Mexico on this beautiful Sunday! Mom's favorite day, Sunday, and here we were with her favorite people. I thanked God we had all made it safely and thought to myself, *God is so good.*

"A slice of heaven" is what we called our favorite vacation spot—and for good reason. I breathed in the delicious smells as I took in the sumptuous spread: bowls of guacamole, homemade salsa, and ceviche were laid out with a big bowl of extra-salty tortilla chips. The chef, Lorenzo, always prepared the best meals for our family and kept his homemade dips sitting out for us at all times.

Mom had the biggest grin on her face. I'd always loved the small gap between her two front teeth when she smiled. That gap was a gift because she would stick her tongue against the back of it and give an ear-splitting whistle to call us in from playtime when we were kids. It seemed we could hear it from miles away. She hated that gap, but we loved it. If it weren't for that gap, we wouldn't have that wonderful memory.

"Gosh, Sarah," she said. "I'm so happy to be here. This place is incredible. Check out that view!"

Mom excitedly waved Dad over, as if he were missing out on something big.

"David! Can you even believe this place? Get over here. It's magnificent."

"Well, yes, I can," Dad said diplomatically. "We've been here plenty of times, and every time I'm here, it blows me away, too."

I could tell Dad was trying to protect Mom by agreeing with her, while also reminding her she had been there many times. He didn't want to call her out on her memory lapse.

One thing I'd always loved about the house in Cabo is I couldn't tell where the swimming pool ended and the ocean began. The pool gave the visual effect of pouring itself into the sea. The far side of the pool deck stuck out about a foot on the other side of a glass wall that stood between the pool and an unobstructed view of the ocean. That glass wall allowed me to look down and realize the house was perched on a cliff, 150 feet above the ocean and jagged rocks, yet it was almost invisible and created a seamless portrait of the surroundings.

Our family was ecstatic to be together: This was a family getaway we hoped to cherish forever. Mom and Dad were snuggled up in each other's arms like newlyweds, staring out into the ocean as if nobody else were around.

"I don't ever want to leave here, David. Look at them. Our children are all here with us. I'm so happy."

"I know, Beck. We are blessed."

"We are. Where are we again? What is this place called?"

"We are in Cabo. One of our favorite places to visit."

Mom knew she had been there before but didn't remember any details of the house or how high it was above the beach. Like a child seeing something incredible for the first time, she viewed it with awe.

Unfortunately, she made childlike choices, too.

THE NEXT MORNING BROUGHT ANOTHER sunny day in Cabo. *Today is going to be a great day,* I thought as I sat down to our buffet-style breakfast.

"Sarah," my dad said, "thanks for taking care of Mom today while I golf. I trust you, and she loves spending time with you. You know that."

"Yes, Daddy, don't worry. Go enjoy your day. You've needed a break for a long time. I've got it under control, and she is in good hands. I love you—have fun!"

Dad and most of the boys left after breakfast for a long day of golf. I was pumped to get outside and soak up the sun. Trish, my older brother's wife, was with us. Always happy, she was intentional about getting the family together for times of reflection, singing, or reading Scripture.

With her wavy hair tumbling over her shoulders from beneath her large sun hat, she was smartly dressed for the beach, and as usual, she wore bright lipstick but minimal makeup.

Mom was dressed and ready for sunbathing.

"Trish, would you mind watching Mom for a minute while I put on my swimsuit? I'll be back in a minute," I said.

"Of course, sister," Trish replied.

Trish, the mother of three young ones, had a servant's heart. She understood what watching a childlike individual like Mom meant.

But while I was upstairs, a scream burst through the serenity.

"Help! Need some help here!"

It was Trish screaming. Panicked, I threw a towel around myself and rushed down. Mom was on the cliff side of the glass wall.

Trish was standing at the glass wall around the pool deck, trying to hold my mom against it. No matter how hard Trish tried to keep Mom from stepping out farther along the ledge, Mom grew fiercer, pushing Trish away. Trish was all that was keeping Mom from falling 150 feet to her death.

Paralyzed and barely dressed, I was too stunned to move. Reagan, one of Mom and Dad's closest friends, ran out of the house. By God's mercy, he had opted out of golf that day and was home.

Walking up to Mom from behind, Reagan, with his trademark calm, attempted to pin her shoulders up against the glass wall.

"Rebecca, I need you to hold onto me. It's not safe for you to be standing here. Please calm down and be still."

"I'm fine! Just . . . just . . ."

Mom couldn't get her words out. Her anxiety swelled.

"Rebecca, listen to me, please. Stop fighting us. We are trying to help you. This isn't safe. You may fall."

For someone in his midseventies, Reagan was extremely fit. He had known Mom for years and was the best person to talk sense into her. But there is no talking sense into a person with Alzheimer's disease; their logic has left them.

Fighting with all her might, Mom was yelling, "Leave me alone! Get off me! Get off me!"

I ran toward her while Fernancio, the house handyman, ran from the other side of the deck, jumping fully clothed into the pool to swim across and help Reagan. Lorenzo came quickly from the kitchen.

"Rebecca, you have four of us trying to keep you from falling," Reagan said. "Stop kicking, please!"

It was taking a village, but Mom wasn't surrendering easily. She kicked Fernancio away, hurting his knee. Trish, shaking, was yelling and begging Mom to stop fighting. "Let us help you!"

I could tell Reagan and Lorenzo were in shock. It wasn't just anyone they were trying to save from falling to death: It was Mom!

After what seemed like an eternity, Reagan and Lorenzo lifted Mom up and over the glass wall. She was finally safe.

Standing there in my blue bath towel, I realized she had nearly died.

Mom was now circling around the pool deck, disoriented. She didn't seem to know who or what she was looking for and neither could she comprehend what had just happened. It was as if her body and mind wouldn't allow her to move or think clearly. Stuck in a moment of complete confusion, she seemed panicked and unable to speak.

Her panic turned to fury.

"I am a *grown woman*!" she shouted. "Everyone leave me alone! What is wrong with y'all? I was just trying to get something! That thing! Are y'all crazy?"

Staring where she pointed, I saw a blue plastic water bottle. It seemed so insignificant, but this bottle had almost cost my mother her life. Eight feet away from Mom, it was floating in the overflow pool under the infinity pool. Because she could not perceive the distance of an object, she thought it was only a few inches away.

I approached her slowly, trying to calm her, but she jerked away.

"Get me out of here," she yelled. "Get me out of this place! I am going home."

She stormed off into the house, her face bright red, with anger and fear gleaming in her dark brown eyes. Her hands were shaking crazily.

The rest of us stared at one another, unsure of what to say or do. Trish, traumatized, went straight to her room and sobbed like a baby. It was all too much.

Reagan was in a state of quiet shock, and Lorenzo shook his head, as if thinking, *I can't believe what just happened.* He could barely speak.

I took off to the bedroom to gather myself. I thought I might throw up. The pit in my stomach had never felt so hollow.

Fernancio had gone to the garage to attend to his knee. Checking on him, I opened the garage door to find him sitting, rubbing and massaging the knee, tears rolling down his face.

"Fernancio, are you okay?" I asked. "Are you injured? I am so sorry. What can I do?"

I went away for not even five minutes, and Fernancio is in the garage crying, Lorenzo is traumatized, and Trish is upstairs weeping. I can't believe I stepped away. This is all my fault. Fernancio is hurt because I left Mom with someone other than myself.

"No, no, Sarah. I'm okay. *Por favor.* It's okay. Only scared. Very. *No problema. No problema,* Sarah."

Fernancio didn't speak much English, but he was able to say "scared," which stuck in my mind the rest of the trip. Fernancio was pretending he was all right, but I could see the pain, fear, and sheer disbelief in his eyes.

What if he had fallen off the cliff? He just risked his life for my mom. He has a family too. He didn't even think about not helping! He just jumped in to save her.

Every single person who helped save Mom was traumatized. They had never seen anyone try to stand on the opposite side of a glass wall and pool deck that was 150 feet high with one hand and the other hand trying to grab a plastic water bottle.

I went to Reagan next. He had tears in his eyes. "She just kept saying, 'Right there, right there! I'm just trying to get that thing. Get off of me!'

She didn't even realize she was hanging off a cliff, Sarah. I've never seen anything like it. I don't know who is going to tell David—you, Trish, or me—but someone needs to let him know. She is dangerous, and she could have killed herself."

Reagan wiped his eyes. "My heart is broken for her, you, David, and your entire family. I've known Becky for forty years, and it's tragic what is happening. Something needs to be done, and David needs full-time help. And I mean soon. Real soon."

I was speechless. I knew all of this, but how could I make that decision? It was Dad's to make.

Mom was fearless, but just like a child, she had no awareness of danger, and she certainly had no concept of distance. She needed someone to protect her, and she needed someone to make decisions in her best interest. She needed to be safe, and she needed to listen and cooperate and understand why we were all trying to help her. But Mom's brain wasn't functioning properly. It wasn't sending the signals necessary to help her comprehend what she was doing, nor was her brain able to make sense of it all.

Not even five minutes had passed, and Mom couldn't tell me what had happened. She sat quietly on the white linen sofa. I reached out and took her hand.

"Are you all right, Mom?"

"No," she said, jerking back her hand. "I don't like being watched. I don't need babysitting—I'm a grown woman."

Mom was mad. But I wondered if she even knew why.

"Do you know what just happened?" I prodded gently.

"I'm a grown woman," she fumed.

"But what just happened on the pool deck, Mom? Do you remember?"

She was frustrated and flustered, unable to tell me what took place. I realized then that my worst fear was true: Her Alzheimer's had taken every bit of her short-term memory.

You can't teach someone or try to explain why something just happened when that person has no short-term memory. So I couldn't tell Mom how much danger she'd been in, or why she shouldn't do something like that again. It was like her words and thoughts had gone into a bubble and—*pop!*—they'd vanished, never to return.

Walking into the house as he laughed with his golf buddies, Dad entered the kitchen where the rest of us stood, staring at one another in silence.

He sensed something was wrong.

"Daddy, there is something we need to tell you."

ELEVEN

PICKING UP THE PIECES

June and July 2016

--◦•❭✕❬•◦--

A S THE SEASON TURNED TO summer, the Dallas afternoon highs reached the nineties. Mom loved her walks, and no matter how much she perspired in the humid heat, she wanted to go several times a day. But Dad put his foot down and said they could go only in the mornings.

My family traveled a lot in the summers. Thad's job usually enabled him to work from anywhere. So when the girls returned from camp, we spent a week in Yosemite with my older brother, David, and his family, followed by four weeks in Colorado with Thad's family. But my mind was in Dallas instead of in Colorado with Thad and the kids.

I had no peace of mind being so far away from my parents, and it took a toll on my body, mind, and spirit. I tried hard to enjoy the hikes, bike rides, and other activities, but a guilt like nothing I had experienced before settled on me. Dad never pressured me to help, and he told me frequently to be with my family and not worry about Mom and him.

The problem was that I really missed my mom. I wanted to be with her. My heart's desire was to spend as much time as possible with her before Alzheimer's took her mind completely. Seeing how quickly the disease was progressing, I didn't want to return to find she couldn't recognize me. Every day and every moment I spent with Mom was meaningful, purposeful, and priceless, and the thought of going weeks without seeing her was gut-wrenching.

While in Colorado, I continued my early morning habit of coffee and quiet time. I prayed fervently that God would give Dad wisdom, discernment, and clarity in making important decisions, as well as the patience and strength to take care of Mom. Begging God for help, I asked Him to preserve Dad's health. Mom's disease was draining the life out of him, and I feared Dad might go down with her.

Thad, the kids, and I returned to Dallas about a week before the girls' soccer tournaments began. Shopping with Mom was at the top of my agenda.

"Hey, Dad!" I said excitedly. "Let me talk to Mom, please."

As soon as Mom grabbed the phone, she said, "Hello? Sarah? I've missed you. Come see me!" She had actually missed me, and it made me feel good.

"Oh, I'm coming, Mama! Are you dressed? Do you want to shop for some new shorts and tops? It's hot outside."

"I'd love that!" Mom was in the best mood. It was so interesting to witness how the thought of my being nearer to her could change her mind-set. She was sad when I was in Colorado, but the moment I returned to Dallas, she became a new person.

Shopping in the mall was great exercise for us both and saved us from the heat outside. We took lots of time walking in and out of stores so Mom would not be overwhelmed.

Chico's became my new favorite store for Mom because almost everything had an elastic waist. Also, the colorful pullover T-shirts were easy for Mom to put on and take off. Buttons were too difficult now— her fine motor skills in her hands and fingers were shutting down.

"Sarah, look at this!" She was holding a fuchsia blouse with some gold hardware on the shoulders. "What size do you think it is? Does it look too big?"

Mom had always been very conscious of size, and Chico's made it easy for me because of its clothing sizes. Pants were labeled 0.5, 1.0, 1.5, and so on. I said, "Mom, a 1.5 is a size 6. That's *perfect.*"

As I brought her more clothes to try on, she yelled over the dressing room door, "This is fun, Sarah! I love shopping." I felt tickled because not everyone is thrilled by trying on seven pairs of pants.

At the checkout, I texted Dad to call and distract Mom while I paid the bill. She had lost the concept of numbers and didn't know if an item was expensive or inexpensive. Still, I didn't want her to fuss about the prices on every single thing.

When Dad called, I handed her the phone and steered her to a corner. I told her it was quieter there, but it was also away from the door so she couldn't wander out while I paid.

I quickly explained the situation to the cashier, telling her, "I'm so sorry to ask you to be fast. I need to pay quickly, or she will question the cost on every little thing. I apologize in advance if she pops off at you or seems edgy."

The lady smiled kindly. "I totally understand. We have customers who come in here all the time helping a loved one. I will be super quick, and please know if you need to return anything at all, it will not be a problem. Just bring your receipt, and I'll be happy to help you."

Her words were music to my ears. Communicating discreetly with others about my mom's disease was awkward. Often I would type notes on my phone and hand it to the clerk to read when Mom wasn't looking. Or I would talk to them when she was in the dressing room or digging through a rack of clothes. I worried about how others would perceive Mom, but I also wanted to protect her and prevent uncomfortable situations. It was mentally draining, but I felt it necessary.

Finished with her call, Mom brought the phone to me and noticed a turquoise blouse exactly like the fuchsia one we had just purchased. "Sarah, I like this. Did we get this one?"

"No, not that color, but we did get that exact shirt in a different color." I showed her the matching fuchsia blouse on the adjacent hanger.

"I want this one," she said. "Let me try it on."

Knowing Mom had already tried on that shirt in another color, I grabbed the turquoise one and said, "Here. This one is your size. Let's just buy it since we already know it'll fit."

She looked at me, puzzled and confused. "We don't know my size. I need to try it on."

I gently disagreed. "We do know your size, Mom. See, look." I took the fuchsia blouse out of the hanging bag so she could see it for herself and said, "It's just like this fuchsia one you tried on."

She stared at it, looked back at the turquoise blouse and then at the fuchsia again. "No. That's not the same shirt. It's a different color."

She could not comprehend that two blouses could be different colors but the same style and size. Feeling my stress rise, I turned to take the turquoise shirt to the dressing room, not realizing she had begun taking off her shirt in the middle of the store.

"Here!" Mom's voice was agitated. "Where are you going? Let me try that on!"

There she was, standing with her shirt halfway up her bra, her belly button and white stomach hanging out, and one arm already pulled through a sleeve.

"*Mom!*" I gasped. "Mom, no! Not in the middle of the store! Dressing room. The dressing room!"

I looked at the cashier in disbelief, and she mouthed, "Don't worry, it's okay." Regardless, I was mortified.

Mom started laughing but was not making the connection. "What? It's just us girls! What's wrong with me trying it on here?"

Suddenly, I burst out laughing. "Mom! We are in a mall with glass windows! My entire life you hardly let me see you in a bra, and now you are totally fine with not only me seeing you, but a complete stranger at Chico's? Wow, Mama. You have come a long way!"

I pulled Mom's shirt down and helped her with the sleeve. She laughed and said, "Well, okay! But this lady doesn't care, do you?" She pointed to the cashier, who smiled sweetly.

"No, not at all. But there are some men walking by, so your daughter is probably right. I think it's best to try it on in the dressing room."

That day was a jumble of joy, laughter, and grief. Mom and I tried on shoes, pants, and shirts, grabbed a Starbucks coffee and a cookie, and even stopped by a salon to have our hair washed and dried. After such a fun day, that night in bed I cried tears of joy and sadness. While I was thankful Mom had no shame about her body, I was sad she was no longer protective of what others might see, and I also despaired at her lost abilities.

Physically slower, she couldn't make decisions, and she would argue with clerks about shoe and pant sizes: "I told you I needed a bigger size. What's wrong with you?" While outings with her could be embarrassing and stressful, or fun and memorable, the emotional roller coaster of being out with Mom taxed me. Sadly, I knew our shopping days were ending, and I began to grieve yet one more loss.

ON A LAZY DAY WITH no agenda, Mom and I relaxed at her house while Dad went to a lunch meeting. While I checked my emails, texts, and Instagram, Mom was piddling around, rearranging books and picture frames on the shelves. We had done our usual walk around the block and strolled through our favorite shopping plaza. We each lunched on a hot turkey-and-cheese panini with homemade potato chips.

Enjoying the uneventful day and Mom's contentment, I realized it was one of those rare occasions when she didn't want to go anywhere.

Suddenly, I heard the sound of glass breaking from the bathroom.

"Mom? Are you okay? What's going on in there?"

"Yeah. Everything's fine. I just . . . I just . . . It's okay. I'm okay." Her voice sounded winded, and I could tell from her tone she was focused on something.

Running down the hall, I put my hand on the doorknob of the bathroom and pressed my ear to the door. "Can I come in, Mom? Are you dressed?"

Even if Mom no longer cared if she was seen undressed, I didn't want to violate her privacy.

"Yes, you can. I'm dressed. I just . . ."

As I opened the door and leaned in, I saw Mom bent over in her white pants, with her hair falling down around her face, picking up broken pieces of glass.

I gasped. "What happened?"

She slowly stood up and pointed to the sconce hanging on the wall on the right side of the mirror. "I don't like the lighting here, so I was, you know, trying to . . ." I saw that Mom had unscrewed a light bulb from the sconce while the light was on. My guess was that it was so hot, she dropped it immediately, although she couldn't tell me what had actually happened.

"Mom, be careful. Here—step over here. I need to get a vacuum. You may get glass in your finger." *Again*, I thought. *Like the time you broke your bowl.*

"I can get it, Sarah. It's just a little bit."

I gently touched her shoulder and looked into her deep brown eyes. "I know, Mom. I know it seems like just a little bit. But please, I'm asking you to trust me and let me get it all for you. I have little kids, and I deal with things like this all the time. Let me help you."

She smiled as she moved out of the bathroom to carry a few pieces of glass to the kitchen trash.

Retrieving the broom, dustpan, and vacuum, I felt a sadness wash over me. There we were, enjoying the quiet ease of the morning, and within two minutes, Mom had nearly electrocuted herself.

In self-condemnation, I told myself, *Wow, Sarah, way to watch Mom. What if she had stuck her finger in the light socket?* And then the killer question: *Who are you to think you can protect your mom from hurting herself? How can you tell your dad she'll be fine under your care?*

Tears rolled down my face once again as I swept up the tiny, sparkling pieces of glass. Each sparkle seemed to represent every close call Mom had had over the last year: wandering off and getting lost, cutting the mole off her chest, trying to finish her cereal out of a broken bowl, and climbing onto a ledge over the ocean. I remembered the day she tried to use a table runner as a rug on her hardwood floors and left the china cabinet in the middle of the room and not against a wall.

I swept, then turned on the vacuum. *Poof!* The pieces were gone. Mom's fine motor skills, short-term memory, ability to reason, concept of time, and names of friends had been sucked up like pieces of glass into a vacuum: gone forever. I had failed as a caretaker, and the thought flitted through my mind again: *My mom is slowly dying in front of my eyes.*

The emotional ups and downs were like jumping from a diving board. As a child, I would jump up and down one or two times so I could get some height from the springs. Then I'd jump as high as I could, flying free in the air with my arms spread out like wings, holding my breath before crashing into the water and plummeting toward the bottom of the pool. I'd use all my power, paddling and kicking to move myself toward the light—and air—at the surface. Proud that I'd overcome the challenges and surfaced for air, I went back, stood in line, and did it all over again.

As an adult child, however, the thing driving me to resurface for air and do it all over again was a cry to God to fill me with His power, courage, endurance, perseverance, and patience.

TWELVE

911

July 17, 2016

⋯◦❊◦⋯

"THIS WAS SO NICE OF you guys to have us over for dinner," said Pedro in his polite, lightly accented English. "We are really so happy we could finally get together."

Pedro was our neighbor who lived across the street. He and his wife, Meredith, were the neighbors who had left homemade desserts on our doorstep the day we moved into our home nine years earlier. We loved being with them, although we weren't able to spend as much time with them as we would've liked because of our age differences and the activities of our children.

Sitting around our dining table with them and their son, we ate homemade chicken parmesan loaded with mozzarella and homemade tomato sauce. Our conversation ranged from their daughter, who was studying at a prestigious ballet school in New York City, to local school-district issues, Pedro's entrepreneurial endeavors, and our shared faith.

After dinner, the four of us moved to one of our favorite rooms in the house. With four chairs around a coffee table and a favorite Colorado painting on the wall, this room was cozy and invited intimate, meaningful conversations.

Pedro asked me about my mom. "Sarah, how is your mom? I don't know if you want to talk about it or not, so it's okay if you prefer not to. I just want you to know that Meredith and I talk about it a lot, and we are really heartbroken for you and your family and for all that you are going through."

I looked out the window briefly with my arms and legs crossed comfortably in my chair and thought about how to answer his question.

"Mom's doing okay. I mean, she doesn't realize what she's lost, you know? She has scared me quite a bit, and I think she's becoming more and more dangerous to herself."

I don't know if it was the glass of wine I'd had at dinner or the overwhelming flashbacks to Mom's episodes that made my throat tighten and cramp. My eyes began to feel glossy and damp, and I took a long pause. I looked over at Thad.

"It's okay, honey," he said. "They understand if you don't want to talk about it."

Pedro immediately responded, "Oh, Sarah, for sure, please, I am sorry. I just want you to know that we care. That's all, and we will continue to pray for you and your family."

Meredith nodded from across the table. "I'm so sorry. Yes, we will be praying."

"No, really, it's okay. *I'm* sorry! Talking about it just makes me emotional because my heart is so heavy, though more for my dad, honestly. I don't know how to advise or help him—and really, I can't make decisions for him. The guilt is unexplainable. I feel guilty if I consider suggesting he place her in care, and I feel guilty if I am not available to help take care of her, and I feel guilty if I am with her and something happens. It's a no-win situation."

I gazed down at my half-empty wine glass and flashed back to Mom holding any kind of glass, whether a light bulb, a cereal bowl, or a coffee mug.

Holding my glass up to Meredith and Pedro, I said, "See this glass of wine? If Mom were holding it, she would hold it like this." I tilted it to where the wine was almost spilling out of the glass. "She has no control over her hands and they shake constantly. She's broken so much glass lately. She also used a pair of scissors to try and cut a mole out of her skin."

They both gasped.

"But I can zoom out and see the big picture a little more than Dad can, because he lives it every single day. He's so wrapped up in the details that it's hard for him. And I tear up and get emotional because the big picture is Mom needs help. And I can't tell you what that means exactly.

"I feel damned knowing she needs help, and I feel damned not having an answer. I am afraid of what can happen. So far, she's avoided getting really hurt, but at what point will something big happen that could take her life? I am living with these thoughts and emotions every minute of every day, and I can't imagine how it must feel for my father. I hate to admit this, but I think Mom needs to be placed."

My eyes filled with tears and my lower lip quivered. "I don't want to take her from her home. She loves being home. She loves Daddy so much. Dad would feel like a widower if he had to place her. But I just don't see any other way out."

Meredith and Pedro were empathetic listeners. This after-dinner visit felt more like group therapy. I felt safe, and every time I looked over at Thad, his eyes were filled with love, compassion, and sympathy. He loved Mom, and I knew this was painful for him as well, though he was being strong for me.

The house phone rang, but since we were deep in conversation, we didn't answer. I turned off my cell phone early in the evening so we could have uninterrupted time with Pedro and Meredith. Then Thad's phone started buzzing in his pocket. The caller: "David Sr. mobile."

"Hey, David," Thad answered. In an instant, Thad's face changed.

Handing me the phone, he said, "Honey, your dad. He needs you right now."

My stomach dropped. "Excuse me, sorry, one second."

The look on Thad's face told me everything: This was an emergency.

"Sarah," Dad said without hesitation. "It's your mom. I don't know what she drank or what she's done, but she is red all over and has a rash everywhere. I mean, everywhere. I think she's having an allergic reaction. She seems calm, but I may drive her to the hospital."

"I'll be there in ninety seconds. I'm coming with you." Abruptly hanging up the phone, I looked at Pedro, Meredith, and Thad, and said,

"I'm so sorry. Mom's having an allergic reaction to something she drank. I need to leave. Thad, I'll call you when I know something."

They nodded, their faces frozen in fear and concern. I raced to the car and pulled out of the garage, hardly looking where I was going. I didn't drive the six blocks to Mom and Dad's house—I flew.

RUNNING INSIDE, I YELLED, "DADDY? Mom? Where are you?"

Dad called to me from their bedroom. "Our bathroom!"

I ran into their bathroom; Dad was standing with Mom.

"Sarah, I just don't know," he said. "She's becoming calmer and calmer since I called you, and I think she will be okay, but look at her. Should I take her to the hospital? She's bright red all over."

Mom chimed in, "I'm okay, y'all. Really, I am okay."

Her cheeks looked sunburned, and her whole body was red. She started scratching one arm. "It just itches here, and kind of all over, but I am not hurting. Just feel warm."

"Dad, did she just take a shower?" I asked. "Could she have taken a hot shower and scalded herself? Sometimes she doesn't taste things, so maybe she can't feel hot water?"

It was then I smelled the strong odor of nail polish. Checking her nails to see if she had been working on them, I saw they were the same color as they were the day before. She had just had a manicure.

Curious and confused, I opened the shower door, but the shower wasn't wet, nor the doors and glass foggy or damp. I scanned the bathroom.

"Mom, did you drink something? Can you tell me what you may have done?"

She calmly brushed a piece of hair out of her eye, then reached her hand back to her hip to rub it. "No, nothing. I don't know. I don't know why this happened. But I'm okay. Just itchy everywhere."

Dad touched my back. "Sarah, will you check her bottom? Will you just check her all over? I want to see how red she really is. I've peeked, but it may be better if you check her all over."

Looking at Mom intently, he told her what I was going to do. "Beck, she's just going to check you on your bottom and chest."

She smiled and gave a small chuckle. It was actually a great icebreaker.

"Mom, I'm sorry. I'm just pulling the back of your pajama pants down and your underwear so I can see your cute cheeks and make sure they aren't red."

"Ha!" she cried. "Hardly cute!"

Mom's bottom was red all over, and I was mystified. What had caused this reaction? The good news was she was becoming calmer by the minute, and I felt like she was going to be okay. But I still feared that she had poisoned herself without knowing it.

Checking her chest and breasts, I could see they were as pink as if she had sunbathed topless. "Mom, does your chest itch? What about your stomach? Or just your arms and bottom?"

Mom seemed to move slowly in her thoughts from head to toe. Her brain could no longer process quickly.

"Well, right here, on my leg, and uh, here, right here, and my rear. It's itchy. I don't know, Sarah. Everywhere really. But I am okay. I really am. I will be all right."

The moment she said she would "be all right," I looked on her countertop and saw two bottles of nail polish remover. One was completely empty with the lid on it, and the other was open and half full. My heart sank.

"Mom. Could you possibly have drunk nail polish remover? I know this was full because I bought it yesterday after we got your nails done. You were out, which is why this one is empty, so we bought you a new one. Do you remember anything at all?"

She thought for a few moments and then said, "No. No, I didn't drink that. That was there."

I know it was there, but if you can't tell us anything that you did and why you have a rash all over your body, how do you know if you didn't drink the nail polish remover? It reeks of acetone in here!

"Dad, come here. Do you smell nail polish remover? That is the first thing I smelled when I walked in here, but when I checked her nails and they looked the same, I blew it off. Honestly, I think she drank nail polish remover."

Dad looked at Mom. "Beck, do you think you accidentally drank this? Are you sure you didn't?"

"I'm sure."

Overwhelmed, Dad walked into their bedroom and sank down on their king-size bed. As I grabbed Mom's hand to lead her out, she pointed to the nail polish remover.

"Sarah," she whispered. "That's it. I thought it was my Diet Coke."

I knew it. What now? Do I call Poison Control?

"Dad, did you hear that? She thought the nail polish remover was her Diet Coke. Do you think we should call Poison Control? I don't know what to do because the color on her face is fading. She's not as red, and her arms are better already."

Dad responded, fairly confident, "No, I don't think we need to call Poison Control. The color has faded quite a bit."

"Dad, are you sure? Should we call Poison Control just in case?"

Dad was her primary caretaker, and I wanted to follow his lead, but I was just as confused as he was in that moment.

I felt unable to protect both of them in their own environment. Things I couldn't imagine were happening. It was overwhelming, and I felt inept as caretaker, protector, and daughter.

Surely Dad thought himself a failure, too. How could he fulfill his role as husband, caretaker, protector, and defender? The guilt had to feel like a mass of bricks on his shoulders.

Mom sat down in Dad's lap in her white terry cloth robe.

"Mom? Are you still itchy?"

"No, not as much. I'm really okay now. Y'all stop worrying about me so much!"

I guess he's right. Maybe we don't need to call Poison Control. I'm not sure I agree with that decision, but I want to respect him.

Dad had one arm around Mom and one arm on her leg as she snuggled in his lap. He looked at me with fearful, sad eyes. Confusion, guilt, and panic seemed to set in all at once. He tried to hold back the tears but couldn't. Mom didn't notice, being cuddled up to him like a five-year-old girl with her head on his shoulder. She actually reminded me of myself as a little girl, curled up in my daddy's lap.

Dad tilted his head back to wipe away his tears so she would not notice them. He shook his head at me. I wanted to rescue him. I wanted to hold Mom for him, to sweep her away so that he could fall to his knees and let the emotions pour out. He held it in all the time, and I knew this time he was falling apart.

"Daddy, it's okay. Mom's all right. I think we need to give her an antihistamine to help the rash and itching go away." Playing the strong caretaker, I focused on business and treating the rash. I wasn't sure it was working very well.

"I was just . . . I was just in the kitchen," he said. "Cleaning the dishes. Loading the dishwasher. She was in the bathroom putting her pajamas on, Sarah." Another tear rolled down his cheek.

"Beck, do you see why I can't leave you here at the house alone? You scared me. You scared me bad. You couldn't even tell me what happened. I can't leave you alone without someone here in the house. Do you understand that?"

Very chipper, Mom said, "Dave, I'm fine! I'm fine now. It was just a small thing. I don't know why you and Sarah are so worried about me. Y'all act like I am a child or something."

And there it was. Her disease was convincing us, and Mom, that all was good, that we could go back to normal now. But after this gut-wrenching experience, Dad wouldn't have it.

"Becky, you are not okay. You couldn't even tell me what caused your body to turn bright red and itch all over. That's a problem. If I had not been here and you had done that or worse, what would have happened? Tell me. If I am not here and something happens, what would you do?"

She tilted her head and thought for a moment. Looking at me, she pointed and smiled, "Well, I would call her. My daughter!"

Dad shut that down. "And if Sarah didn't answer her phone, and you can't get hold of her, then what?"

"I would call you and tell you, and then you would help me from wherever you are."

Dad rolled his eyes, irritated. He had moved from despair to frustration.

"Oh, really? And if I was on a golf trip, or at the driving range, or in a business meeting, how could I help you? By the way, what is my phone number? Or Sarah's? Can you tell us?"

Of course, she couldn't.

I came up with another scenario. "Mom, let's say the house caught on fire or someone broke in the house. What you would do?"

"I would run out that door!" She pointed to the bedroom door. "I would go out that door and outside and get help."

Carefully, I played the devil's advocate. "Mom, you can't run past a robber. Who would you call from your bedroom phone? What is the emergency phone number you need to call if there is ever an emergency? Not mine, or Dad's, but the number for the police or ambulance or fire department. Can you tell me that emergency number?"

She stared at me and grinned, as if she knew she was supposed to know the answer but didn't. "I don't remember," she said and laughed.

Dad and I were not amused. He was heartbroken and annoyed. I tried to be gentle. "Mom, you would call 911. That number calls the police immediately, and you always want to call 911 first, okay?"

Mom started laughing, and Daddy and I couldn't understand what she thought was so funny. "Y'all are treating me like I am a child! I was home alone for years, David, when you were out working. I am *fine*. You two! Y'all make me laugh."

"I'm so glad you think we are funny, Mom. Now, tell me, what's the number you call if there is an emergency?"

She rolled her eyes. "9-1, uh, 9-9. Shoot. I forgot. Tell me again?"

I had to get up and walk out of the room. Going straight to the bathroom, I slammed the door shut and locked it. Slapping my hands down on the marble countertop, I burst out crying. I was angry, frustrated, and bitter at the fact that I couldn't even teach Mom three digits to remember. *911.*

I cried out to God in silence. *God, do something! When are You going to bring us help? Where are You? Why are You taking so long? How long do we have to go through this? Please give my dad some rest. Please.*

I sent Thad a text from the bathroom, "All okay. Sorry didn't call earlier. She drank nail polish remover, but she's okay. I'll stay a little longer until Dad is in a better place and I feel I can leave. I love you."

He responded, "Praise God she's okay. Take your time. I'm sorry, honey. I love you."

"Praise God she's okay." Those words stuck out to me, and they almost irritated me. Easy for Thad to say! But at the same time, I felt convicted. Sitting on the toilet with both hands over my face, I began to pray.

I'm trying to praise You, God. Praise You when things are good and praise You when they are bad. You are my stronghold. You are my rock, my shield, and my shelter.

God, please deliver Daddy from this pain and give him rest. You are his refuge, and You promise Your deliverance. I'm standing on Your promises right now. Take this from him and me, and show us Your way. Please, God, reveal Your purpose and plan for all that You are allowing to happen right now. I don't understand it and I'm trying to be positive— but Lord, this is so hard!

I need Your strength and courage this very moment to go back in there and not be angry at Mom. I'm angry at her disease, not her. She's innocent. Don't let me be angry with her. Please help me stand up right now and go love on the both of them the way You love on me. I'm trying to trust You, God. Please help me trust.

Amen.

THIRTEEN

THE CRASH

August 2016

-·❖·-

"HOORAY!" ELIJAH BELTED OUT AS he stepped off the airplane. "We made it. Hello, Colorado!" The kids were excited to experience their favorite mountain activities again.

Elijah tugged at my sleeve. "Mommy, Mommy—can we *please* go get a snow cone?"

Two seconds later, Emery said, "No, Mommy! Can we *please* go to the breakfast café first? I'm so hungry and really want my favorite smoothie and their pistachio sausage."

I looked over at Thad as he mimicked the kids. "Mommy! Mommy! Can you *please* take me to Paradise Bakery so I can get a few scoops of mint–chocolate chip ice cream?"

I laughed. We all laughed. Then Frensley chimed in, "Yeah, Mommy! Can you *please* take me to get truffle fries at The Tavern?"

Life was great at that moment. The dry, fresh mountain air heated up my face and skin without a drip of sweat running down my chest, unlike in Dallas. I looked up at the sky. *Thank you, Lord, for this break. It's beautiful. God's country.*

As we loaded the rental car at the airport, I turned around and said, "All right, kids—and yes, Thad, that means you, too! Let's go unpack, and then we will go into town for lunch and hit all your favorite spots. Let's get settled in first. We have a week, so let's enjoy every minute together."

We turned onto the dirt road at the entry gate to my in-laws' place, where the Texas flag waved. As we started to unload, I noticed a massive American Indian teepee—about 25 feet tall and 25 feet wide—installed on the back lawn. Walking inside the teepee, I immediately felt cozy, surrounded by soft Navajo printed blankets and beautifully covered chairs.

I'd found my place for solitude and quiet times with the Lord. I could come here early each morning and pray fervently for Mom and Dad and our family and children. In fact, for the next seven days, I did just that with my hot coffee, fleece robe, and slippers.

The next morning, before walking out to the teepee, I came across something on my phone written by Andrew Bonar:

> "In order to grow in grace, we must spend a great deal of time in quiet solitude. Contact with others in society is not what causes the soul to grow most vigorously. In fact, one quiet hour of prayer will often yield greater results than many days spent in the company of others. It is in the desert that the dew is freshest and the air is the most pure."

Great solitude, for an hour, in the freshest dew and air, was exactly what I needed and what I'd found. There was no doubt in my mind the Lord was calling me to Him, especially that week. I wouldn't understand how much I needed it until later.

OUR DAYS WITH THE KIDS were packed with biking, hiking, swimming, golfing, rafting, a day camp for Elijah, and even a few soccer lessons for the girls. We had dinners out with other families and we cooked at home. The kids canoed in a pond, caught a few fish, and Thad played a round of golf with his buddies. It was as if I were trying to fit in as much activity as possible to make up for lost time with my family. I even researched puppies online, thinking I'd surprise the kids with a dog since I had been so mentally unavailable lately. I must really have been losing my mind if I thought I had time to take care of a puppy.

"Hey, kids! Daddy and I thought it would be fun to go to the club and swim. Elijah, you and Daddy can drive the golf cart around and hit a few golf balls, and we can shower there and have dinner at sunset. How does that sound?"

All three kids yelled simultaneously, "Awesome!"

Thad and I knew they would love it. It was one of our favorite things to do as a family. There were M&Ms around for the kids, and the girls loved the "spa shampoo," as Emery called it, in the ladies' locker-room showers.

Not long after we arrived, I could hear the kids playing Marco Polo in the pool. "Marco!" Emery yelled. "Polo!" Frensley yelled back. They went back and forth, laughing and screaming. As I sat in my chair, sun hat in place, I listened to the voices of the kids playing, the sound of babies crying, and the splashing of water as the kids each tried to make the biggest splash.

"Mom, can I please have a snow cone? Pretty please?" Elijah was obsessed with snow cones.

"Sure, honey. Why not? Enjoy!"

His hazel eyes lit up, and his long eyelashes nearly touched his eyebrows. "Really? Yes!" He gave a big fist pump toward his itty-bitty waist, as if I'd never let him have a snow cone before.

He looked over at Emery, who was on the opposite side of the pool, and walked quickly toward her. "Mom said I could have a snow cone!" Emery looked over at me and mouthed the words, "Can I?" I gave her a thumbs-up. They ran to the concession stand, eagerly waiting in line to order their unnaturally flavored rainbow snow cones.

Feeling so carefree that day, I said yes to nearly anything and everything. Love was in the air. I was sunbathing in one of my favorite places, and I was with my husband and children. Thad was next to me reading a book. I reached over, grabbed his hand, and whispered, "I love you."

He smiled back with his charming dimples and gave my hand a squeeze. "I love you, too."

That night, as we sat at the dinner table overlooking a beautiful sunset, I thought back to the summer before. We had invited Mom and Dad to Colorado, along with two of their favorite couples. We had celebrated Mom's seventieth birthday and had sat at this same table overlooking God's one-of-a-kind sunset. Mom hadn't even known it was her birthday. Even though we had wished her a happy birthday several times that day, when she saw the special flower arrangements at our dinner table that night and the gifts at her spot, she asked, "What's this for?"

Now, as I looked out, I smiled at God's sunset. It was not a coincidence we were sitting at the same table. It was His reminder that He was present. He heard everything I said to Him, and He knew my every thought before I even spoke it. *I love You, too, Lord. Thank You for my front-row seat tonight to see Your beauty. I know You have me exactly where you want me.*

THE NEXT MORNING, MY ALARM went off at 5:20 a.m. Donning my robe and slippers, I headed to the kitchen for my cup of coffee. I couldn't wait to get in that cozy chair in the teepee and seek God's heart and all that He had to say.

Settled in the teepee, I opened one of my favorite devotionals, *Streams in the Desert,* and read: "We pray for patience for many years, and when something begins to test us beyond our endurance, we run from it. We try to avoid it, we see it as some insurmountable obstacle to our desired goal, and we believe that if it was removed, we would experience immediate deliverance and victory."

These weren't the words I anticipated reading and hearing.

Hesitantly, I read on. "Turn from your running and submit. Claim by faith to be a partaker in the patience of Jesus and face your trials in Him.

There is nothing in your life that distresses or concerns you that cannot become submissive to the highest purpose. Remember, they are God's mountains. He puts them there for a reason, and we know He will never fail to keep His promise."

I was like the mighty oak being tested by the storms. Although I prayed fervently for Dad and for deliverance, I had never fully surrendered my mom and dad to God and asked Him to take them for me. I had prayed for patience, but had I fully submitted to His purpose?

Things hadn't been going the way I wanted them to go. I wanted help, and I wanted it immediately. I wanted God to free my father so he would live a longer, healthier life. He needed more breaks and time for himself. I wanted Him to heal my mother and make her well again. God was asking me to accept this situation, and I was not willing to accept it. I was only willing to ask Him to change it and provide the help I thought was necessary to bring peace.

That morning in the teepee, I cried for what seemed like hours, going through an entire tissue box. I opened my hands and fell to my knees, asking God to free me from my attempts to fix things, and I apologized for not seeing our family's situation through His perspective. I wanted Him to teach me, but how could He teach me if I was only waiting for the answer I desired?

I released my parents to God. As difficult as it was, I released my dad and any decisions that needed to be made about Mom to God. I couldn't make decisions for my dad, and I knew God loved Dad even more than I did. I pleaded with God to give me balance in my life. I began to understand at a much deeper level that He truly does work everything for good, no matter how chaotic or out of order life may seem. I thanked Him for carrying the burdens that lay ahead so that I wouldn't have to. They were no longer mine to carry, but His, and I felt a welcome sense of relief.

Two days later, Thad and I joined our friend Amanda and a few others on a long hike up a mountain, or so we thought. It turned into a run because Amanda ran the whole way. We could see her every second or third turn, as her white visor peeked through the tree branches.

I wasn't sure I could pick up the pace to a full jog, and there were so many times I nearly gave up. But thank goodness I didn't. I can't explain why I felt the need to finish this run without stopping. Perhaps I had been through so much pain mentally and emotionally over the past year that I wanted to feel like I could accomplish something challenging, that I had some control over something in my life, even though I knew God was in control at all times. I had no idea what it would feel or look like at the very top, but I knew I wanted to get there as fast as I could, no matter how painful it was or how winded I might feel.

The "hike" was amazing—I'd never seen views like the ones we saw that day. The trail went up peaks and through white-barked trees, then careened down into valleys and past streams, skirting fields full of wildflowers. There were flowers everywhere, in every vibrant color of the rainbow: crimson, rose, peach, rust, gold, sapphire blue, cobalt, daffodil yellow, and, my favorite color, purple. We went from one field of amazing flowers to the next, the terrain always changing. The scenery changed so much that we never knew, from one moment to the next, what we would see in the open fields.

It was hard. There were moments while jogging uphill that I thought, *I'm not strong enough for this. I don't have what it takes.* Every time my feet hit the trail, the fears and doubts rose inside of me. But every time I thought I wouldn't make it, I'd take a deep breath and pray, *Help me, God. I can do all things through Christ who strengthens me.*

Thad and I made it to the top. My legs shook, my feet swelled, and my arms ached. I had doubted myself from the beginning, but now I felt like a champion for running almost the entire hike, not letting the voices of fear and doubt win. As I stood breathing heavily on the mountain, the air never smelled sweeter. I looked out at all of God's wondrous creation and felt a warm, blissful gratitude pour through me. He had given me so much.

That same afternoon, I received a call from Dad. "Hey, Sarah. Remind me when you come back to Dallas?"

"On Monday. Are you okay?"

"I'm okay. I'll be fine through Monday. When you get back, we need to sit down and talk. I'm ready to look at some places for your mom. I need help. I can't do this anymore."

My face felt warm, and I started to feel a little nauseated. "Uh, okay. Wow. Want me to call Ginny and see if she can stay with Mom while we visit?"

"That would be great. I'm sorry to have called you, but I just needed to tell you." He was honest and to the point.

Shortly after we hung up, my mother-in-law, Joan, just back from the farmers market, walked into the kitchen. The kids were sitting on bar stools at the kitchen island, snacking on homemade kettle corn.

"Kids, why don't y'all take your popcorn outside and play some soccer or swim while I help Mia unload some groceries?"

Mia is what the kids called Joan. When they were little, she would say, "Come to Mia!" and the name stuck.

Joan was a soft-spoken woman of faith who always thought before she spoke. Her mother was also diagnosed with Alzheimer's disease, but not EOAD like my mom. Joan knew the disease's toll on a loved one or spouse. I felt the need to share Dad's call with her about looking for placement homes. I was so discouraged. I needed the confirmation that this step was the right one and reassurance that we had exhausted every other option in Mom's care.

"Joan, my dad called. I think he's crashed and hit his wall. He told me he wants to sit down and talk about visiting memory-care facilities." My eyes watered and my neck ached. The look on Joan's face was so empathetic and loving that I could tell she agreed with his decision.

"Sarah, your dad loves her so much. He would never make a decision that wasn't best for your mom. It is such a hard disease." She wrapped her arm around me and gave me a hug. I did everything I could not to sob on her shoulder, but I couldn't help myself. My tears began to soak through her white cotton shirt.

Stepping away, I grabbed a soft paper towel to dry my eyes.

"It really does wear down the caretaker," she said. "He can't do this alone anymore. Honestly, I think this is what he needs. I know it's hard, and I know there doesn't seem to be a perfect answer, but I do know that you and he and so many others have prayed for God's guidance. Perhaps this is God calling him to release your mom and accept that there are professionals out there who truly do know what they are doing. They are experts with this disease."

I sat down on a bar stool, leaning my elbows on the island. "I know you're right. It's just so hard. He wants to take care of her through sickness and health. You know my mom. How in the world would we place her? She's tough, she's strong, and she's young. I can't imagine her living in her own room in a memory-care facility with a bunch of eighty-year-olds! I don't even know how we would get her there."

"You don't need to worry about the how right now," Joan said. "What's important is that your dad gets help for your mother. And Sarah, he will be able to take better care of her when he is more rested. When we are exhausted, it is very difficult to take care of others. Think about how tired you get sometimes taking care of the kids day in and day out, and then imagine your dad, at seventy, taking care of your mom twenty-four hours a day, seven days a week. He needs rest and needs to know it is okay to receive help."

She looked out the kitchen window at the mountains, staring heavenward as she contemplated what she wanted to say. The words she said next penetrated my heart.

"I choose to believe that placing her doesn't mean he's gone back on his word to love her 'in sickness and in health.' He will still take care of her, no matter where she lives. He still loves her! He just needs assistance and to know she is safe. He won't be leaving her. He will actually be taking *better* care of her because he will get a mental break and be able to love her more fully for the rest of her years."

For the first time, I realized Daddy would still love Mom and be her one and only, no matter where she lived. Joan was right: Placing Mom in a home didn't mean Dad would stop caring for her. It meant the opposite. He'd be acting out of complete love, making sure she got the care she needed.

Joan gave me another hug and told me how much she loved Dad, Mom, and me. She told me she hated what we were going through. It brought back memories of her own mother and her difficult move to Dallas from Houston and into a home. It was as if she were reliving moments in her life as we talked.

"Please pray for Dad, Joan. I don't feel like I can tell him what to do, but I can tell you that I have prayed *so* much for clarity and for him to make the best decisions for Mom. Honestly, I am not scared, because God is answering my prayers, but I am not sure I am prepared for the answer. 'Be careful what you pray for' is what's on my mind right now!"

We laughed at the truth of that statement. Then we stared out the window, quietly absorbing the beauty of the mountains, wondering what God had in store.

FLYING HOME WITH THE KIDS, I realized I was dreading the days ahead. Frensley, Emery, and Elijah wore headphones. The girls had a dual connector plugged into Frensley's iPad while they watched *Miracles from Heaven*, and Elijah was watching a faith-based football movie. My heart warmed, knowing they had chosen religious movies to watch. At the same time, my heart was heavy knowing that soon they would probably refer to Pop and Beauty's house as just "Pop's house." Beauty and Pop went together in their eyes, so the thought of their separation and its effects on the children weakened me.

I went to the airplane restroom. The moment I shut the door and turned the lock, I leaned over the metal sink and wept. I stood there, one hand on each side of the sink, while the plane bounced through the clouds. Tears fell into the sink as I reached for tissue to wipe my cheeks and runny nose.

Then I had a talk with God.

God, maybe You should just take her home. Maybe I should have been praying You would just bring her home to You. I don't know if I can watch my parents live separately. They have been married almost fifty years. Lord, I don't think I can watch this. They live together. That's their house. They have never not lived together since their wedding day. How can they be in the same city yet sleep in different places? They are married, not divorced. She's not dead. She's alive. I don't know what's best, God. You let her die and bring her home to You and her family? Or move her away to a new place where she is safe and You can love her there? It's too much. I can't, God, I just can't handle this heaviness.

Was He even hearing me? As I felt a headache coming on, an announcement came over the loudspeaker.

"This is your captain speaking. We are beginning our descent and ask that each passenger buckle up and prepare for landing."

I stared at myself in the mirror. For a moment, I wondered which hat I would wear once when we landed. Mom hat? Caretaker hat? Daughter hat? Self-pity hat? Leave-me-alone hat? Life-is-too-much hat? Walk-with-fear hat? Anxiety hat? Sadly, the trust hat did not pop into my head as an option.

The second I unlocked the restroom door, I had a choice to make. Three precious children waited for me with no understanding of what was running through my mind, and I needed to be strong and courageous and act normal. I thought about Thad, who was driving our car home from Colorado. I wondered if he was out of the mountains yet.

Then I laughed at my reflection in the mirror. *Wow, Sarah. No makeup, swollen eyes, and greasy hair in a bun. Welcome back to Dallas! Mom hat it is.*

I CALLED BIG GINNY A few hours after we got home, but her phone went to voicemail. I left a message.

"Ginny, I need to talk to you. We desperately need your help this week.

Dad wants to go look at facilities for Mom. He is crashing, and he texted me that he can't do it anymore. I think he's hit rock bottom, and I need to help him as soon as possible. Is there any chance you can occupy Mom for several days? I want to line up two days so Dad and I can see as many places as possible. And please pray for Daddy. I can't believe it's come to this."

She texted me back a few hours later. "Absolutely. Just tell me where to be and when. This won't be easy for you and your dad, but I do think it's the best thing for everyone."

Best thing? How does she know that? Why does she say that? Joan thought so, too. Dad is ready. I'm not sure I like the "best thing," but what other options are there?

I stopped at my parents' the next morning. Dad looked like he had aged two years since the day I'd left. I felt like I needed to tape a sign on him that read "Very Fragile: Do Not Touch."

"Hey, Mom!" I called brightly. "I've missed you. Let's go get our Starbucks iced chai."

She was more reserved than usual. I wasn't sure why until she turned to Dad and, afraid to leave him behind, said, "Are you okay here?"

At that moment, I realized that she was clinging to Dad more than ever and that she'd become more reluctant to leave him, even to go somewhere with me.

To me, he subtly gave away his true feelings of, "Please go. I need to sleep for hours."

But in his love for her, Dad, in undeniable patience and graciousness, said, "Don't worry about me, Beck. I'm going to take a little nap and rest. You go have fun with your daughter. I know you have missed being with each other."

I hugged Daddy goodbye, and I whispered in his ear as Mom headed toward the front door, "Hang in there, Dad. Ginny is available, and we will get through this together. Help is on the way."

• • •

MOM AND I WENT BACK to my house, grabbed the kids and their swimsuits, then headed to the club. I wanted the day to be full and long so that Dad could rest and spend time alone.

One of Mom's favorite things to do was dip her feet in a swimming pool. We picked an area that had four lounge chairs under a large umbrella as Frensley got towels.

"Hello, Mrs. Smith! How are you today? Hello, Mrs. Bearden!" It was so nice to be back and welcomed by the club's sweet staff. They knew my mom, and they also knew her need for chilled nonalcoholic wine or virgin margaritas.

Edgar smiled at me and turned to Mom. "Mrs. Bearden, would you like something to drink?"

She turned and looked at me. "What are you having?"

"I'm going to get an ice-cold Arnold Palmer! It's tea mixed with lemonade, and they put a mint leaf in it. Would you like to try that, Mom?"

"Sure, I'll have that."

I set two chairs in the shallow part of the middle pool where I could dangle my feet in cool water four or five inches deep. On a hot August day in Dallas, it was the perfect spot to be.

Mom started kicking and splashing her feet in the water like a little child. "Look! Splash! It's fun! Feels good."

Sitting in her big black sun hat, she had gotten her shorts sopping wet. I always traveled with an extra pair of underwear and shorts for her, never knowing when she might have an accident. But this day, it was no accident—it was fun in the sun.

Frensley, Emery, and Elijah would swim up to us or jump in, making the largest splashes they could for Beauty. She would judge who had the best splash, and it was one of her best days, and ours, that summer.

We had two Arnold Palmers, a glass of "wine" and a "margarita." She kept repeating, "This is the nicest hotel I've ever seen!" Although her ability to recognize places was slipping away, her love of family was not.

I sent Dad a text about three hours later.

"Hey, hope you are okay. Thinking about you and want you to know how much I love you. Mom is having a blast at the club."

Dad loved to respond with emojis. I received a thumbs-up, a smiley face with hearts for eyes, and then, "Thanks, Sarah. I'm so tired. I'm sorry to drag you through this with me."

Drag me through this with him? He wasn't dragging me through anything. This monster of a disease was dragging our entire family through it together, but Dad and I were taking the brunt of it because my brothers couldn't be as available.

"Dad, don't ever say that again. You aren't dragging me through anything. God has a plan. He will reveal it one day. All I know is that I will love on her as much as I can. We have each other, and God will give you the strength you need to get through this. Remember, He won't give us anything we can't handle."

As I typed those words, I thought back to my reflection in the airplane mirror. I remembered the prayer and the questions I had asked of God, then realized I had forgotten at the time the very words I had just shared with Dad. He promises to give us only what we can handle. That day on the plane, I had cried out to Him, "I can't. I just can't."

I also thought back to the day Dad called me in Colorado. I realized it wasn't a coincidence I'd gone on such a beautiful hike that morning. With God, nothing is ever a coincidence. As I ran through open fields of wildflowers, I had the distinct feeling that anything could happen. Sometimes the path was easy, sometimes it was hard; sometimes the fields were empty, and sometimes they bloomed with colors that took my breath away.

Many things can appear to be challenges or tests—but you can find love in all of it. Love gets you to the top, and it gets you to the bottom. It gets you through the hills, the streams, and the valleys. Sometimes the terrain is calm, and sometimes it's difficult. But if you cloak yourself in love, you can make it to the top.

Still sitting in the pool, Mom and I heard Elijah yell, "Look at me!

Look at me, Mom!" Elijah sprang off the diving board. "Did you see that, Beauty? Did you see my splash?"

"I sure did! It was a big one!" Mom turned to me. "He's so cute. I love him so much."

"I know you do, Beauty. And he loves you big. All our kids do. Thanks for spending the day with us at the pool. I hope you always remember you are *so* loved."

She grabbed my hand, then turned back to watch the diving board. She scanned the slide, the swimming lanes, and the baby pool. Looking at me again, she squeezed my hand and said, "This is the best. Thanks, Sarah. I love you, Daughter."

FOURTEEN

WALLS WITHOUT WINDOWS

August 2016

─•❖•─

I T WAS A TUESDAY. THE second Ginny drove away with Mom, Dad jumped in his car to meet me at our first appointment. Knowing it would be difficult, we left my car at the first assisted-living facility and rode together to the rest of the appointments that day.

I looked around as Dad approached the reception desk. The lobby had tan walls, dark wood ceilings and trim, and gold curtains hanging from their thick rods to the floor. A tall flower arrangement stood on the entry table, and a large sitting area with tan leather couches and wood-trimmed chairs was nearby. Next to it, set off by columns, there appeared to be a game room with square tables and decks of cards, puzzle boxes, and dominoes.

"Hello. I'm David Bearden. We have an appointment with Mary."

Dad, unshaven, tried to smile, but his body language was anything but happy or relaxed. He held a stapled packet of paper along with information he had printed from the Internet.

Dad and I sat and looked at each other. Shaking our heads, we were thinking the same thing: *I can't believe we are here. We have taken the first step.*

But this facility didn't ease our minds.

It feels too quiet. The wood trim is too dark. Too much brown leather furniture. It's depressing and boring. Nobody is around. Nobody's playing games. It's dead in here.

"Dad, this place is depressing. I can't see Mom living here."

He spoke in a low tone. "It just doesn't feel right. Maybe it's just me not wanting to do this. Will all places be like this?" He paused and looked at me with tears in his eyes. "Lonesome is how I think it looks and feels. My first impression is that no, I don't see Mom living here. I don't think I can leave her someplace like this."

Then a tall, pretty woman came around the corner to greet us.

"Hello, Mr. Bearden, and—tell me your name again? Is it Sarah? You are Rebecca's daughter, correct?"

"Yes, ma'am. I am her daughter." I spoke softly as my heart beat a little faster.

She turned the palm of her right hand upward, like Vanna White on *Wheel of Fortune*, and she motioned us toward the thick brown columns. She took us to the square tables that I'd pegged as the game room.

"I know this is probably not easy for the two of you to be here. I see from your online paperwork that Rebecca has EOAD. Is that correct?" She looked directly at Dad.

"Yes, that's correct."

Dad wasn't one to embellish or give extra details unless asked.

"Tell me a little about Rebecca. Is she incontinent yet?"

I turned to Dad as he looked down and twirled his thumbs. "That hasn't been an issue at all yet. She can use the restroom by herself, and she has not had an accident, at least not that I know of."

She smiled. "Just so you know, Mr. Bearden, not all people with Alzheimer's are incontinent, but it is a very high probability at some point that she will be. There are many different causes for incontinence, and it's our job to help them retain a sense of dignity. I understand it is not an easy topic to talk about."

As she took notes, she continued with her questions.

"How is her short-term memory? Can you leave her at the house alone, or has she wandered off and gotten lost? I am trying to gauge where she is in the disease and if memory care is the only option for her. As you may know, we also have assisted-living floors, so we always want to make sure our potential residents are placed in the proper area to help them have a better quality of life."

"Her short-term memory has definitely become more of a problem. Sarah can spend several hours with her one morning or afternoon, and an hour or two later, Rebecca won't remember being with her at all."

I was so proud of Dad, because I knew he did not want to be there. However, I noticed as he told Mary more about Mom, he brushed over things I felt were important.

"She doesn't wander off," he said. "I mean, she does like to go on her walks, but I go with her, or I follow her, so she still knows where she lives and how to get around."

Doesn't wander off? But she got lost, and I found her! And didn't the SMU police bring her to you? That is called wandering off and getting lost, right?

Knowing it wasn't my place to answer for Dad, I didn't interrupt or answer questions directed to him. However, I was wondering whether he was afraid to admit she had gotten lost, or if perhaps he had forgotten about it. Or, maybe he was in denial or not seeing things clearly out of sheer exhaustion. Whatever it was, it didn't sit well with me.

Then Dad said, "Well, once. She did wander off once, and it really did scare her. Sarah saw her and called me. I think Beck remembers it because when I bring it up to her and remind her she can't go for walks alone, she remembers and expresses how scared it made her feel, and she hasn't done it since."

I respectfully added to that comment.

"Mary, like Dad is saying, she did wander off, and it did scare her at the time. But isn't this disease one of those things where Mom may make a spontaneous decision to do something, whether she remembers what may have happened before or not? For example, couldn't she walk out again on her own and get lost if she's done it once or *twice* already?"

Mary was taking notes, but she looked up at me when I said "once or twice." I'd placed the emphasis on "twice."

I tried not to look at Dad, not wanting him to think I was trying to prove a point or be disrespectful. This was such a delicate matter and conversation, but I also wanted to hear more from a professional.

"That is correct, Sarah. Once someone with Alzheimer's wanders off or gets lost, a red flag goes up. In the moment, they think they know where they are going. They are in their own neighborhood or a familiar place. And, in a flash, they are disoriented. They become confused, and therefore they also don't know to ask—or are unable to ask—for help. Terrible things can happen when someone gets lost because of traffic and weather conditions and things like that. They may walk alongside a curb and trip or fall into the street, or they may cross a street without looking out for cars. They are like children, and it's our job to keep them safe and protected. In many cases, if one is lost for twenty-four hours or more, there is usually serious injury or death."

After more questions, Mary said, "Well, it sounds to me that your wife does, in fact, need to be in memory care. She is past assisted living. What I would like to do is give you a tour. Do you have time for that?"

Dad turned to me and gave my knee a gentle squeeze. "No, I am sorry, but we do have two more appointments today. But I thank you very much for your time."

He was done. *Scratch this place off the list*, I thought. He couldn't get out of there quickly enough. And I didn't blame him. I wanted to at least like the feel of Mom's new home.

It wasn't just the ambience, but the lack of activity and how quiet it was downstairs that bothered Dad. Mary was helpful, and the facility was reputable, but Dad trusted that the right place for Mom would *feel* right to him.

We sat in his car, taking it all in.

"I don't know, Dad. This all seems so surreal. Is it making you question what to do?"

"Well, yeah, but what else am I supposed to do? I can't do it anymore."

He rubbed his eyes. He was so emotional and doing everything in his power to maintain his composure.

"Dad, there is something you need to know. Your children support you. We love you. David, Gabriel, and me. We all love you. You have to remind yourself you wouldn't be here if God didn't lead you here. You have prayed for His guidance as much as I have and probably even more."

He patted me on the leg, whispered "Thank you," and we drove away from that depressing place.

THE NEXT APPOINTMENT WAS A twenty-minute drive from the first place. We were stunned by the difference as we walked toward the main building.

"Wow," I said. "This place looks really nice."

Surrounded by a park with benches, teak tables, and chairs with patterned umbrellas, it was a new building of dry-stack stone with large windows.

Dad and I walked into an atrium where there was a reception desk with granite countertops, a warm fireplace, and tall ceilings—the opposite of the first place. Behind the reception area, there was a hair salon and spa, and through the back window, colorful flowers surrounded a beautiful green lawn.

As the elevator doors opened, several people stepped out, smiling and happy. One lady even came out with her small dog on a leash.

"I mean, Dad. Totally different!"

After checking in, we were directed to the waiting area, where we sat in two large swivel chairs flanking the fireplace.

"This place seems pretty incredible," he agreed. "It feels so much better than the last place. I can't even believe the difference."

Christie sat down with us, asking many of the same questions Mary had. Then she began our tour.

As we walked on the back lawn, she told us the history of the place.

She showed us all the buildings, some new and some old. The one we had first entered was their newest remodel, which explained the updated look and feel. We turned a corner and walked up to double glass doors.

"This is our memory-care building. As you can see, we use a code box to keep the residents safe. Only family members and caretakers are allowed to know the code, and we have cameras recording at all times for safety."

I noticed two cute women, probably in their eighties, staring at us through the doors. One was waving at me, and the other was trying to push a keypad on the inside. I smiled, waved back, and mouthed, "Hello." Dad waved, also. We continued to stand there and listen but were distracted by the women.

Christie said, "Oh, goodness, I am so sorry, but it would be a good idea if we turn around right now and pretend we don't see them standing there, then head to the other entrance. I apologize."

It wasn't until I heard the words "pretend we don't see them standing there" that I realized what was really happening.

Those precious women were trying to get out. One had her purse over her shoulder like she had someplace to be. She was dressed in a soft pink shirt with a beautiful strand of pearls around her neck. Waving and smiling at me, she started to knock on the glass doors. As I stared into her green eyes, she began to knock a little louder. So much happened so quickly that I had no idea what was going on until we were told to turn our backs on them and walk away, leaving them standing there, banging on the doors and watching us leave.

All I could picture was my mom. My beautiful mom, smiling and waving and knocking on the window for someone to open the door so she could walk outside and smell the fresh air. Would someone smile back at her? Or worse, turn and pretend she wasn't there? All for good reason, of course—to keep her safe—but she would never know or understand why. In Mom's eyes, she would be trapped and abandoned.

As we walked away, Dad said, "So those two women were trying to get out? And they can't? They can't walk around here in this courtyard?"

"That is correct. They have a very strict schedule, and they get out occasionally when the caretakers are with them. Many times, people with Alzheimer's are still living the life they had before, or at least trying to. Some think they need to get to work, and some think they are going on a trip or traveling. We have one lady who was an airline attendant, so she often tells us she is going to miss her flight if she can't leave. It's not easy, but you get used to it. It's our job to keep them safe from wandering off without a health-care professional by their side."

What the hell? Is this a freaking jail?

Dad and I looked at each other, both puzzled. I felt burdened and terribly guilty that those two women thought we had abandoned them.

"Now we are at the other side of the building," Christie was saying. "As you can see, this side has a code and keypad as well, for safety."

Yes, I see it. Thanks for pointing that out again. Are we going to abandon anyone else and pretend like it's no big deal? What if that was my mother? She would want to know the code and not understand why she couldn't have it.

As we entered the building, all I could see were gray concrete walls.

Where are the windows that look out at the green grass and flowers? Where are the granite countertops and sitting areas around the fireplace? What about the salon? Where did that go?

"This is our memory-care building. It's strictly for residents who require 24-7 care and is where Rebecca would be staying. I'm going to show you a room around the corner that is empty and available, if you choose to move her here."

Are you kidding me? This is where my *mom would be? Hell-with-a-double-l no! This is a jail cell.*

I was doing everything I could to stick with the tour, to stay with Dad and not have a meltdown. This was insane. This wasn't home. This wasn't a better quality of life. This was a lockdown life with no freedom.

"Here is the room. The bathrooms have recently been remodeled, and there are outlets for cable television as well. As you may notice, the lights above the bed location are lower because these used to be hospital rooms."

This is a remodel? It's a stainless-steel sink with a shower curtain, a handi-cap shower rail, a bench in the shower, and "hospital-bed lights." Lord, I need some help here! Please calm me down—I think I might lose control.

And then I heard the words, "The great news is they do go out to the other building where we first met for movies and music classes. We have an incredible activities leader who does all sorts of fun exercises and games with them. So they do get out—it just needs to be scheduled."

Okay. Maybe she would get out more often than I think. I mean, Mom needs out. She needs fresh air. She needs a courtyard. She is not an indoor woman.

We continued our tour, but I could not get past the low ceilings and windowless walls. Everyone was so friendly, and the residents seemed happy, but I just couldn't picture my mom there.

Then around the corner, I saw hope, the hope she would have one friend. There was a woman within a few years of Mom's age who had recently been placed. We asked about her and learned she had EOAD and a few other problems. When Dad and I saw her beautiful brown hair, cute outfit, and fit physique, he turned to me and said, "That one would be her friend. I can see them being buddies."

This precious woman was holding another resident's hand, leading her to their next activity. She was like a volunteer on staff, serving and encouraging her to participate. For a few minutes, I felt much better about the place. I saw hope and joy and happiness in this resident, who looked pretty, wore makeup, was freshly dressed, and seemed to love "volunteering" like Mom.

"Isn't she great?" our tour guide asked as we watched her walk away with the other resident. "She has come such a long way. It took about two weeks to get her settled in, but now you would never know it. It's not an easy process, but if you hang in there, the residents can—and most will—get to a place of peace and contentment."

We looked around some more. But once everyone walked away, the walls started closing in again. The lack of windows, the older-looking buildings, and the steel sink and hospital-bed lights resurfaced in my mind.

Mom would turn this place upside down if she were here. There is abso-lutely no way she could live here. You think your residents are happy? Wait until Becky Bearden shows up. She will have them all breaking free! She'd have them going this way and that way and ganging up on every caretaker in here. She's a strong *woman. She'd find a way out, and not just that— she'd rescue every single person here.*

I laughed out loud at my thoughts and shook my head. Dad turned to me and said, "What's so funny?"

My eyes rolled at him. "Oh, I'll tell you in the car."

FIFTEEN

BEAUTY AND ELEGANCE

August 2016

-•⊂✕⊃•-

D EAR HEAVENLY FATHER, I DON'T *know what to pray for this morning. I'm scared and anxious. You tell me to be anxious for nothing, and with everything by prayer and thanksgiving, let my requests be known to You. I thank You, God, for opening the door for Dad and me to visit these potential homes for Mom; but God, I'm anxious and worried. I am worried about placing Mom, taking her away from her home, and I'm scared of how we would do it. I can't see Mom living anywhere but her own home.*

Lord, please help us. Daddy and I are tired. We are emotionally broken. We don't want to drive around and look at these places that seem so depressing. We have prayed for Your will, and we have asked for Your guidance, and I know in my heart You are guiding us, but Lord, please guide us to the place You want Mom. You love her more than we do.

God, please go before us and stand beside us today. Help us get through this day visiting two more places. Give us strength, God. Thank You for loving us, Mom, and our family so much that You will give us the best option possible for her.

In Your holy name, amen.

. . .

MY PRAYERS WERE BIG, ESPECIALLY the second morning, when Dad picked me up again to tour assisted-living and memory-care facilities. The first one was a place we had toured before—this was the facility Daddy and I had visited when they first moved to Dallas. One of his friends had advised him to at least take a look, in case there was a waiting list. It was the farthest from home, about a thirty-minute drive. When you walked in, it felt like a step back in time.

Walt Disney World and Disneyland do a great job creating the ambience of their greatest movies, including the city where they're set. Adventureland has Cars Land, which places visitors in the familiar setting of the movie, with the beautiful mountain backdrops of Cadillac Ranch along Route 66. The stoplight intersections and the street lampposts enhance the town. The scenery is incredible.

Walking through this facility felt a lot like that. It was created to give the Disney experience to its residents, with amenities including a barbershop and salon, a theater, and a "Sweet Shoppe." Mom always loved sweets and a good movie, so we thought we should visit this facility again after two years. Because Mom was now in a new stage, we thought it might appeal to us the second time around.

We walked in and saw "Main Street." Oldies music was playing and black-and-white family photos were hanging on the walls. The facility had different neighborhoods branching off of Main Street. Each had its own wing, based on the level of dementia. There was one large area, as if on a movie set, and three different hallways branching off with key-coded doors to separate wings. The "neighborhood" for Mom, of course, would be the lockdown neighborhood, but at least it didn't feel like she was trapped in a place with no windows, and she could visit Main Street and still be safe. The idea was genius. Dad and I loved the way it felt— until we walked around Mom's potential living quarters.

Our tour guide entered the code, and as we stepped through we saw a large trash can filled to the brim. Straight past the trash bin were two couches and a few chairs. On one couch, a lady was sound asleep with her walker next to her, and on the other was a man sitting and talking to himself. Beside him, another man, sitting straight up, was fast asleep with his chin to his chest. No helpers were around. Just a quiet room with three residents in their eighties either asleep or babbling.

As we walked by the kitchen area, we saw a few people sitting at a table with their snacks. We waved at them, but none raised their hands in reply. Sitting there in their wheelchairs, their faces appeared vacant, as if they were placed there without knowing why.

The rooms were clean and new but small. One lady sitting outside an empty room was staring at a wall. Our tour guide said hello but the woman stared blankly as if she hadn't heard a sound or even seen us.

I hardly heard anything else our tour guide said. Dumbfounded, once again I couldn't believe we were walking around these places thinking Mom could live in one. No friends, no one her age, no activities, and a lot of mental illness. *What if Mom just sat and stared and slept?*

Dad and I were taken into a conference room after the tour, and we had a few minutes to ourselves.

"I don't know, Sarah. Seems like another no. I just don't think I can do it. Not here." Dad was waiting for my feedback. I knew he was making a statement, but by the look on his face, it was also a question.

"I agree. I thought this would be it, honestly, with the Sweet Shoppe, the barbershop and salon, and jukebox and fun music. But clearly she would be the youngest one here, with most people way past her stage. Mom will need more interaction and activities. She has to stay busy and feel like she is doing something. This isn't it. I don't see it either, Dad. I'm sorry."

Dad quickly canceled the interview, "Thank you for your time. We have another appointment, but I will take the folder and materials home to look it over and get back with you soon."

Alrighty then, God. One more stop today.

• • •

"WELL, DAD. THOUGH YOU'VE BEEN to this one, I haven't seen it. All I can say is I've heard great things about it. It's newer, and I know you're concerned about their level of experience, but let's just go in with an open mind. You can do this. God has a plan for Mom. We just need to be patient and keep following His lead."

"I know," replied Dad. "The last time I saw it a year and a half ago, it was under construction. At least now I can see the memory-care building. Who knows? I did reluctantly put a deposit down. I knew there was already a wait list and that a deposit would give us first priority, so we'll see. Maybe this will be the one. I just don't know anymore."

"It sure would be convenient, wouldn't it? It's literally five minutes from our houses. Almost too good to be true," I said.

We both smiled, even though it was all we could do to take another tour.

After parking in front, we walked into the new covered entryway of The Tradition. The automatic glass doors opened to reveal four white leather chairs around a coffee table, on which sat a beautiful arrangement of fresh flowers in a blue and white vase. Crossing the foyer, we walked toward a warm fireplace trimmed in white wood. Windows on each side faced a lovely courtyard with Japanese maple trees, flowers, green grass, and a fountain. Like the other place, the lovely outdoor area was refreshing and inviting. An antique grandfather clock, similar to the one we had while I was growing up, ticked away against the wall. We instantly felt a warmth and strange familiarity in these surroundings. It felt like I was in a home. God's home.

We sat down in a room with a pot of purple hydrangeas, my favorite flowers, on the side table. Looking down the hallway, we could see more windows overlooking the fountain and lawn, and we noticed benches for the residents' use.

A lovely woman, Janet, a few years younger than my mom, came out of her office.

"Hello, Mr. Bearden. Hello, Sarah. It is so wonderful to see you again, David, and to meet you, Sarah. Please, let's sit over here for a few minutes and go over our plan for today, then see if you have any questions. I know this is very tough for the both of you. Please know how sorry I am for all you are going through, and if there is *anything* I can do for you or your family, don't hesitate to call. I also love to pray, so I would be honored if you would like me to pray about anything."

I couldn't explain the look in Janet's eyes, but I felt the presence of the Holy Spirit. Her skin glowed, her smile was joyful, and her voice was tender and soft. She had compassion, and she really cared about us and our situation. This was not just a business transaction for us: We were heartbroken, and she empathized with us. Her eyes never drifted away when we spoke. She listened, didn't take notes, and spoke the truth. She was gentle, kindhearted, and exuded love. She brought peace to our broken hearts.

I immediately started crying. "I'm so sorry, Daddy. I'm sorry, Janet. I'm so tired, but I already love this place. Thank you for taking the time to meet with us. I can't explain it, but this place feels like home. It has felt so comfortable since we first came through that front door."

I wiped the tears from my cheeks. "I love the way it's decorated. It looks like a place Mom would live. The blue and white lamps, the traditional mahogany chairs and the formal side tables remind me of my childhood home. The colors are so soft and calming. The yellows and greens—she loves that soft green. Her home in Houston and now her home in Dallas have that same green. Even the curtains over there on that window look like Mom. Don't you think, Dad?"

"She would love the way it's decorated, that's for sure. It really does remind me of her."

Janet, gracious and speaking softly and kindly, gave us a tour of the entire facility. It had a physical therapy room on the first floor, and to the left was a hallway leading to the first-floor assisted-living area. There were four floors in all, three for assisted living and the fourth for memory care.

Down another hallway, there was another sitting area with two couches, a coffee table, brightly lit lamps and another fireplace with a large mantel. There were picture books to look at and an arrangement of square tables covered with puzzle boxes, cards, and games.

They even had a private "family" dining room with a round antique table and ten chairs painted a soft mint green. I felt like I was stepping into my mom's old dining room in Houston.

With my mouth open and eyes wide, I turned to Dad and shook my head in astonishment. He smiled. "I know, Sarah. This is *so* her! Mom would love it here."

Trying not to get his hopes up, he looked at Janet, "Would Becky be allowed to use this dining room? Could we bring our family here to eat? I already know now by looking at other places she will be on the memory-care floor, so what is the rule or procedure for memory-care residents? Are they allowed down here?"

"Yes, absolutely," she said. "We do it all the time. We just have a caretaker bring her down here whenever you request it. And if you want to have your family here for dinner, you just call me, and we mark it on the master calendar. As a matter of fact, we have a resident here whose family uses it once a month for dinners, so we welcome that."

Dad turned to me. "I really like this place. That is good news."

Janet walked us to the main downstairs dining room. It was fully staffed and seated about 150 people. The staff all had smiles on their faces, were professionally dressed, and knew the residents by name.

I noticed one man pouring ice water.

"Hello, John! How are you today? Would you like your favorite peach tea this afternoon?"

He knew exactly what John wanted. Janet hugged several people on our tour, calling each of them by name. There was movement and activity, people coming and going. Nobody was asleep on a couch. And there were windows everywhere.

Janet guided us to another area and told us about their happy hour. "We have a piano player come every Wednesday at 4:00 p.m. Our residents love him. Your mom is always welcome down here, as long as a caretaker or a family member accompanies her. Some of our assisted-living residents drink wine, but many of our residents drink nonalcoholic wine without knowing it. Their families tell us beforehand, and we get to know each person individually so that we are sure about their beverages. I don't know if that has been a struggle for Rebecca or not, but some of them can go through a drinking phase."

Dad and I laughed, as she had disarmed us. "Oh, man, have we ever! We have a few stories, that's for sure. She would definitely be the nonalcoholic resident," Dad said with a look of pure relief.

Janet led us down the next hallway. "This is our salon. We have a nail station, and we have a lady who comes to do hair. Many of our residents have standing appointments for nails and hair and things like that. It's our goal to maintain their dignity."

Sharing another glance with Dad, I grabbed his hand and squeezed it. "She can always have her hair done, Daddy. Mom would want that. And just think: no nail polish remover in sight. She can't swallow it or ruin her fresh manicures."

"Boy, that's the truth. Yes, she would be in here each week, Janet. We would want that for her," Dad said. When Mom was first diagnosed, Dad had promised he would never let her lose her dignity. To the best of his ability, he would do everything to take care of her, to honor and protect her.

Janet smiled broadly. "May I take you upstairs to memory care now? I know it's not easy, but I hope you go up there knowing she does have this downstairs as well, so please do keep that in mind. There is no doubt Rebecca would be our youngest resident on memory care, so again, I know this is not easy as you look around at the residents. Let me assure you, however, that we have *wonderful* caretakers. They love our residents with all their hearts, and they really do take amazing care of each one. I go up there all of the time. It's our desire to know every single resident in this building, regardless of what floor they live on."

Janet took us up the elevator to the fourth floor. We stepped out into a tiny hallway where a receptionist sat behind a desk. A few steps to the right was a door with a keypad and a small window that looked into a living area with couches and chairs.

"Anyone who comes to the fourth floor must have a code. Once you open the door, you have about ten seconds to come through and shut it behind you or an alarm goes off. This keeps the residents from trying to sneak out or escape. So if it goes off because we didn't make it through in time, you will know why."

I loved Janet. She explained everything. She was very thoughtful, careful to not mislead us or leave out any information that might be important.

Walking into the memory-care floor, I heard someone say, "Come on, Renee, you can do it!"

Music was playing. Then I heard some caretakers yell, "Yay, Renee! You did it!"

"What is going on over there?" I asked.

"It sounds like they are doing a craft or 'bowling'—something fun. But let's go see. They do a great job keeping the residents busy up here, but they also give them the freedom to opt out if they want to. It's important to us and the caretakers that we don't make anyone do anything they don't want to do. We want to give them a sense of freedom in their decisions, if that makes sense."

As we walked in that direction, she showed us a large calendar hanging on the wall.

"This is the activities calendar. They switch it out every month, but you can take a picture of it or look at it at any time to see what they will be doing each day, and to see what outings are scheduled. They do take them out once or twice a month on a small bus to get shakes, burgers, ice cream. The residents love it!"

She can get out in a car? Go get a burger? A shake? With caretakers and be safe? Amazing!

"Hello, sweet Judy." Janet gave her a hug. "How are you today? You look so beautiful in your purple."

"Ohhh, thank you so much! You are so nice!"

Judy was wearing a purple silk top, and her hair was clean and styled so beautifully. She wore glasses and had on light pink lipstick. Her nails were a soft pink as well. She looked as if she had just left the salon downstairs. I was impressed with how "put together" she looked, especially at her age. She must have been in her mid-eighties.

Janet went to the next person. "Good afternoon, Lucy. I see you look happy today."

"Teehee! Thank you! I am," responded Lucy.

Janet walked us over to the kitchen area where much of the action was taking place. A caretaker named Louie was dressed in a cowboy hat with a fake snap gun around his waist. He called himself Billy Bob.

"Howdy, everyone! I'm Billy Bob. And today, we are going to *bowl*! Who wants to bowl?"

Having the energy of a ten-year-old, he was actually sweating from working so hard. As he pushed wheelchairs out one after the other, the patients rolled big plastic beach balls into large bowling pins, knocking them over. Every time someone would knock a pin over, all of the caretakers would yell, "Yayyy!"

Dancing, entertainment, arts and crafts, and other activities like bowling all seemed to happen in the dining room, and there was something for everyone.

The kitchen was beautiful. It had a long countertop and a large stainless-steel refrigerator and sink that were clean and shiny.

Janet showed us the empty bedrooms. They had fairly spacious floor plans with high ceilings in all the apartments. The closets were roomy, and there were individually controlled air conditioning units with thermal windows throughout. The bathrooms had raised vanities and walk-in showers with a seat.

Only four rooms were available, but since Dad had placed a deposit over a year ago, he could have first pick if he placed Mom here. Two of the rooms were on the small side, and one was larger but overlooked a construction site. The last room overlooked a beautiful courtyard with trees and a fountain. It was a closed-in view, in that she couldn't see buildings outside except for the other balconies that also faced the courtyard.

Janet looked at Dad. "What are you thinking, David? Do you like the rooms? Does any room stand out for you?"

"Well, yes. This one. The other is a little larger, but not that much larger. And honestly, Rebecca loves to look out a window, and this by far has the best view. I think I would pick the one with the best view before considering size. What do you think, Sarah?"

"I'm in complete agreement. I don't know how much space she really needs, and when Mom looks out and sees a fountain and flowers and trees, I think it will bring her a sense of peace. I'm with you."

Janet showed us the other three hallways. Each room had a shadow box hanging outside of the door or to the right of the doorjamb. She explained we could fill the shadow box with pictures and memorabilia, or whatever the family felt would make the resident feel loved and at home. There were four sitting areas, two of which had televisions, and a large patio outside that had several round iron tables with chairs and flowered cushions. The patio was safe because it had a large glass window that would not allow residents to walk to the edge, but it was large enough to make them feel like they were outside.

Janet entered the code as we exited the fourth floor, and I left with mixed thoughts. One: *Is this the place You have for Mom, God? It's beautiful.* And two: *I can't imagine Mom living here and not in her home. Are we really at this point, Lord?*

Then I heard Janet say, "It's like a home in a way, right? I hope you feel that, because that is everything the owner intended this to be. A home outside of home for all who live here."

Okay, God. Maybe this is Your place for her, and maybe it's not a place. Maybe it can be a home.

WE FOLLOWED JANET DOWNSTAIRS. AT the reception desk, Dad turned to her and said, "As you know, I've already filled out some paperwork and I placed a deposit a year and a half ago. What do I do now? If I do this, can I hold the room I like for her?"

She told him he needed to fill out a few forms for that specific room, sign a contract, and then decide when he wanted to move her. A social worker, other caretakers, and Janet would work with us on the logistics of getting her there and what was to come.

He would sign a few forms? Sign a contract? That's it? Is he doing this?

Dad and I got in the car and headed home.

"Are you going to do it?" I asked. "You sound like this is it."

"I loved that place. I haven't seen anything like it, and I haven't heard of anything better. It just feels right for Mom. If there are only four rooms left, I think I need to at least hold the one I like for Mom and pray about it for twenty-four hours. I guess this is probably it, honey."

"Okay, Dad. I trust you, but I'm scared. This is all so crazy."

"I know. I just have to remind myself how hard it's been. I've got to get some help."

"I know, Daddy. And I've been praying. It's just that when you pray for so long, for years, then all of a sudden it feels like overnight help comes—you almost aren't prepared for it. It's unexpected." I took a breath. "When would you do this?"

"I don't know, but I can't hold out too much longer. And Sarah, I don't think I can do it. I don't think I can place her myself. You may have to help me. I'm not sure I can take her and leave her. I don't think I'm strong enough to do that."

"I'll help however I can. Are you thinking a week, two weeks, a month? I'm sorry—I am just a little in shock and overwhelmed."

"Whenever it's convenient for you, I guess. Maybe within a month? I don't know. Again, I need to pray about this."

I texted my two brothers and sisters-in-law, asking them to pray for Dad. I told them I thought he'd found her home. When Trish asked me the name of it, she went on its website.

I received an astonishing reply that read: "Just have to share . . . on the front page of the website it reads, 'BEAUTY is everything.' On another page, it reads, 'A place of BEAUTY and Elegance.' Love you, Sis. BEAUTY is in God's hands. Will be praying."

SIXTEEN

DECEPTION

August 4 to August 10, 2016

--•»※«•--

Dear Friends,

I am emailing you because you have been alongside me through my journey of my mom's Alzheimer's disease. It is with a heavy heart that I request your prayers for our family at this time. These last several days have been very painful. My dad and I visited several memory-care homes for Mom, and he has decided it is time for her to be placed. The move will happen either Thursday or Friday of next week. With Thad and the kids traveling to Colorado, it will allow me a full three days to help with the move, transition, and all of the unknowns that go along with it.

I can't tell you how devastating this is for us, yet we do know and accept this is the best thing for my mom. I just ask that you pray for strength, courage, patience, and peace as we go through these next several weeks. I can't really explain my emotions at this time; however, I know God has heard our cries and has Mom and us in the palms of His hands.

My mom does not *know that she is going to be placed, so I ask that you keep this to yourself if for some reason you run into her or my dad (not that you would say anything in the first place, but I just want to be clear).*

I love you all, and I am deeply grateful to each one of you and thankful for your prayers during these past few years (and especially this past year), and I thank you for being there for me and for always checking in to see how Mom, I, and Dad were doing. You have lifted me up so many times without even knowing it! Your encouragement has given me so much strength this past year. I feel blessed to call you my friends.

Love, Sarah

I sent that email August 4, 2016. The day before, Dad and I had come to the conclusion that it was best for me to be available for Mom's move, which meant missing my mother-in-law's seventieth birthday in Colorado with the family the following weekend. With the family gone, I could help Dad with the placement and stay at his house so he would not be alone. While wearing only the daughter hat this time, I was afraid guilt would become the lining of every hat I would wear in the next few years. Though we knew we were making the right decision, at a deep level it felt like a betrayal. My heart was shattered.

Dad tearfully told me he could not place Mom. There was no way he could leave her somewhere. We also knew we could not tell her. She wouldn't understand, she would throw a fit, and it would potentially tear her and Dad apart.

Almost all memory-care facilities have a transition period in which the resident must settle in before their loved ones can visit. Because the time frame varies as each resident adjusts and acclimates, we did not know how long it would be before we could see Mom again.

We met with the head nurse of memory care and the social worker who would help with the emotional pain of placement. The social worker was there to be Mom's advocate. She helped caretakers understand and recognize the emotional reactions from the illness and helped the families and the patient navigate through the confusion and emotional distress.

We sat in a conference room at a rectangular table, with two tissue boxes—one for me and one for Dad—bottled water, and paper and pen for taking notes.

At the head of the table sat Macy, the head nurse and a beautiful brunette whose big smile came with a dimple on each cheek. Compassionate and empathetic, she understood the pain and fear we felt about the upcoming days.

"I know this isn't easy," Macy said. "This is and will be one of the most difficult things you will do in your entire life. David, I'm so sorry, and I want you to know that we will give Rebecca the attention she needs. We will love her and spend time getting to know her. I ask that you trust the process."

Her eyes did not leave Dad's eyes. "Most families start to question the process, and if you can just trust us and give Rebecca time to adjust, I can assure you she will be fine. You will get through this, and so will she. It won't be easy, though."

I looked at Dad. He could barely speak. He didn't cry in front of others, but he couldn't stop rubbing his tearful eyes. He nodded his head in agreement and tried to smile, as if to say thank you, but he simply couldn't speak.

Shelley, the social worker, spoke next. "David and Sarah, this staff gives their hearts to the residents and most would tell you they feel called to take care of those with dementia and Alzheimer's. They have all been trained and have years of experience. I am here not only for Rebecca but also to help you navigate through any confusion and answer any questions or concerns."

Reaching over, I grabbed my fifth tissue. Tears rolled down my cheeks.

"I don't want to do this. I don't know *how* I am going to do this," I told them. "We can't just tell her we are leaving her here. It's not an option. Daddy and I understand that, but how do I get her here? How can I possibly walk her into this place knowing I am leaving her here? It's like I'm lying to my mom and dumping her in a new place with no explanation. I'm taking her from her home. How do people do this?"

I cried harder as I pictured dropping Mom off and not seeing her for weeks. She would be so confused, wondering where I had gone and why I had abandoned her. I envisioned her banging on the doors and wanting out. My mind was so clouded by the image I couldn't think of anything else.

Shelley grabbed my hand and gave it a soft squeeze.

"I will help you both. Again, there is no easy way, and you must know in your heart that you are not abandoning your wife, David, or your mother, Sarah. Let's work together on a plan you feel is the best for Rebecca. You know her better than anyone else."

That's true, we do. Which is why she may need to be drugged to get her into this place.

"Shelley, you're right, we do know Mom. And this is going to sound crazy, but maybe the only way we can get her here is if she's given a Valium or a glass of wine or something. She is so feisty! I've tried 'volunteering' with her at Friends Place, but she lost control when I walked away for just five minutes. It was a disaster. I can't tell her we are going to 'volunteer' and bring her here. She would never set foot in this place."

Shelley reassured me. "We have seen everything. We have seen people drop their loved one off with no issues. We have also had families bring their loved one in after giving them something to sedate them. Not to the point of coming in asleep, obviously, but if a little bit of wine helps or even half a Valium to relax her, it won't hurt her. I would suggest calling her doctor to see what she thinks."

I looked at Macy. "How long do you think it will be until we can see Mom again? My friend who placed her dad didn't see him for two weeks. Do you think that will be the case for us?"

"Honestly, there is no way to predict that. It will probably be a few weeks, yes, but based on what we are hearing and have learned about your mother, she may be more difficult. It could be longer, maybe three to four weeks. It's hard to say until she's here."

Three to four weeks? That's forever!

"Really? You think it could be that *long* before we see her again? I mean, we are all she has right now, and you are suggesting that after I drop her off, she may not see Dad or me for three to four *weeks*? I just don't see how this is going to work. You are going to have a mess on your hands. She is strong, and during her lucid moments, she's convinced that there's nothing wrong with her!"

"I understand," Shelley said. "But as Macy said, if you can trust the process and know we are doing our very best, she can get through it and she will be safe."

She looked into Dad's eyes. "David, you will also get the rest you need. You will *want* to spend time with her instead of being so worn down that you dread taking care of her."

To both of us, she said, "We know how much you love Rebecca. We also understand her age is challenging and that she will be the youngest resident on the floor. We will apply the form that you both filled out and use her gifts and talents in her daily activities, such as planting flowers, serving others, setting tables, dancing, and music. We want the best for her and for your family."

I held Dad's hand. Then we hugged Macy and Shelley, thanking them for caring and helping us through this process.

The meeting had lasted about an hour and a half. We had the placement day scheduled and a plan in place. Once Mom was there, they would put her in the respite room for a few days so she would think it was temporary. It looked like a hotel room, the idea being that the staff would eventually move her into her permanent room once she'd adjusted to her surroundings.

Once she was in the respite room, the movers would bring her things to her room two days later. Macy and the caretakers would distract and redirect Mom to make sure she did not see the movers or us. A few days later, they would transfer her into her room, where her own decorations, towels, artwork, clothes, and bed would be waiting. We believed a slow transition would diminish the abruptness Mom might feel with this move. Of course, Mom might not rationalize it that way. All logic was gone at this point, but this transition plan made us feel better.

As we walked out of that meeting, I realized we would have to take things day by day. We could not predict how long it would be before we saw Mom or how the placement would go. I knew the only way I would get through this was by the strength and grace of God. He would need to carry me through each moment, from the first day to the last. I could not do it without Him.

I CALLED ON A FEW friends for help, including Jennifer, who had helped me unbox Mom and Dad's things when they first moved to Dallas. She was an organizer, worked fast, and had a heart to serve and help others. She also had a son in high school who had started a moving service with a few friends. Since we were only moving a few large items, we felt these boys could do the job quickly and affordably.

I also called Carie, my childhood best friend who lived in Corsicana, Texas. Our parents went to college together, and although we grew up in different cities, our moms made it a priority to keep our friendship tight. I didn't think I could deal emotionally with moving Mom's smaller things, but Carie would know what Mom would like. She quickly agreed to come to Dallas and help out. "You know you can count on me. This is so hard, and I'm heartbroken for you all. I love you, BFF," she said in her soft-spoken, small-town twang.

Carie always called me her BFF. And she really was my best friend forever. She knew me, and Mom, inside and out.

And she was the only friend who could make Mom stop griping. If Mom complained about something or got worked up over a minor thing, Carie, who had been a nurse, would simply say, "Now, Becky. Quit your whinin'! You have a great life, and I don't want to hear one more word, you hear me?" Mom would burst out laughing.

I made the second call to my other dear friend, Little Ginny, the daughter of Mom's close friend, Ginny. Little Ginny and I were like sisters because of our moms, and we'd grown even closer since her move to Dallas years ago.

"We are doing it. Mom is being placed Thursday. I need you with me because I just can't do it alone," I told Little Ginny.

She did not even hesitate.

"I don't know what I have that day, but it's officially off the calendar. I will be there without question. Tell me where I need to be and what time. You know you are doing the right thing, don't you? It's going to be tough, that's for sure, but it's time. Your dad can't do this alone anymore, and neither can you."

I broke into tears over the phone. It seemed like crying was the new me. "I know. It's just that . . . I don't know how I can leave her. I think I have to sedate her, which feels deceptive."

"Well, of course, she has to be sedated," Little Ginny said. "We know how strong and independent she is, and the professionals know how to do this in the least upsetting way. What did your dad say?"

"He agrees. It's hard to feel like we are basically drugging Mom, but he knows it will be the only way. We think I will need to take her somewhere, have some food and a little wine. If that doesn't work, then I'll slip some Valium into her drink. Oh my gosh, it sounds so scary."

"Giving her a glass of wine or a little Valium is not going to hurt your mother," Little Ginny said. "It's just enough to relax her before we walk in. Will it just be us?"

I told her Dad and I had discussed calling Lisa, a caretaker we really liked, but Mom refused to spend more than a few hours with her. Mom had even reached the point of having Dad cancel Lisa's visits. It wasn't that she didn't like Lisa. She didn't want *any* caretaker or "friend" coming over anymore. But of all the caretakers, Lisa was the one Mom liked the most.

"I think we will ask Lisa. It would be nice to have someone experienced with us. I want to take Mom to get her hair done so she will be pretty when she goes in. Then maybe Lisa can meet you, Mom, and me for lunch, and we will celebrate. Hey, your birthday is less than a week away, right?"

That sounds weird. "Happy birthday, my dear friend. Let's go place Mom as your birthday gift!"

"I know that sounds terrible. Great birthday gift, huh?"

Little Ginny laughed.

"If Mom thinks we are celebrating something," I said, "then we will all have a reason to order wine. You know, she finally stopped drinking, so I hope just a little wine will be enough. But I feel so bad using your birthday as an excuse to have lunch and celebrate."

"Don't be ridiculous. I can see past that, Sarah. This is about peace and rest for your dad and safety for your mom."

I knew with Carie and Little Ginny by my side, I could do it. Our three moms were college friends, and we three shared a special bond. They were my soul sisters and are even to this day.

Dad spoke with Lisa, and now the whole team was on board.

THURSDAY, AUGUST 11, WAS FAST approaching. I scheduled Mom's hair appointment for 9:30 that morning. While Tona, Mom's hairdresser, colored and styled her hair, I would meet Little Ginny at Dad's, then we would drive together to pick up Mom. From the salon, we would join Lisa at the restaurant. After lunch, Lisa would ask us to visit some of her "friends" at a nearby care center.

It was all a lie. Once again, I was nauseated just thinking about the manipulation and deception, with Mom the innocent victim.

Why this disease, God? Why this way? How is this love? I hope You forgive me one day, because I don't know if I can ever forgive myself. I trust in Your plan, although it is hard to see the light at the end of the tunnel. We have prayed and we are walking by faith, but the lying and manipulation and deception seem anything but right.

I was a traitor to my own mother.

SEVENTEEN

ABANDONMENT DAY, PART 1

August 11, 2016

⟶⊰⟫✕⟪⊱⟵

THURSDAY MORNING, AUGUST 11TH, I woke up at 5:00. Grabbing my coffee, I headed straight to my prayer room. Each morning, I would spend an hour alone with God before the kids awoke and the busyness began. Today of all days, I needed God to take over. Already weak and emotional, I was not ready for this day.

I sat with the girls during breakfast. Without giving them much detail, I told them what was going on. Elijah was still asleep and too young to understand anyway, but the girls were eleven and twelve years old.

"Girls, I love y'all so much. Please pray that God gives me the strength and courage to help Beauty into her new home because it won't be easy. I'm sorry I can't be with you in Colorado this weekend for Mia's birthday, but I know you will have so much fun. Take good care of your brother and dad."

Emery looked down at her breakfast and asked, "Mom, will Pop be all by himself now?"

"Well, eventually he will be home by himself, but I am going to stay with him tonight and this weekend and next week. When you get back, I know he would love for you to stay with him, too."

I knew Emery, our sensitive child, was thinking about it too much.

She and Mom, so much alike, had a unique connection, different from those of the other grandkids.

"Em, look at me."

Her big brown eyes locked onto mine without blinking.

"Pop will be okay. Beauty will be okay, too, because this is the best thing for her. It will take time for her to adjust, but she can do it. Pop can't care for her alone anymore. You have witnessed things that have been extremely difficult for him and me—for all of us. But he is a strong man and has lots of wisdom and courage. Please don't worry about Pop, all right?"

She had tears in her eyes but nodded her head. "Okay, Mommy. I just don't want Pop to be alone."

Frensley, deep in thought, had a distant look in her wide hazel eyes. I knew she wanted to share what was on her heart.

"What is it, Frensley?"

"Well, I just . . . how are you going to get Beauty there? I mean, are you going to tell her or what? She's going to be so mad at you, Mom!"

We both laughed, and then Emery smiled and backed up her sister. "Yeah, Mom, she's going to be *so* mad!"

"It won't be easy, but y'all don't worry about the details of today. What is important is to be grateful that God is in control. He will go before me and before Beauty. I trust Him. We can cast all of our fears and anxieties on Him. He will drive this train for me today. He will get me through."

I was strong for the girls, and deep down I was terrified. But it had to be done, and I had to believe He would help me through the coming hours.

After dropping Thad and the kids off at the airport, I went straight to Mom and Dad's house to pick Mom up for her hair appointment.

Okay, God. Here we go. You are my rock and refuge. You are my shepherd. Lead me, please.

"Good morning, Beauty! Are you ready to get all pretty today? Time to get those roots touched up."

"Yes, let me grab my purse."

Mom always carried a purse, and whether at a nail salon, hair salon, restaurant, or hotel, she always wanted to hand a few extra dollars or a $20 bill to those serving her.

"Oh, Mom, you don't need a purse today. Dad's already paid, and he's given me some money so you can tip—no need for a purse."

Mom looked so beautiful that morning. She was wearing a turquoise outfit that showed off her olive skin, and her nails were manicured from the day before. She was tan from walking around the block with Dad, and her makeup and bronzed cheeks enhanced that. She had managed to put on her metallic rose-and-bronze eye shadow perfectly; the corners of her eyes were even lit up with a smudge of shimmery soft pink. I could also smell the perfume I'd purchased for her years ago. Awed by her beauty and that she looked so put together, I struggled again with placing her. I doubted for a moment we were doing the right thing.

Dad, pale as a ghost, walked up behind Mom. Pain and heartbreak were written across his face. He was doing everything in his power to keep his game face on. The reality of all the brokenness engulfed Dad.

He knew when she walked out of the house it would be the last time he'd see her go out their front door. The night before was the last for them to sleep in the same bed in their home, and that morning had been the last time they would sit in their living room having toast, turkey bacon, and coffee together. It was also the last time he watched her pick up pecans from the sidewalk as she walked to the car.

His pain gave me chills. All I could think about was driving away and my dad falling to his knees in agony, crying out to God over the loss of living with his wife. Overnight, he would practically become a widower.

Sarah, you have got to be strong for him. No fear. Be strong.

"You ready to go, Mom? Give Dad a hug. We don't want to be late."

Barely able to watch them hug, I wanted to weep and go hug her with him.

"I love you, Beck. Don't ever forget how much I love you."

Mom kissed him on the lips.

Dad gently patted her on the back, then looked at me tearfully as Mom walked away. I just wanted it to end.

Barely able to lift his hand to wave, I knew he was thanking me, and I knew there was no way he could have placed her.

Mom threw a pecan out toward the street, turned around to Dad and waved, then said words burned forever in my mind.

"I'll be back later! I love you!"

Oh, Mom. You won't be back here. I'm so sorry for what we're about to do.

All Dad could do was stand there with a fake smile. Then he shut the door and faced the cries of his pierced heart.

"GOOD MORNING, REBECCA," TONA SAID as she bent down and gave Mom a tight hug. "I'm so happy to see you!"

Tona was beautiful. She had big blue eyes and long, blondish, wavy hair. Her body was lean from yoga and exercise. Having battled cancer and other health problems, she stuck to a healthy diet. Her zeal for life was incredible.

We couldn't just leave Mom with anyone, but Tona had experience with Alzheimer's disease after going through it with her grandmother. She knew how to speak to Mom, engage her in conversation, and redirect her when needed. Mom trusted Tona, so I could leave and come back for her.

I went back to Dad's to wait for Little Ginny. He was somber, his eyes lifeless and full of tears. He could barely talk.

After sitting in silence awhile, I said to him, "Daddy, everything is going to be okay. God is in control, and He led you to this decision. So as painful as it is, you are doing the right thing."

He looked down, wiping his eyes the entire time.

Leaning forward I said, "I know, and everyone else knows, that this is not the path you would have chosen for Mom. You are being obedient to God and trusting His ways and plan for Mom and you. You are following His way because it is the only way. You taught me that!"

Dad smiled and looked up at me as he wiped his eyes again. "I know all that you are saying is true. It's just the guilt and sadness. The lies. The feeling of abandonment. She doesn't deserve this, and I don't want her to ever think I have neglected her."

We sat silently a few more minutes. I couldn't argue with those feelings or say anything to make them go away.

The doorbell rang. It was Little Ginny, which meant it was time to pick up Mom.

Opening the door, I mouthed to Little Ginny, "He's not good."

She came in and hugged him. "Hey, David. I'm really sorry for today. I know this is terribly painful, but I promise you this will be the best thing that could happen for Becky and you."

"Thank you, Ginny. And thank you for doing this. I'm sorry that you are in this position, but I just couldn't do it. I really appreciate you being here for Sarah. She couldn't do this without you."

"I would do absolutely anything for you two. You're family!"

I hope it's okay to leave him alone. Will he be okay by himself?

I had mentioned to him days ago that maybe he should call my brother Gabriel to stay with him, but Dad, always a private griever, turned that offer down.

We hugged for a long time. "Daddy, I love you. Are you *sure* you're going to be okay? I can call Gabriel or someone to be with you."

"No, no. I'll be fine."

"Just pray for God to take over. That's all we can ask. I am walking by faith and not by sight. I feel totally blind as to what the day will bring."

As we parted, he said, "Just remember, Sarah. Moment to moment. Just like the disease. Just be in the moment. God will do the rest."

LITTLE GINNY AND I, TOGETHER in her car, headed back to Tona's salon.

"Ginny, I am so grateful you are here. I am so nervous, I'll definitely be having a glass of wine at lunch!"

"*A* glass of wine?" she said. "How about two?" We both laughed. But I knew that drinking a glass of wine was not going to heal my broken heart. Only God could do that.

Little Ginny's smile was so big. She had the high cheekbones and infectious laugh of her mother. She was so close to me that she knew when to laugh and when to be serious.

I had arranged for us to meet Lisa at P.F. Chang's in the mall, where Mom had gone several times with Big Ginny. I didn't want to take her to a restaurant in our neighborhood, but someplace where it was unlikely we'd run across friends who might disrupt the mission.

"Did you bring a Valium?" Little Ginny asked.

"I just hate the thought of drugging my mom. It's so terrible," I said.

"You aren't *drugging* your mom, Sarah. Let's be real. It's a very low dose, just enough to take the edge off. Do you see what I'm saying?"

"You're right. I may need you or Lisa to help me do it, though, if it comes to that."

I looked out the window as we drove past the neighborhood houses, the Starbucks that Mom and I liked, and the girls' school where we carpooled together.

Will I get to take her to Starbucks again? Can she ever carpool with me again? Can we go on walks outside again? Will she even be allowed to get in my car and go anywhere with me?

Ginny's voice snapped me out of my thoughts, and I felt her soft hand on top of mine. She gave me a gentle squeeze.

"Hey, it's going to be okay. You just need to get through the next several hours, then you can cry and weep and do whatever the heck you want. But for now, you need to be strong and focus on your mom. Not the what-ifs or the weeks and months ahead. You need to take care of business today."

"MOM! YOUR HAIR LOOKS SO good! Tona is the *best*."

Little Ginny chimed in, "It looks amazing. Your color is perfect."

"Really? It does? I haven't even seen it! Where's a mirror? I want to see what you girls are talking about."

Mom had seen it. She had been in front of the mirror for an hour and a half. But, as usual, she couldn't remember things minutes later. Anytime we complimented her hair, she would tell us she hadn't seen it yet and immediately look for a mirror. I always carried a mirror in my purse so she could inspect her hair, lipstick, or makeup.

After she'd admired Tona's handiwork, we three climbed into Little Ginny's car. "Where are we going to lunch?" Mom asked.

"We are going to one of yours and Mom's favorite places—P.F. Chang's!" Little Ginny said.

Mom paused. "P.F. Chang's? I'm not sure I know that one. Where is your mom? Will she be with us?"

"No, she is out of town. But we will do it again. Besides, we have to do it again because she's missing my birthday. This is a birthday lunch— we're celebrating my birthday!"

"Oh, I love birthdays!" Mom said. "Well, we do need to celebrate!"

As we laughed and joked in the car, I felt disgusted with myself.

How can I be joking and laughing as I'm about to manipulate her into a memory-care facility? Possibly even about to drug her? This is sick. God, I'm so sorry I'm trying to have fun and pretend it's okay when I'm basically lying to my mother. Help me, please!

Then I saw these words in my mind, and there is no doubt they were from God.

Stop thinking so much. I know what your mom needs. She loves to laugh. Let me give you this day to laugh together. She loves being with her daughter. Enjoy this time with her. I have a home for her. You are following My plan, so be joyful that I am your strength and will make all things good. I know your heart, Sarah.

I struggled to not burst into tears. He was speaking to me. He was driving the train. I had asked Him to take the wheel, and He had it. But feeling guilty in this gut-wrenching situation revealed to me my fear and lack of trust even as He led me.

He knows my heart, I kept telling myself. Crazily, I had told my own dad the same words, but I didn't realize how much I needed to hear them spoken to me. And not just by anyone, but by God.

EIGHTEEN

ABANDONMENT DAY, PART 2

August 11, 2016

--•❧❦•--

A S SOON AS WE ENTERED P.F. Chang's, we saw Lisa waiting for us.

"Well, hello, Rebecca! I'm joining you ladies for lunch."

Mom was happy to see Lisa. I just wished she had been as happy to see her five days a week for ten hours a day. So here we were.

Mom grabbed Lisa's hand and hugged her.

"Good to see you. I didn't know you were here. Do you know my daughter? And her friend, uh, uh, Ginny?"

"Well, yes, I sure do. I met your daughter a while ago when the three of us had lunch at Sarah's country club."

"Oh, that's right. I forgot about that."

Mom was so good at pretending she remembered anything, but of course she had forgotten.

At our table for four, Little Ginny was quick to make friends with the waitress, asking her for the wine and cocktail list for the "birthday" celebration.

"Oh, yeah, girl," Lisa added. "We will take that drink list. We are here to celebrate!"

Usually I told restaurants in advance about Mom's Alzheimer's, but I had forgotten to make that call today. I wanted the wait staff to understand why she might get snappy or confused about what she ordered.

"Excuse me, ladies. I am going to run to the restroom." Looking at Lisa, I winked, grabbed my phone, and left the table.

I spotted the manager and asked him to let our waitress know about Mom's condition. I also told him that we would be ordering a few drinks and that it was okay for Mom to have alcohol.

In the restroom, I took three deep yoga breaths. I prayed over and over for God to be with me. My hands, feet, and knees were shaking. In my anxiety, I could feel my chest heating up and breaking into hives. I felt like I might pass out.

As I sat back down at the table, Little Ginny looked at me and said, "I'm ordering a pinot grigio. What are you having?"

I quickly scanned the wine list. "I'll take the chardonnay."

Then Mom said to the waitress, "I'll have what she's having."

"Yes, she would like the chardonnay, also. We are all celebrating today!"

Celebrating what? Celebrating locking your mom up on the fourth floor of memory care? Taking her away from her home?

Needing to change the focus of my thoughts, I turned to Lisa and said, "I'm so glad you're with us today. Now tell me about you. How have you been?"

HALFWAY THROUGH LUNCH, MOM HAD barely sipped her wine. Ginny noticed, tapping my leg under the table and nodding toward Mom's glass.

Quickly, I took my glass of wine and said, "Let's make another toast. To Ginny, my soul sister whom I love so much. Happy birthday!"

Mom grabbed her glass, and we all clinked ours together and took a drink. Mom slowly put the glass to her lips for a small sip, if that. I was starting to think that Mom might need that Valium after all.

Lisa raised her glass not even two minutes later. "Let's make a toast!

To Ginny! Happy birthday, Ginny." We clinked our glasses together again and took sips. Mom took the tiniest sip, her glass still half full.

Under her breath, Little Ginny said to me, "She's never going to drink that glass, is she?" We laughed, nervously.

I had to laugh because nothing was going as planned. We had already toasted Little Ginny's birthday at least five times.

The waitress came over. "Is everything okay over here? Would you ladies like another drink?"

Lisa ordered another, and when hers arrived she lifted her glass again.

"Ladies! Another toast. Happy birthday, Ginny. I'm so happy to be here with you gals. Cheers!"

Mom took another small sip. Under the table, I texted Little Ginny and Lisa. "We need to give Mom the Valium. I'm going to hand it to one of you under the table. Please crush it up in her wine when I take her to the bathroom."

Their phones vibrated on the table. Lisa read hers, glanced at Mom and then looked over at me. She nodded at me and put her hand under the table. I felt like a drug dealer.

My hands were shaking under the table as I handed her the pill.

"Hey, Mom, would you mind coming to the bathroom with me? I need some help."

While in the ladies' room, I noticed the label on Mom's shirt was hanging out the back of her collar. Reaching over to tuck it in, I realized her shirt was on inside out. We laughed hysterically, which helped relieve the anxiety over her drink being spiked. I fixed up her shirt, and we walked back to the table.

I eyed the chardonnay to see if I could detect the crushed Valium. There were granules at the bottom of the glass and a small white cloud just above them. I stared at the wine, which was once perfectly clear and now clouded with medicine—a glimpse into Mom's once-clear mind now clouded by plaques and tangles and medicine. As we made one more toast, I tearfully watched Mom swallow her chalky wine without knowing what was in it.

Oh, God. Please forgive me. This doesn't feel right at all. It's so deceptive. It feels terribly wrong. I'm really sorry.

Little Ginny saw my sadness and reached over. "Hey, it's all good. Okay?"

I shook my head yes. I smiled at Mom; she smiled back and seemed so happy.

The guilt was eating me alive.

OUR BIRTHDAY CELEBRATION FINISHED, IT was time to pay the bill and head to Mom's new home.

Mom had finished her glass of wine. Noticing a little powder left at the bottom of her glass, I wondered if she'd had enough Valium.

She seemed normal as we left the restaurant. She walked the same and didn't seem the least bit tipsy.

Oh great. We can't go yet. There is no way.

As we got in the car, I panicked. Little Ginny was driving. Our plan was to ride together to the memory-care facility to meet some of Lisa's "friends."

I texted Lisa from the back seat. "Lisa, we can't go there yet. Mom is totally sober. We need to stop somewhere and have another drink! Please tell Ginny there is a Central Market with a bar, and we can get a glass of wine there."

Lisa read the text. "Ginny, let's stop at Central Market," she said. "We should get a birthday treat! We forgot to do that at the restaurant. A slice of cake or a macaron. What do you think?" She turned to me in the back seat. "What do you think, Sarah?"

Before I could answer, Mom piped up, "It's your birthday, Ginny? Well, let's celebrate!"

My jaw dropped. Mom's forgetfulness still left me surprised.

"Sure, let's do it," I said. "Ginny, we can get dessert and a glass of wine to celebrate your birthday!"

Looking at me in her rearview mirror, Little Ginny raised an eyebrow, "Well, okay! Let's do it."

When we arrived at Central Market, Mom said she wanted a glass of red wine.

Red. Oh my gosh, that's it. Red wine, not white!

Ordering us both a glass of red wine, I just couldn't drink. Mom was the only one drinking. The rest of us toasted and faked a sip, but Mom gulped hers down.

"Wouldn't you know it," Little Ginny whispered to me. "Red wine is the ticket."

I noticed Mom's hands as she held her wine. The beautiful red from her manicure the previous day matched the red of the wine perfectly. The two colors were so gorgeous together that I felt compelled to snap a picture of her fingers touching her wine glass.

Taking Mom's hand in mine, I told her I loved her. I needed her to know how beautiful she was.

After several gulps of wine, Mom slurred her words ever so slightly. "It's time to go," I mouthed to Lisa.

"Well, ladies, are y'all ready to leave?" Lisa asked. "Since I work right next door, I thought it would be fun to stop by. I'd love for you to meet my friends."

Mom was thrilled. "Let's go!" With that, she gulped the last of her wine. My eyebrows raised in shock at how quickly she finished her wine, and she knew she was busted. We all burst out laughing. "Wow, Beauty—don't think I've ever seen you do that before."

One of my favorite things about Mom was her laugh. Her nose scrunched up, her eyes teared up, and she made that ugly happy face when you laugh hard. When she laughed like that, it exposed the small gap between her front teeth.

Thank you, God. Thanks for letting me experience my favorite thing about Mom, her smile and laugh, one last time—for who knows how long. I needed that.

• • •

WE WALKED THROUGH THE FRONT doors of the care center. My
hands were sweaty and my heart was anxious.

But there was Janet, ready to show us around. As planned, Lisa would
play along, like she had been there before.

As Janet introduced herself, she made her way to me. "Janet," Lisa
said, "this is Sarah and her mother, Rebecca, and Sarah's friend, Ginny."

Janet stuck her hand out. "Hello, Sarah and Ginny. Hello, Rebecca.
I'm Janet. It's so nice to meet you. Have you ever been here before,
Rebecca?"

Mom smiled and said, "Oh, yes! We love it here. Sarah, me, and
David have been here. We eat here a lot."

I gasped. I had to look down because I didn't know how to play along.
We eat here all the time? What?

Thankfully, Janet kept walking and leading the conversation so I
didn't have to reply.

Janet pointed to the private dining room. "Rebecca, do you like to
entertain? We love to entertain here, and we have this beautiful dining
area and private dining room to host parties and things like that."

Janet had read everything about Mom. Every detail we wrote on
paper, she had down pat. She knew exactly what to say, how to make
it more appealing to Mom and how to engage her in a conversation. It
blew my mind.

Mom looked at Janet as she slowly walked and looked around. "Yes, I
love to do that. David and I have done that here. Before. We had a party
there. In that room there."

This is amazing. Why and how does she think she's been here before?
Thrown a party here? God, this is so You! Thank You for taking over. I can't
speak. I'm so scared.

After we toured the first floor, Janet said, "Shall I show you ladies
upstairs?" She looked directly in my eyes. I knew it was time.

"Yes, that sounds good, thank you."

We got on the elevator. My heart was pounding. My body felt weak, and I wanted to just stay on the elevator. Maybe it would get stuck and the doors wouldn't open. Maybe we could go back down and pretend this didn't need to happen.

Please, God. I'm so nervous. Please help me right now. I can't do this. I don't think I can do this. God, I feel like I'm going to vomit. I'm shaking. Please, please, please help me right now. I can't do this.

As the elevator bell dinged, I looked up and saw the number four in red lights. As we exited, I saw the door with the security keypad. As Janet entered the code, Lisa and Ginny put on their game faces.

"Rebecca, I'm so glad you are here to meet some of my friends," Lisa said. "You will really love them."

Mom smiled. "Yes. Me, too."

As we walked through the door, Janet started to walk toward a group of people. I noticed Mom slow down. Walking a little behind me, she looked at me and began to turn her head from left to right very slowly.

"What's the matter, Mom? We are just here to see Lisa's friends."

She said, "But I've done this. I've helped people. I don't want to be here long."

"I know, Mom. I understand."

Friends Place. She's thinking of Friends Place. She's already tried to volunteer with me, and she thinks it's the same thing. She doesn't want to be here but will do it for a few minutes. Shoot, God. I don't know when to leave. You have to guide me. I don't know whether to step left or right or forward or backward. You are my feet. This is it. I can't do this anymore.

We approached a group of residents being led by a caretaker in filling in the blanks of songs and famous sayings.

"Hello, everyone. How are you? Hi, Bart! Hello, Lucy! How are you today?" Janet said.

I waved at them, and Mom waved, too. Lisa went to talk to a few of the residents, and Mom followed her. I noticed that Mom was by far the youngest one in the group. Most of them were in their eighties, sitting in wheelchairs or with walkers beside them.

Mom went from one person to the next. She bent down to hug one woman in a wheelchair and then moved on to the next, grabbing her hand and smiling. "Hi, I'm Rebecca. How are you? You are so beautiful."

I was enamored with Mom. The gifts that God had given her were coming alive by being around others. She loved to serve, to hug people, to bring joy and light. She wanted to make them feel loved and purposeful.

I turned to Little Ginny, saying, "I think it's time. I think I have to leave now. I think I need to leave when I see her loving on them, so she won't notice I'm gone."

"Let's go. You can do this," Little Ginny said.

I took one last look at Mom. In her sleek turquoise outfit and sporting a new hairdo, she was *Beauty*. She bent over another woman in a wheelchair, cupping her soft hands over the lady's. I knew her hands were serving as the hands of Jesus that day. I would walk with faith from that moment on and trust God that He would take care of her.

Little Ginny and I rode the elevator down in silence. I shook and felt queasy. Suddenly my knees buckled, and I fell to the floor. I wailed with grief, pain, and anger. I was too weak to stand up, and I couldn't catch my breath. Little Ginny kneeled down, put my arm over her shoulder, and said, "Sarah. Oh, Sarah. It's okay, Sarah. Come, hang on to me."

As the elevator dinged and the doors opened to the first floor, Little Ginny carefully helped me out, carrying every burden for me. I thought of Jesus hunched over, carrying a heavy wooden cross for every human being. Little Ginny painfully, yet with unexplainable strength and courage, carried me to safe ground.

Short of breath, I cried out, "I need a restroom. Help me find a restroom, please, Ginny."

Not ten seconds later, I went straight to a stall and slammed the door shut. My entire being, fully clothed, sank to the toilet seat. I sobbed and sobbed and sobbed. I couldn't control myself. Every emotion poured out, my tears like tidal waves. In pain, I cried out to God and yelled. I don't even remember what I said.

As I stood up, I leaned against the cold metal door and cried some more. I heard someone whisper to Little Ginny, but I was too over-whelmed with guilt to comprehend the words.

I blew my nose several times, and as I opened the door, I was met by a beautiful black woman. She opened her arms wide then hugged me, holding on firmly.

"Oh, honey. It will be okay."

I lost control again. I cried on the shoulder of a total stranger, feeling weak yet loved. I wanted to fall down again, but she held me up. She just let me cry, rubbed my back, and said, "It's okay, sweetie, it's going to be okay. Bless your heart, it will be okay."

After I started to calm down, she grabbed my shoulders and said, "What is her name? What is your mother's name?"

"Rebecca. Rebecca Bearden. I didn't want to do this. We didn't want to do this. We didn't have a choice." I started to cry again, unable to hold back the tears. "I abandoned her up there! She didn't know. She doesn't know what's going on. She will wonder where I am. She's going to look for me!"

Turning to Little Ginny, the woman asked, "What's her name?"

"Sarah."

"Sarah, honey, my name is Stacy. I am a nurse here. I promise you, I will look after your mother. You have my word that I will check on her. Look at me. You have my word. I see how much you love her. I will love her, too."

As I looked into Stacy's eyes, I saw love. I felt love through her hands, her hug, her eyes, her shoulders, her voice.

From that point on, I called her my angel. God purposely had her in that restroom with us. He knew what I needed at the perfect time, and He provided.

NINETEEN

THE PHONE CALL

August 11, 2016

··❧✖❧··

LITTLE GINNY AND I WALKED over to the fireplace of the sitting area and sat speechless in the leather chairs. Our mission was complete. My eyes were swollen from crying, and my head was pounding. The grandfather clock chimed 4:00, but I didn't want to leave. I could have slept in that chair from mental exhaustion. My emotions were so raw, and neither of us knew what to say.

"Do you want me to text Lisa to see how your mom is doing? I can let her know we are still downstairs," Little Ginny said.

"Sure. I guess so." Putting my forehead in my palms, I slowly massaged from the top of my hair all the way down to my neck.

"I can't believe it, Ginny. I just can't believe my mom is officially here. She won't be home anymore. I can't wrap my brain around it."

"I know it's hard to call this home right now, but it will be. She will be happy here, Sarah. It is *so* beautiful. It's very Becky. You have to trust the caregivers. They are going to help her get settled in. The hardest part is over."

Little Ginny's phone dinged. "Lisa is on her way down now."

A minute later, Lisa turned the corner and sat in the leather seat beside me.

"She's still talking to the residents, and she didn't even realize I'd left," she said.

"Did you notice how old everyone is?" I asked. "Do you see how *she* is the one trying to comfort them, yet she is one of them? She is going to flip out when she realizes she is with them for days and weeks to come. I just can't stop thinking about how she will *flip out* when she realizes she can't get out."

"You can't think that way," Lisa said. "They are professionals. They take over from here and will do their job and will do it well. You brought her here for your dad, and now she is safe."

We sat in silence a few more minutes. I turned to Little Ginny.

"Thank you. I don't know how I could have done this without you." My eyes welled with tears again, and I began to cry. "And Lisa, just having you here as a professional caretaker gave me so much more peace. I'm still in shock. We've dropped her off and abandoned her, and she doesn't even know it yet."

"Sarah, I'm sorry," Little Ginny said, "but I can't listen to the word 'abandon' anymore. You are not deserting your mother. You are *loving* her by giving her a better quality of life. You will see her again, and you will be doing her makeup again, and you will be dancing with her again. Stop believing the lies in your mind."

I grabbed her hand.

"Thank you. You always tell me what I need to hear. I don't like it sometimes, but you are usually right."

"Well," said Little Ginny, breaking the ice, "can we talk about the red wine being the ticket?"

I laughed. "I should have gone with my gut and just ordered the red at lunch. Oh, well—leave it to Mom to keep us in suspense. She never makes anything easy, does she?"

Little Ginny laughed and boldly said, "No, she does *not!*"

Lisa leaned in. "Sarah, I was hesitant when you said y'all were placing your mom in the first place. But when you told me she drank nail polish remover and tried to cut a mole off her skin, I knew she was a danger to herself. I've been around people with this disease, and I'll be the first to say it can be *very* scary. I'm really proud of you, dear. I really am."

"Thank you, Lisa. I told you Mom is sly. She can make you believe she's okay. And she looks so great for her age, which makes it that much more confusing."

Looking around, I noticed the pink and purple hydrangeas on the coffee table arranged in a blue and white vase. The entryway was quiet. Mom's new home gave me a sense of peace and comfort.

I turned to Little Ginny, "I guess we should go. I'll text Dad and let him know Mom is here."

We took Lisa back to her car. Hugging her goodbye, I told her thank you several times. Now that Mom had twenty-four-hour care, I wondered if we would see her again.

"Lisa, I don't know what this means. I don't know what will happen in the future, but it's my hope that you see Mom again one day."

I could see the sadness in Lisa's eyes.

"I hope to see her again, too, Sarah. I love your mom. I really do."

We hugged tightly. It was a difficult goodbye.

I CALLED DAD AND ASKED if he was okay and if he needed any food. He said he wasn't hungry and told me to enjoy some time with Little Ginny. He knew I needed to decompress.

Little Ginny and I ordered salads and split a margherita pizza at Taverna. Exhausted, I felt like I could fall asleep at the table.

As we reflected on the day, I was reminded how God steered the ship. He had carried me through that day, step by step, and taken me from place to place. As if floating, I could hardly comprehend our movements.

I immediately thought of a Bible verse in Isaiah: "But those who hope in the Lord will renew their strength. They will soar on wings like eagles; they will run and not grow weary, they will walk and not be faint" (40:31 NIV).

That was how I felt that day. I had hoped and trusted that God would lead the way, and He had given me wings like an eagle and renewed my strength. We were able to run the race and not grow weary or faint.

• • •

WHEN LITTLE GINNY DROPPED ME off at Dad's, the house felt empty as I walked through the front door. I wanted to call out, "Hey, Mom" and see her turn the corner and greet me with a hug. This change felt so permanent.

I walked toward the kitchen, where Dad was sitting at the table alone. The whiskers on his face were full, and his eyes were swollen and glassy. His sadness made me feel as if we had just attended a funeral.

Putting my purse on the countertop, I saw one of my favorite pictures of Mom in a frame above the built-in desk. Dad had moved it to a more visible place. She was wearing her Kilgore Rangerette uniform and was posed against a streetlight in New York City, her back leg kicked up while standing in the snow. Mom had performed at the Macy's Thanksgiving Day Parade, and she looked joyful and energized.

Dad stood up to give me a hug, and, as he did, I noticed a box of tissues at the table.

"Hey, sweetie, how are you?" he asked.

I didn't want him to let go of me. It felt so safe to be in my daddy's arms. I started bawling.

"Oh, Daddy, that was the most difficult thing I have ever done in my life."

I heard him snort and sniff and knew he, too, had tears. He was trying to be strong for me, but we were both drained.

Holding on to me tight, his voice cracking, he said, "I know it. I can't thank you enough for doing this for me. I just couldn't do it, Sarah."

"I know, Daddy. God gave me strength, and it's done now. I'm just sad and tired, and I feel a wretched guilt. I can't get past just leaving her and not telling her why."

"Daddy, do you think she will remember *I* was the one who put her there? Do you think when I see her she will be so angry with me that she will slap me? What if she hates me? It's like me dropping off one of the kids at some stranger's house and not telling them why or when I will be back."

My dad's wisdom began to pour out.

"Your mom can't rationalize, honey. Her mind can't think logically. If we told her, she wouldn't understand. Even when she occasionally recognizes her memory is failing, she doesn't understand the severity of the loss and the difficulties it places on the family."

I nodded.

"A child is different," he said. "A child may not understand the big picture and why, but you can tell them and they trust you because they're dependent on you. It's that childlike faith. Your mom gets paranoid and doesn't trust *anyone*. She wants to make her own decisions and be completely independent. I don't blame her—she's seventy years old!"

It made sense to me. You could teach a child a lesson, but you couldn't teach Mom because she wouldn't remember a few minutes later. Even if I had told her, she would have manipulated me into thinking she was fine, and then forgotten moments later what either one of us had said. Some things are better left unsaid.

AROUND 9:00 IN THE EVENING, I went up to take a shower and check in with Thad. I hadn't spoken to him since the morning. He had texted me during lunch to tell me he loved me, that he was praying for me and that they had arrived safely in Colorado. But being so focused on the placement, I never responded. He was relieved to hear the placement had gone well.

Daddy and I reconvened around the breakfast table. He had picked up a few appetizers from Dive, a local fish restaurant. Though neither of us was very hungry, we had a few healthy bites.

"I'm hurting so much, Dad. I can't even begin to understand your broken heart right now."

"It's broken, that's for sure. It's hard to walk into our bedroom and bathroom and closet. Her things are everywhere. And we haven't even started gathering her clothes and bed and the other things that will be moved on Saturday."

My cell phone rang, and it was a Dallas number I didn't recognize.

"Hello, is this Sarah?" asked a woman on the other end.

"Yes, this is she."

"This is Betty from The Tradition. I have Rebecca here, and she says she needs to speak with you."

Suddenly, my heart beat rapidly and my face turned bright red. With huge eyes, I looked at Dad and he *knew* something wasn't right.

"Who is it?" he mouthed.

"Uhhh, Betty, I'm so sorry—can you hang on just one second?"

Hitting the mute button with shaking hands, I started to cry.

"Daddy, it's Betty from The Tradition. She says Mom needs to speak to me. What do I do? I'm terrified! What do I say?"

"What? Mom needs to speak to you? Why in the world are they letting her call you? Gosh, Sarah, yes, go ahead and talk to her. Just see what she wants. Tell her I am out of town visiting my brother."

He raced to his bedroom to see if he had missed a call from the care center on his phone.

I clicked the mute button again.

"I'm sorry, Betty. Uh, yes, I . . . I guess I can talk to her. I didn't think I would be speaking to her this quickly or that she was allowed to call me."

"I'm sorry, but she keeps insisting. Thank you—one second please."

Great. She keeps insisting, so you give in that easily and have her talk to me? The one who left her there? Oh God, please help me . . . please, God . . .

"Sarah? Sarah, are you there?"

Hearing my mom's voice on the line, I wanted to sob. I wanted to tell her I was so sorry and how much I loved her. My mother. My best friend.

"Hi, Mom. I'm here." I didn't know what else to say.

"Sarah, oh, thank God! I'm at this place. This place, with these people, and they won't let me leave. Where are you?"

"Well, I'm . . ."

Mom cut me off.

"Where's your dad?"

"Uh, Dad's out of town visiting his brother."

At this point, I felt like throwing up. The phone was slippery from my sweat-soaked hands.

"Oh, sure. Great. He's out of town," she said sarcastically. "Where are you? I need you to pick me up. I'm at this place, and they won't let me leave."

"Uh, Mom, I . . . I can't right now."

She cut me off again, panic and frustration in her voice.

"Sarah, listen to me right now. I need you to get your keys, get in your car, and drive to this place." I heard her say to Betty, "What's the name of this place again?"

I don't even think she heard the name—she just kept talking. "I need you to get in your car and come pick me up *right now*. You hear me, Sarah? Right. Now."

"Oh, Mommy, I'm sorry, but I can't. I love you, Mom." My eyes filled up with tears. I didn't know how much longer my voice could remain calm and collected.

"Sarah! No! Sarah! Listen to—*Sarah*. Don't do this to me. Don't *do this* to me!"

Oh. My. Gosh. She knows. She knows she's been dropped off. Does she know it was me? God. Help me.

"Mom, I'm sorry, but . . ."

She cut me off. "*Sarah*. If you don't come get me right now, then don't ever call me your *mom* again."

Tears streamed down my face. She had disowned me and would never forgive me for what I had done. All I could do was cry silently as I kept hearing, "Sarah? Sarah, are you there?"

"Yes, Mom, I am here. I love you."

"I am going to tell you *one last time*. If you don't come pick me up this minute, you may never call me your *mom* again, and I will never call you my *daughter* again. Come get me. I have to go. The lady here needs to make a phone call."

Suddenly, Betty got back on the phone. "Thank you, Sarah. I'll be in touch."

Click.

Silence.

I was stunned at how articulate and clear my mom's speech was. She hadn't been that clear in over a year, possibly longer. She knew exactly what she wanted to say, how to say it, and when to say it. The only thing she couldn't figure out was where she was. She just knew that she wanted out.

All I could think about were those women at the facility we'd visited, banging on the glass doors, wanting out. I had turned my back on them. I couldn't rescue them. But this time, it was my own mother.

What in the world am I doing to her? God, how can I turn my back on her like this? She is begging me to get her out, just like those women! The difference is, those women were smiling at me, but Mom is pleading with me to rescue her, and she's confused and full of pain.

Dad turned the corner as I wept like a baby. I tried to tell him about the conversation, but I couldn't get the words out as I choked on the tears.

Dad sat next to me. "Sarah, I am so sorry. I had a missed call. They tried to call me first. When you were on the phone they called me again. The head nurse apologized and said she was very sorry they had to call you, but there was a mix-up with the topical gel prescription. They are supposed to have it to rub on Mom's arm to calm her down. Apparently, the pharmacy delivered it to the wrong floor, and they have been trying to locate it. She was causing a disruption with the residents; they thought they could kill a few minutes having her talk to you. I don't know what to say. I am *so* sorry."

"Calm her down? We *told* them to be prepared for her, and I am pissed off they would even *think* to call me! They are supposed to be the professionals, Daddy. Not us! I just placed her for God's sakes, and they want the person who placed her to calm her down? Are they out of their minds?"

Dad nodded in agreement.

I sobbed even more.

"I think they are out of their minds," Dad said slowly, "because Mom has made them feel that way. We knew this would happen. Not the phone call, but . . . I can only imagine the trouble she is giving them. I'm frustrated because I went to the pharmacy the other day myself, and they told me they would deliver it for me. It was hard enough for me to go back over there and sign the papers."

"She told me not to call her Mom anymore, Dad! She told me if I didn't come pick her up, I am not her daughter anymore!"

I couldn't get those words out of mind. It didn't matter what Dad— or anyone else—said to me. I'd been the one on the other end of that phone. I was the one who had heard her voice. She had been stern, angry, scared, anxious, trapped, and yet also discerning about what was really happening to her. She *knew* deep down she was being left there, and she had let me know.

That was the worst phone call I have taken in my entire life.

I LOVE YOU WITH
ALL MY HEART

August 12 to August 14, 2016

-•◦✕◦•-

THE NEXT MORNING, I WOKE up to the sun shining brightly through the blinds of my parents' guest bedroom. The house was quiet, and I could hear the birds chirping from the large pecan tree outside the window. I didn't want to move. It would be another emotional day: emptying drawers and moving furniture, among other things. I had clothes to sort and errands to run. She would need new underwear, socks, a toothbrush, soap, shampoo, and fresh pajamas.

She loved P.J. Salvage pajamas. Soft and colorful, they came in all sorts of prints. But most of the tops were button-down, and Mom could no longer button her pants or tops. I needed to find pajamas just as soft that she could pull over her head without buttoning or tying.

Smelling coffee from downstairs, I wondered if Dad had gotten any sleep. We had both been up late, distraught over Mom's phone call. Despite four hours of sleep, I still needed to start the day and be strong for Dad. The next day he would watch her things be taken out the front door and loaded onto a truck, another goodbye to many loved possessions. He had already packed up her favorite paintings and crosses and her Rangerette yearbook.

I headed downstairs to join Dad in the cozy living room, his first morning without her.

He held a cup of coffee, his Bible open on his lap. He admitted to not sleeping well either.

In the kitchen, I popped a coffee pod into the machine and flashed back to Mom. I still remembered the time we went to Starbucks when Frensley was about eight months old. Mom liked her coffee extra hot, and as we sat around the small table to eat our fruit and yogurt, Frensley reached for Mom's coffee—and spilled it everywhere, including all over her own chubby baby legs.

Frensley screamed bloody murder. Terrified, Mom and I grabbed her from the highchair and threw her into the restroom sink, turning on the cool water. Luckily, she was fine, but it was a story we would laugh about for years when ordering extra-hot coffee or zapping a cup in the microwave for an extra forty-five seconds.

As I sat down in Mom's favorite chair, Dad closed his Bible.

"I miss the little things already," he said, "like cooking her turkey bacon or pouring her coffee. I can't believe she's not home anymore."

"It's so surreal," I said. "Do you think she remembers how she got there yesterday? I pray she doesn't. That kept me awake all last night."

"I don't think she will. But, if she does, *you* have to remember we did it out of love."

"I get it, I guess. I discipline my kids because I love them, but it's also in hopes they learn from it. Mom won't ever learn a lesson from this. She'll never know why. I just hope she knows when we see her again how much we really do love her and she doesn't resent us. I hope I didn't destroy her love for me."

"Sarah, your mom will always love you. Do you know how hard it was for me to hold you on my hip when you were a baby? Mom wouldn't put you down! She went to the bathroom with you, cooked with you, took naps with you. If I ever had a chance to hold you, it was a miracle."

I smiled. I'd heard him tell that story many times, and he'd shown me pictures of her holding me all through my toddler years.

Mom had had a stillborn baby two years before I was born. My sister, Jessica, died during labor, and they never knew why. Years before, Mom told me she had known during labor their little girl wasn't going to make it. She had felt and heard God say to her that she would have to give her baby up. She even wrote about it. Yet she was in such peace.

Mom and Dad both said it was because of Jessica's death that Mom would not put me down.

"I suppose that's why Mom is my best friend," I said. "She never left my side. You're right: She loves me big."

Looking around the room, I thought about the things that needed to be done. I would need to wear both my business hat and my daughter hat.

We discussed all of the different things to pack: the rug, bath towels, pillows and bedding, as well as artwork and chairs and an ottoman.

I called Carie to confirm the moving plans. "Hello, my BFF," she said. "You and Dad doing okay? I've been thinking about you all mornin'."

There was something about Carie's drawl that made you want to melt in her arms.

"I'm not sure how to answer that. Actually, we're not well. Last night was unbelievable. Mom called me."

"What? Why in the *world* did they let her call you? I can't believe what I'm hearin'!"

It broke Carie's heart to hear the words Mom had spoken.

"Listen, BFF, I'm going to be there around 3:00 or 4:00. I'm bringing you and David dinner, and I'm preppin' it right now. That time work okay?"

"It can't get here soon enough. I can't wait to hug and be with you."

"Awww, honey, me too. Don't you worry. We will get it all done. I'm also bringin' us some Cabernet, so you better get out Becky's finest wine glasses!"

I dressed while Dad left to run a few errands. I think he needed to get out of the house. Meanwhile, I was ready to get to work and tackle the next twenty-four hours.

Later that day, Carie arrived.

"Hey, David. I'm so sorry. I know your heart is broken to pieces."

Dad gave her a big hug.

"Well, thank you. It is broken, but there's not much we can do about it. It needed to happen. How's ol' Bobby doing?"

Bobby was Carie's father and Dad's fraternity brother. As much as I tried, I could not pry any stories out of Bobby about Dad in college. Their bond remained firm no matter the distance or the time that had passed since they'd last spoken.

"You know Dad. He's the same old, same old. You should go to Fairfield some time. I know he would love to see you and cook you a few steaks."

Carie made herself at home, unloading the groceries, turning on the oven, and searching for pots and pans. I loved that about her. She knew we were family, and she acted like family.

As Carie prepared dinner, I sorted Mom's clothes in her closet.

She loves these shorts, and these. Oh, and those blue cropped pants, where are those? Let's grab her black workout pants. They make her look slim and are easy to put on. How many outfits is that? She probably shouldn't have too many to choose from. Awww, her favorite shirt.

I started crying in the closet. I sat on the floor and I wept. I squeezed her black pants and held them to my heart, bowing my head into them as the tears rolled down. These were clothes we had purchased together, and now I might never shop with her again. The memories of Chico's and her taking her shirt off in front of the cashier—it all flooded back, and it was all too much.

Pulling myself together, I gathered her shoes, her flip-flops, and a pair of tennis shoes. I began neatly packing her clothes.

When I went into the kitchen, Carie saw I had been crying.

"Oh honey, let me give you a hug. You're gonna get through this, I promise. Your mama is safe now, Sarah."

"I know, it's just . . . " and I wept on her shoulder. Through my tears, I noticed Carie still wore Quelques Fleurs perfume, smelling just like she did when we were fifteen.

Carie put a baked Brie with puffed pastry and jalapeño jelly out to eat while we sipped on our wine. Dinner followed, with freshly baked okra in a delicious teriyaki sauce, butternut squash with rosemary and cinnamon, and chicken, also marinated in teriyaki, with a little lemon on top. It was the best home-cooked meal Dad and I had eaten in months.

We sat around the table talking about Mom and our memories with her. Carie and I recalled one hilarious story from our time in college.

"Sarah, do you remember when we were talkin' about thongs? And your mom thought it was a *sin* to wear a thong! She was convinced that they were devilish or somethin'. Do you remember?"

"Oh, my gosh, yes!"

Dad asked, "What? Thongs?"

Carie went on, "Oh, *yes*, David. I nearly fell over the ottoman I was laughing so hard! You know how I like to yank Becky's chain? Well, she thought wearing a thong was a sin and that it was devilish, so I said, 'Becky, are you kidding me? It is a *thong*. And you know what? You might kinda like wearin' it!'"

"I didn't need to hear that!" Dad exclaimed.

I was laughing so hard. My nose crinkled, and making that ugly laughing face, I felt like my mom.

Carie kept us rolling in laughter with her stories. It felt so good to laugh. Daddy and I had been through so much the past few weeks, from the day we first set foot in a memory-care facility.

After dinner, Carie pulled out some labels with my mom's name and room number on them. She had asked for Mom's room number a few days ago, but I never thought to ask why.

"Let's get to work. I'm gonna iron all of these labels onto Becky's clothes. The last thing you want is for someone else to be wearin' her cute clothes. We want to make sure the housekeeper knows exactly where these clothes belong."

Dad and I looked at each other in disbelief—it was something we'd never thought about.

There was enough work that by the time Carie and I were finished, we were exhausted.

We shared a room, each in our own bed. Donning her sleep mask and employing her lavender oil drops and Aquaphor, she completed a bedtime routine that hadn't changed in twenty years.

We lay there with the lights out.

"Carie, I don't know if I can go with you and Jennifer tomorrow to set up her room. I'm worried she might see me, but I also want it arranged the way she would love. That is part of the reason I chose you—you know exactly how Mom would decorate it."

"Let's just see how you feel in the mornin'. You don't have to go. Jennifer and I have it all under control. If you want to go, then go, and if not, that's okay too."

"I'll just see then. Goodnight, BFF. I'm so thankful you are here."

We fell fast asleep.

ONCE AGAIN, I WOKE UP to the sun shining through the blinds of the same window, with the birds chirping in the pecan tree.

Jennifer, her son, and a few high school boys were on their way with a pickup truck and trailer.

I feel sick. God, this is too much. I don't want to see her things go. Why did it have to go this way, God? Why?

Jennifer came in and we all got to work. Soon, the last load went onto the trailer, and the cars were packed with boxes, pillows, lamps, frames, and knickknacks.

I glanced at Dad and saw his tears.

Holding up a finger, he said, "Just a minute." He went into his bedroom and quickly reappeared with a pillow that read, "I love you with all my heart."

His voice cracked as he said, "Here, Sarah. Take this. She will know what it means."

That pillow was the last of Mom's items to go.

• • •

OUR PLAN WAS IN PLACE. Carie wore a baseball cap to be incognito in case there were any Mom sightings. While Mom was around the corner at an activities session, Carie, Jennifer, and the boys used the back elevator that, luckily, was next door to Mom's room.

I had decided to go after all, but as we removed boxes from the cars and loaded the dollies, I felt paranoid—especially when I saw several windows overlooking the loading dock.

"Carie, what if she sees me? Should I stay in the car? What if that's the respite room? I'd feel funny sitting here watching y'all do everything for me."

"Sarah, didn't you say they were taking her around the corner?"

"Yes."

"Then stop worrying. I can promise you they aren't gonna let your mom look out a window, especially overlookin' the loading dock!"

But I couldn't overcome the idea that Mom might see me, and I grew more anxious.

What if she sees me from a window and starts banging on it? What if she wonders why her stuff is coming in? What if she recognizes her bedframe and this side table?

Jennifer walked up.

"What if she can see me?" I said in a panic. "I want to help, but—"

"Sarah, stop." Jennifer chuckled at me, but I didn't think it was funny.

"No, Jennifer. I'm serious."

"Sarah, honey, she's not going to see you," Jennifer said, smiling.

"I'm just not sure. I'm doubting everything and freaking out."

"Well, then stay in your car. All I know is we got work to do." And off she walked.

Her comment felt empty, as if I shouldn't feel what I was feeling. But, she didn't mean to sound rude. She was there to move a lot of things within an hour. Her son and his friends had another moving job that afternoon and needed to work quickly.

In my rearview mirror, I saw Jennifer and Carie conversing in low tones. Carie walked to my door.

"Bearden, listen. Your mom isn't going to see you. But if *you* think she will, stay in the car. Have you forgotten that God is taking care of you and your mom? Do you *really* think God will allow her to see you right now? If you wanna help, then get out and help. If you wanna *not* trust God and be paranoid, stay in the car." And Carie, too, walked off.

She's right, God, and I'm sorry. Of course I want to trust You. I want to help. Please protect me and keep Mom where she needs to be so she doesn't see me.

I left the car and helped unload furniture and other belongings onto a cart bound for Mom's room.

Carie and Jennifer texted me pictures of her room since I didn't dare go upstairs. As I made suggestions about this table or that blanket, they moved things accordingly.

After an hour or so, they came downstairs and showed me more pictures.

"It's so beautiful. Oh, look—you even hung the sconces! I wish I could see it in person."

"Do you want to see it?" Jennifer asked. "We can take you up there."

Carie chimed in. "Why don't you come see it? I think seeing it would make you feel better. You can be in and out in two minutes. Have faith, sweetie. She's not going to see you."

"I'm scared, but okay. I do want to see it."

We went up the back elevator, and as the doors opened, I peeked around the corner and sprinted four or five steps to Mom's new home.

The minute I stepped inside, I sighed with relief and gratitude.

It was so quiet. Jennifer and Carie didn't say a word. Putting my hand to my mouth, I looked from wall to wall as tears fell down my cheeks.

"I can't believe y'all did this in just an hour. Oh, her *Jesus* painting. I *love* it there!"

I turned to Carie and Jennifer, and they both smiled.

"Is there anything you want us to change? If so, now is the time," Jennifer suggested.

"It's perfect. Thank you so much."

My heart raced as I walked into Mom's bathroom. Her white monogrammed towels hung from the rack, and new white bath mats were placed on the floor. Her green tissue box cover matched so nicely with her white-and-green trash can. Mom would feel at home.

Pulling myself together, I took a few pictures for Daddy to see and for me to remember. Not only was Mom and Dad's favorite pillow in the center of her bed, there was a large cross hanging on one wall, a painting of Jesus washing a disciple's feet on another, and a framed Bible verse on the third. God filled the room with love.

This is love. I know it hurts, Sarah, but this is love.

TWENTY-ONE

REUNITED

August 15 to September 23, 2016

-•❉•-

THAD AND THE KIDS ARRIVED home from Colorado on Monday, August 15th. The first day of school was two days later. Though it was time to put on my mom hat, in reality it felt like a facade. Underneath was a heavy layer I would wear for months: despair. Hitting rock bottom, I was now very angry at this disease.

I wanted to be strong for the kids during their first week of school—to let them know everything was going to be okay. But I had no strength. I could barely move. Thoughts roared in my head.

Will Mom be able to stay? Were they able to calm her down after that phone call? How long before they call us and say, "We're sorry, but it's not going to work"?

Thad knew my struggle, but even he didn't grasp the depth of my pain. For those on the outside, including my family, "things should be better now." Mom was placed, Dad and I had relief, and I could focus more attention on my husband and children.

But that wasn't the case. It felt like my mother had died. My father, in my eyes, was a widower now, living by himself. And it happened overnight. Thad was going through it *through* me, but he was going to the office every day, planning work lunches, scheduling dinners for us with friends, planning our travels, and so on. Life continued for Thad and the kids—but for me, life had stopped.

Going to the carpool line for the first time without Mom was extremely painful. I couldn't even turn on the radio or check my phone for emails or text messages. Daydreaming about Mom was all I did. Blowing bubbles, drinking our Starbucks, listening to sermons, and thinking of the times Mom spotted the same plastic bag stuck in a tree branch day after day. I missed her. I missed spending time with her in that carpool line.

Macy, the head nurse of memory care, texted us updates once or twice a week. "David and Sarah. Mom is hanging in there. She still wants to go home, but she is manageable. The good news is that she is easily redirected. The bad news is redirection doesn't last very long! Please feel free to call or text me anytime."

All Dad and I could do was wait for the phone call telling us we could finally see Mom. One week went by, then two, then three, each week more tortuous than the last.

Finally, we met with Macy and Shelley in the same conference room with the tissue boxes and bottled water on the table.

"I know you were hoping to see Becky by now and I am sorry it has already been three weeks," Macy said. "But we will continue with updates on her and go from there with any questions or concerns you may have."

"I can't believe it's been three weeks. It's been the longest three weeks of my life," Dad said, grabbing a tissue out of the box.

"I know, David. She is getting better. Becky is easily redirected, and she's getting more involved with different activities. The first week and a half, she didn't want to do anything at all. But she's now helping plant flowers on the patio, and she helps at meal time serving drinks and setting tables."

"Macy, what did she do or say for that first week and a half?" I asked. "And I need to know this: Does she remember I brought her here?"

"She does not know you brought her here. She thought she went shopping in Snider Plaza and walked over here by herself, and now we won't let her out."

Tears of joy and relief ran down my cheeks. I felt a crushing weight lift off my shoulders.

"The first two weeks, she was confused," Macy said. "She was very angry at us, and we did use the calming gel several times. She somehow got the ankle bracelet off three times. We don't know how in the world she did, but she did. You are right. She is a *strong* woman!"

We couldn't help but laugh.

"She has a new friend named Ellie," Macy continued. "Ellie is older than your Mom, but she's very mobile, physically fit, and still speaks very well. The good news is Rebecca has a friend she loves to be with, and it has kept her busy and her mind occupied. They hold hands in the hallways, and it is absolutely precious. The bad news is she and Ellie have tried twice to escape. Ellie got hold of the code, and they tried to get out. So, while they are good friends, they are double trouble."

Again, we all laughed.

Dad sighed. "I am so glad she has a friend. That makes me feel much better knowing she has someone. And I'm not surprised she's tried to escape. We told you that you would have your hands full with Beck!"

Macy chuckled. "That we do. But she is very sweet. She has taken to me very well. She is feeling closer to me and trusting me more. She just needs more time to get into a routine, and she needs to establish a closer relationship and develop more trust with the other caregivers. Then we can talk about when you can come for a short visit. Shelley will explain more in a bit."

Needs more time? Establish more trust with the caregivers before we can come? For a short *visit?*

"Macy, what do you mean she needs more time?" I asked. "She's been here three weeks now. Is 'more time' a week? Two weeks? Can you give us an idea? Because I thought we would see her around the three-week mark."

"We want Rebecca to be in a place where she trusts us when you or David leave after a visit. We want her to feel comfortable and at home here. If we need to redirect her when you leave, we want her to trust where we are taking her. This kind of thing takes time, and for your mom, it takes extra time because of her personality. We don't want to go through the first week all over again, which is why it's important to trust the process and let us get her fully settled. I know this is very difficult to hear. I know you have been waiting, and you want badly to see her."

"I really want to hear everything she is doing. Can you take me through the day with her?" Dad asked.

"She typically wakes up around 8:00 or 8:30 in the morning. She gets dressed by herself, then she comes out and sits at the same table every morning. There's a group of them—she sits with Bart, Ellie, Lenore, and Pat every morning for coffee together. It's very sweet."

Dad sighed. "I'm so happy to hear that."

"They eat breakfast, and then around 10:00 or so, everyone goes back to their room, usually to brush their teeth or do whatever they need to do," Macy said. "Then a caregiver goes to each room to get them ready for activities. For example, today, Rebecca did a chair exercise class with the instructor, though last week, she wouldn't have it. So that's better! After exercise class, we took them outside on the patio to listen to music and plant a few flowers in pots. We've noticed she really loves messing with the flowers. She will move them all over the hallways and decorate."

That was *so* Mom.

"And then it's time for lunch. They eat lunch followed by either a craft or—Becky doesn't really like crafts, we've noticed."

"Oh, no, she does *not* like crafts," I said. "I am not a craft mom, either, so I guess I can thank her for that."

Macy smiled. "So sometimes, if it's a craft, she will wander off to her room, which is fine. She has played bingo with us. We also have a game where we bowl—"

"Oh, yes, I remember the bowling! 'Bowling with Billy Bob,' a.k.a. Louie."

"Exactly. And after those activities, we have entertainment come in two to three days a week from about 3:00 to 4:00. It may be a piano player, a singer, or an accordion player, but we try to do something musical because music brings back a lot of memories for the residents. And then it's time for dinner."

Dad's face had softened.

"I'm happy to hear all of this, Macy," he said. "I just keep envisioning Becky waiting for me and wondering when I will come back. But if she's active and busy, it will help these long weeks go by faster."

"I understand. She's getting better, and more and more active with each week. This is another reason why we think it's best to wait. The last thing we want is to undo everything we've worked so hard to do."

Then it was Shelley's turn. "First of all, I want to tell you how much I *love* Rebecca. She is such a delight to be around."

Dad smiled. "It sounds to me like she is still her beautiful and loving self."

"She is, David. My job is to meet with Rebecca once or twice a week and gauge where she is on an emotional level and help the caregivers and families understand what is going on in Rebecca's mind. I'm like a facilitator or a therapist. It's my job to get her to talk and express her feelings. Like Macy, I work to establish trust and rapport with Rebecca. Once Rebecca divulges things that are playing in her mind, I am able to guide you and the caregivers to help her have a better quality of life."

I liked Shelley. She looked like she could be one of Mom's friends from Houston.

I had to ask. "Shelley, based on your conversations with Mom—and I know Macy said she thinks she walked over here from the shopping plaza—has Mom said anything to *you*? Has she mentioned her daughter left her here?"

"No, absolutely not. She hasn't mentioned that one time. It's a blessing, really. So be grateful for that. She will never know you dropped her off here, Sarah."

"Thank you, because"—I started crying again—"I haven't been able to live with the pain and guilt and despair of leaving her here. I can't take my mind off that day. She called me the first night, and I—"

Macy interrupted me. "I am so sorry you had to receive that call the first night. I want you to know I was not there—there was another head nurse that night. The one thing I hope you will hold onto is that your mom does *not* remember how she got here, and she does not remember that phone call. She loves you, and she talks about you to me all the time."

Although I felt some relief hearing those words, I still held so much pain and guilt, I couldn't speak.

As we came to the end of our meeting, I wanted to confirm once more how long Macy thought it would be before Dad and I could see her again.

"So you think it could be two more weeks, possibly three? That's five or six weeks total. And Mom and Dad's fiftieth anniversary is September 10. Will he get to see her for their anniversary?"

"I can't make any promises. Again, we don't want to undo what we've worked so hard to do, and she's coming along slowly but surely. It's not easy, but I am asking that you trust the process."

Dad told Macy there was no pressure over their upcoming anniversary.

"I know Beck doesn't even know what day it is. Don't worry if she's not ready yet. I don't want to mess anything up, either."

"Dad, you're right," I said. "It's just that I know you and Mom have never been apart for more than two weeks since you were in the Navy."

He'd told me several times through the years how hard it was to be apart back then. It broke my heart knowing he may not see her on their fiftieth wedding anniversary.

We felt comfort and solace walking out of that meeting, and we anxiously waited for weeks five and six to come.

MOM AND DAD'S FIFTIETH ANNIVERSARY came and went. Dad had a huge basket of fruit and chocolates delivered to Mom with a simple note: "I love you, Beck. I'll see you soon. Love, David."

Six days after their anniversary, Dad received a phone call.

"David, it's Macy. Would you like to see Rebecca tomorrow? I think it's time. No more than one hour—that is all she can handle right now—but if you are ready, I think now is a good time."

Dad was more than ready. He was advised to let her do most of the talking. He was prepared to tell her he was going back and forth to Houston for work, but otherwise he would wing it.

It bothered me that I wasn't invited to see Mom. I didn't understand why I had to wait, but Macy said it was best for Dad to come alone. If we came together, there was a high probability she would think we had ganged up on her or were spending time together without her, thus causing more anxiety and confusion. Macy also knew it would be an emotional reunion between Mom and Dad, and it would have been too much for Mom to handle if we were both there. It made sense, but it was certainly a shot to the heart.

The day Dad saw Mom was difficult for me. I dropped the kids off, went to yoga, then made up errands to keep me busy. All I could think about was how much I wanted to hug my mom.

I anxiously waited for Dad to call. My phone rang while I was sitting in the carpool line.

"Dad! How did it go? I've been dying to hear from you!"

Dad paused on the other end. "It went well. But it was *so* emotional, Sarah. She cried and cried and cried. She told me she thought I had left her for another woman."

"What? That *kills* me. What did you say?"

"I told her she was my one and only, and we have been married for fifty years. I grabbed that pillow I gave you, and I put it in her lap. She loved it. It made her smile."

"What else? Tell me everything!"

"Honestly, I'm pretty wiped. There were a lot of tears. I was there about an hour, or a little less, and they helped redirect her so I could leave. Leaving was the hardest part. I don't know how you did it, Sarah. I can't thank you enough."

"Oh, Daddy, we're a team. I understand if you don't want to talk right now. I'm sorry I got all excited. Hearing you and knowing you got to see her gives me hope for my visit. I pray it will get easier and easier each day you go."

"I'll call you when I am thinking more clearly." He hung up the phone.

Dad and I spoke again that night. I felt weak all over hearing about Mom's rapid decline and listening to him wonder if her decline was inevitable and would have happened anyway, or if the placement and being in memory care had accelerated it.

Emails of encouragement flooded my inbox over the next few days. The love and prayers of so many friends gave us strength and courage to get through each day.

Six weeks and four days after abandonment day, I got the phone call.

"Hey, Sarah. Are you ready to see Mom?"

TWENTY-TWO

KEEP THE FAITH

September 27, 2016

--•❉•--

"GINNY, ARE YOU READY TO see Mom? I need you with me. I'm so nervous. Call me back!"

I knew Big Ginny could break the ice and get Mom laughing, as well as take the pressure off me to lead the lunch conversation. Macy said it would be best if I went upstairs to see Mom first, alone, for about thirty minutes, then have Ginny join us for lunch. Mom had been asking about Ginny, so it was the perfect time to bring her into the picture.

Ginny called me back. "Are you kidding me? I feel like I've been in a jail cell not seeing Becky. I will definitely be there, and I'll bring her some treats for the whole floor."

The thought of seeing Mom made me increasingly anxious. My chest became hot and broke out in hives, and my heart pounded whenever I thought of our reunion. I was also terrified of the moment she saw my face. Would she remember who left her there? My mind raced with horrible scenarios.

As I got in Ginny's car for the visit, I told her I was terrified. I wore my long cross necklace in hopes that it would remind Mom how much God loved her.

"Do you think when she looks at me, she'll be angry? What if she remembers? Or what if she's so angry that she slaps me? That phone call—she said if I didn't pick her up, she would no longer call me daughter. What if—"

"Sarah! Stop it with the what-ifs. Your mother is *not* going to remember how she got there. She doesn't even know how long she has been there or what day of the week it is. She isn't going to remember what happened six weeks ago. Especially since you'd given her two glasses of wine and a Valium!"

I let out a long breath. "Okay, okay. I will try to relax. Deep breaths."

Ginny smiled. "I brought her a little gift. I thought it would be fun to walk in there with a big ol' box of doughnuts!"

"That would be hilarious! Yes, break the ice with some doughnuts. You can come in with that loud voice of yours and give her a doughnut—she would love that."

Ginny and I drove through a Dunkin' Donuts, ordering enough to feed the caregivers and residents.

Macy met me in the lobby to walk me up. She told me that she'd reminded Mom only an hour before that I was coming, but that she'd most likely forgotten. Macy also warned me, as Dad had, that Mom had declined. She explained that it was a combination of the disease's progression and the medicines she was taking.

"What do you mean, the medications?" I asked.

"Well, we had to up her dosage for anxiety, and the medications can affect her cognitively. However, at this point, they are necessary. We will begin to lower her doses as she becomes more used to her surroundings. I know it's hard to understand. Remember, Sarah, your mom has early-onset Alzheimer's, and it progresses more rapidly than if she'd been diagnosed later in life."

"I understand," I said gently.

I asked her to take photos of Mom and me when we saw each other for the first time in weeks.

"Of course. I'll take them with my phone and text them to you."

"Thank you so much. I just want to document as much as I can through these next few years," I said.

The elevator dinged and, looking up, I saw the number four in red lights again: déjà vu of that horrible August day. Taking a deep breath, I stepped out.

"It's going to be okay, Sarah. She will be so happy to see you. Just be yourself," Macy said.

I was short for words. *God, please be with me. Please let this be peaceful and beautiful. I have missed her so much. Please, God, bless this time with Mom and me.*

Macy grabbed the handle on Mom's door and turned it. "Knock, knock. Becky? I have a visitor here to see you!"

Through the bathroom door I heard her say, "Huh?" Then, as I walked toward her standing in the bathroom, our eyes locked.

"*Mommy!*"

"Sarah! Oh, *Sarah*!"

I hugged her tightly. Being taller, my whole body leaned into her as I held her like never before.

She could barely speak. "Sarah, oh, Sarah. Where, where have you, Sarah?" She started to cry. I knew she was asking me where I had been.

I put her face in the palms of my hands as if she were a small child. "Oh, Mommy, I have missed you. I love you so much, Mommy."

Mom could barely open her eyes through the tears. She held my hands as I held her face, and I kissed her on the cheeks, nose, and forehead. I didn't want to let go. We stood in her bathroom for what felt like five or ten minutes, just holding each other.

"Mom, I love you! Oh, Beauty, don't cry. I am here now, and everything is going to be okay."

I grabbed her hands and led her to the chairs in her room.

I noticed her right hand was shaking, and she tried to talk but couldn't. Her emotions had overtaken her. I grabbed a box of tissue and wiped her nose.

She looked at me as I held her shaking right hand. "Sarah, where have you, where, Sarah?"

The look she gave me with her squinty eyes was one of confusion.

She wanted to know how, when, why, and where, but she couldn't say the words.

"Mom, you are safe. I love this place. Look at your room! It is beautiful!"

"You do? You like?"

"Yes, Mom. I really do! You did a great job decorating it."

It's all I could think to say. I wanted to see whether she would agree that she had decorated it or knew I was making that up.

"Well, I tried. It's small, but . . ."

Thank You, God. She thinks she did it!

"I mean, Beauty, it's really lovely in here. I love what you have done. You and Pop really picked a winner!"

Please let her agree, God. Please don't let her know it was me who brought her here. Please, God.

"Well, he likes, uh, likes. But, where is? Where is he?"

"Dad is in Houston right now. He is going back and forth for work. He'll be back soon."

"Oh, okay, yeah, okay. Sarah, where have you? I have missed you. Much."

"Oh, Mommy. I have missed you, too. I am back in Dallas now. We've been in Colorado most of the summer, and school just started for the kids, so I am finally back and can see you more."

"Oh, right. Yes, Colorado. How are? How are they?"

I knew she was asking about the kids. Through her eyes, I could see her heart melting when I talked about them.

"They are great, Mom. They can't wait to see Beauty and Pop's new place. They are going to love it here!"

She rolled her eyes and gave a small sarcastic laugh. "Well, it's not big. Not much, you know, not much for them."

"Oh, Mom, there is plenty for them to do. You have cards and board games and puzzles out there, and Elijah can throw a football anywhere. He doesn't care!"

Macy was still in the room. I hadn't even been aware that she was snapping pictures. She tapped me on the shoulder and said she would let us visit privately for a few minutes. Then she gave me a wink to let me know she would bring Ginny up.

Mom looked different. Her face was a little swollen, and her eyelids were droopier; she had aged in those six weeks. She wore a beautiful cobalt-blue-and-white top with splashes of turquoise, along with matching pants. Her hair was straight and not styled, but it was clean. I'd helped Dad line up appointments for manicures and pedicures every two weeks, to maintain her dignity, and her nails were freshly painted. I wanted to fix her makeup, though, and brighten her eyes.

I told her about my summer, what grades the kids were in, and Emery turning eleven. We talked about how she and Dad had been married for fifty years, and how I prayed Thad and I would have the blessing of being married that long.

Our time together was incredibly meaningful. It was emotional, but the depth of our love for each other had not changed. We had lost weeks together, but it seemed like we gained them back in those few minutes. I missed hugging her, and I missed brushing her hair and putting on her mascara and lipstick. I wanted to never forget that moment.

Hearing Ginny's voice from around the corner, I said, "Mom, someone's here to see you. Shhh, listen."

Mom lowered her eyebrows and tilted her head like a puppy.

"I think I hear Ginny!"

Mom's eyes got big. "Ginny? Let's *hide*!"

Within seconds, Mom had jumped out of her chair and hopped over to the wall on the other side of the bathroom door. She knelt with her hands on her knees. When I came over to whisper something to her, she put her finger over her mouth and said, "Shhh! Let's surprise!"

I can't explain the joy it brought me to see my mom so giddy over her best friend. I felt like I was playing hide-and-go-seek with Elijah! I turned my phone on video—I had to document this moment.

We heard a knock on the door and the words, "Doughnuts! Hello? I brought some doughnuts!"

Ginny turned the corner with a chocolate doughnut hanging out of her mouth and chocolate icing smudged all over her lips. Mom squealed with such excitement that I thought she might wet her pants. She tried to jump up and down but couldn't because her knees were turned inward. And she didn't know what to do with her hands to let Ginny know she had a chocolate mess on her face—wave, clap, or point.

But Ginny just planted a giant kiss on Mom's lips with the chocolate icing all over her mouth. It was the most special moment between two friends, reunited as if nothing had changed. On that day, not even a brain disease could diminish their love for each other.

AS WE SAT DOWN WITH Mom to eat lunch, I was in shock over her decline. Her hands continued to shake, and she struggled to get the soup spoon to her mouth. She had a hard time cutting her chicken because she was holding her fork upside down, and knives weren't allowed for safety reasons. Thankfully, Ginny kept the conversation going so I wouldn't have to talk much.

I wanted to help Mom eat, but I thought my offer might offend her. What Ginny did next was priceless.

"Here," she said. "I'm going to put my straw in my soup and just drink it through the straw. I don't want the noodles anyway! I just want the broth. Who needs a spoon when you have a straw? It's definitely less messy."

Mom looked over at Ginny's soup with the clear straw sticking out of it.

"You should try it, Becky."

Mom grabbed the straw out of her cranberry juice, stuck it in her cup of soup, and slurped down the entire cup of chicken broth. I couldn't believe it. *Genius, Ginny!*

It took Mom an hour to eat soup, chicken, green beans, and dessert. Her fine motor skills just weren't the same.

When it was time to say goodbye, I gave her a hug and told her I had to leave for carpool. I realized when I said this she might want to go with me, so I added, "Then I need to take a group of girls to soccer practice."

The lies. The constant lies. That's one thing I did not miss for six weeks: having to look my mom in the eyes and lie.

Macy redirected Mom as we left. She told her she needed help with something, and as Mom waved at me and walked away, I headed quickly to the memory-care door. Suddenly, as I looked at the keypad, it was déjà vu, that moment of turning my back on Mom and not looking back.

As Ginny and I stepped into the elevator, I started to cry again.

"Oh, Ginny. I miss her so much. Why does she have to have this disease?"

Again, the emotions poured out. I went into the same restroom I'd gone into the day we placed Mom. Just like then, I shut the door and wept. Only this time, I had Big Ginny instead of Little Ginny taking care of me. As I cried, I could hear my mom's words from the past: "Sarah, I really wish you would call Little Ginny when you visit New York and get to know her. You girls would love each other so much."

God, thank You. I love our Ginnys. What would I do without them?

WHEN GINNY DROPPED ME OFF, I was numb. My spirit exhausted, I went to my room, got in bed, and curled into a fetal position. I cried so hard, feeling terribly alone. There were so many emotions running through my brain, my thoughts were cluttered. Memories with Mom began to take over, especially the hours we spent together driving to and from gymnastics. And the conversations we had and her guidance and mentoring through those hormonal teen years.

That night, I realized she couldn't console me anymore. I could no longer talk to her about things that bothered me or get her advice. It wasn't the same anymore and never would be. Although we laughed and smiled and hugged and had fun that afternoon, it was like a piece of me died when I left Mom. Part of my soul was still at the lunch table on the fourth floor, never to return.

My insides were screaming, "Save me!" I shook and cried, blood rushing to my face, and the pressure felt like it was going to burst through the top of my head. I couldn't stand it. This dark spirit of anger and self-pity was stalking me and wouldn't go away.

After my meltdown, as I began to doze off, I heard the words, "I love you, Daughter."

Those were the words Mom said to me often, and God used them then to speak through her to remind me how much He loved me.

Faith is not about making God do what I want, but rather it is about me knowing that what God does is good. As I lay there in a fetal position, I reminded myself that *God is love*. I fell asleep, knowing that He would equip me to stand on my two feet again and run this race with courage. It wouldn't be easy, but I would lean on Him, not on my own understanding.

TWENTY-THREE

FRIENDS ARE THE BEST

September 21 to September 30, 2016

-•❖•-

T HE DAY AFTER SEEING MOM, I awoke to my phone exploding with text messages from friends and family members. I could barely get out of bed that morning, but never had I experienced such an outpouring of love from friends in my entire life. Fresh flowers were delivered to my porch, along with cards filled with scripture. Their messages gave me the courage to stand on my feet again.

Jennifer stopped by late in the morning. She was elated I was able to see Mom, and there I was—depressed, complaining, and sad. I couldn't express any excitement because the negative had overtaken the positive. That dark spirit was stalking me again.

Before Jennifer left, she urged me, "Focus on what is good. You finally got to see your mom, and you are acting like you have no faith. You are forgetting what Jesus did on that cross. Jesus begged for it to be over on the cross, but He did what He had to do. I love you, but you can't let Satan win this pity party. Focus on the good and not the bad."

I was so angry. How could Jennifer say something like that? She'd said it so boldly that it caught me off guard and hurt my feelings. *What kind of friend says something like that after I wait seven weeks to see my mom?*

But hours later, as I typed an update to friends and family, I realized her words rang true.

Yesterday was so emotional, and I had a massive breakdown when I got home. I literally cried out to God that He would breathe life into me because I am feeling so down and sad. I can't handle watching this disease take my mom in such a slow and cruel way. I feel weak, and I feel like I can't do anything. I slept from 8:30 p.m. to 6:30 a.m. last night, and I feel like I could sleep for days. I'm tired of everyday stuff and just want to grieve, but as a mom and a wife, you have to go on, right? I almost feel bitter and resentful. So many emotions that I can't express in words. I don't want sympathy. It's just how I feel, and I want to be raw and honest with you all and not mask anything! But this is not a pity party. I've had one already with Him, and then a friend had to slap me around a few times to make me come out of it. She said, "Focus on what's good, Sarah. Jesus begged for it to be over on the cross, but He did what He had to do."

I read something today:

> *"He is the great generator of the power plant at the center of my threefold being, working in the midst of my physical being, including my brain and other parts of my nervous system."*

That is my prayer for today. That He would be my power plant. I need Him to walk in me and for me, because I simply can't today.

This journey is my own. And many of you are going through your own journey. It is my prayer that Jesus will shine through everyone's personal journey. How can people see His grace, goodness, and light if we can't be authentic and real, if we hide behind our struggles? I am not hiding. This is real-life stuff, and I am in deep pain. I won't compare anymore and think mine isn't as bad as hers or his, or think to myself, "I can't ask them to pray for me again." If I had not asked for prayers, then I would not have experienced the incredible blessing of my phone exploding yesterday with so many scriptures, prayers, and words of encouragement!

Thank you for sharing this journey with me and for praying with me and for my family. I can't allow myself to be ashamed of asking for prayers anymore because I and we desperately need them. Thank you for your encouragement and reminders that you want to pray. Thank you for your amazing messages and love you pour out. I am so overwhelmed with gratitude, it has brought me to my knees.

So I leave you with my "update." It was painful, emotional, and joyful. It was tons of tears and lots of laughter. It was worry and concern, yet peace about where she is. It was delightful. It was special. It was a moment I will never ever forget. It was love. She is loved, and she loves on them: The staff absolutely love her there. Love was in the air everywhere, even in the hymns played over the speaker during lunch. I watched her inability to hold her fork or poke her food, and I saw her wilting before my eyes, but what I am clinging to is the pure love of the Holy Spirit that was there during our time together. He never left! He was present every second. He spoke words through me, and He brought her peace. I'm in awe of His goodness even during such pain. Thank you to the friend who reminded me last night that this could help people and that she wants to be a part of this journey with me, and thank you to the friend today who got in my face and told me to focus on what was good and not bad. I needed y'all, and He knew it. His timing is always perfect.

Love, Sarah

God became my source of strength the day after I saw Mom. The responses I received from that update were overwhelming. People were inspired, encouraged, and blessed by His goodness toward our family. He wasn't only drawing me closer to Him but was drawing *others* to Him. There really is purpose through pain.

My friend Tavia, one of the strongest women I know, called me later that day. Tavia has a faith deeply rooted in Him and the most generous heart. She spoke the truth with love, and she spoke about her love for God boldly and unashamedly.

"Sarah, I have something I want to run by you, and I hope you will say yes. I want to set up meal deliveries for you and Thad over the next several weeks. So many people want to help but don't know how, and I know meals would serve you during this time."

I hesitated. "That is so sweet, Tavia. Thank you, but I'm okay. I'm not sick, and I can drive and get out and run my errands. Thank you for offering, but we are fine."

"But, Sarah, here's the thing. You don't want to have to even *think* about what to cook for your family, much less go to the store. I could email a small group of friends and have meals delivered for a week or two—however long it blesses you."

"Gosh, I don't know. I feel bad accepting meals from people. That's what we do when someone has a baby or is very sick."

"You are emotionally sick. You are in pain, you are hurting, and you are tired. So many of us want to do something in addition to prayer. Please let us do this, even for a short time."

I hesitated, but I heard the love in her voice and felt her heart's desire in wanting to serve our family.

"Thank you, Tavia. I am tired." I began to cry over the phone. "This has been so hard, and I'm trying to stay strong, but I am very fragile. Thank you for stepping up like this. Your friendship is such a blessing. You inspire me to be a better friend to others. Yes, I'd be so grateful for food. Thank you."

"I'm so glad you said yes! Aves and I will bring you dinner tonight."

That evening, Tavia and her youngest daughter delivered chicken teriyaki bowls and delicious kale guacamole. Aves and Emery were close friends, and the moment Aves saw Emery, she ran up and hugged her like she hadn't seen her in weeks, even though they were just at school together that day. Just like her mom, Aves had a way of lifting people up, making them feel special and loved.

Emery, through the glass of the front door, watched Tavia and Aves drive off. "Mom, I love Aves. She's always happy and makes me feel *so* good."

"Well, happiness is a choice, and Aves chooses to be happy as much as she can. You can, too. We can all choose happiness."

As I scooped dinner onto the plates, I was grateful that I didn't have to think about what Thad and the kids would eat. All I had to do was throw away the to-go bag and containers and put the plates in the dishwasher.

The next day, another meal was delivered, and the next, and the next, and the next. We had meals for two weeks, and it was the best gift anyone could have given me during that time. The way my close friends rallied to serve our family encouraged and uplifted us. I was reminded that we all serve a common purpose: to love others.

ONE DAY, I RECEIVED AN email from the Alzheimer's Association about the upcoming Walk to End Alzheimer's. Thad and I had been donating annually, so I was on their distribution list. The Dallas walk was in only a week and a half, and I felt conflicted about participating. It would make Mom's disease that much more real, and I wasn't sure I was emotionally prepared to walk in her honor. I decided to text Little Ginny, Carie, and Jennifer.

"Girls—want to walk? It's next Saturday. What do you think? We could get dinner and a hotel room the night before and not worry about trying to get there early the next morning with the crowds. Thoughts?"

All three of them responded almost immediately: "In!"

I asked Little Ginny to send the date to her mom to see if she wanted to walk. And Big Ginny, too, was in.

Scrambling over the next several days, we had shirts made that said, "God is Good," and came up with our team name, Beauty's Cuties. I booked a room at a hotel downtown, and Thad agreed to keep the kids and take the girls to their Saturday-morning soccer games.

It was surreal. I wasn't in denial, but at the same time, surrounding myself with caregivers and other families in support of Alzheimer's was making me face and accept Mom's disease as well as embrace it, which I wasn't fully prepared to do.

Sending out an email through the Alzheimer's Association, with a short video that included pictures of Mom, I asked friends to pray for the walk. The email also requested donations in honor of Mom, but I preferred prayers to dollars.

Macy called on Monday, September 25. "Hey, Sarah. Would you like to see your Mom again? It will be a week tomorrow, and she's asking for you! We think it's okay for you to return again. If all goes well tomorrow, I think you can start coming up here as much as you'd like."

"As much as I'd like? Thank you, Macy!"

I began to feel more hope. I had seen Mom, my friends had delivered meals, texts and emails with scripture from friends flooded my phone, and I was signed up to do the Walk to End Alzheimer's. Fresh flowers had been delivered to my front door several times, and a few friends left surprise gifts, such as a devotional book and a package of gluten-free flour and chocolate chips for making cookies with the kids.

The love overflowed, and I felt like God carried me through those weeks of heartbreak, walking each step with me. He was giving me the courage I had asked for and the strength to carry on. He was serving me through the hands and feet of my very own friends. The more I thought about the shirts we would wear on Saturday, the more I believed that God IS good.

TUESDAY, I MET MACY DOWNSTAIRS at the center. Although nervous, I felt prepared about what to expect: possibly more tears from Mom, questions about where I had been, and evidence of more physical decline. Though I wasn't sure how Mom would be, I knew I was much stronger.

You can do this, Sarah. You already have, and God is with you.

"Knock, knock. Mommy?"

"Sarah! Where have you been? Oh, Sarah!" Mom hugged me tightly.

"How are you today? You look *beautiful*. Wow, who did that makeup?"

"My makeup? Me, I guess? I don't know. Let me see!"

Mom went into the bathroom to check herself out. She looked beautiful. A caregiver had done her makeup and made it look so natural—soft and dewy.

"Who is that woman?" She stared at herself in the mirror. "I don't know who that is!"

"Mom, that is *you*! I pray I age as beautifully as you have."

Mom turned and hit me on the shoulder. "Oh, you!" She let out a sound like I was crazy to say she was beautiful. She put her arms around my neck and pulled me in tight.

"I miss you, Sarah. I miss you so much."

I grabbed her face again with my hands and saw tears in her eyes.

"Mom, don't cry. I'm here now! And I will get to come see you more and more because the kids are back in school."

With my thumbs, I wiped the tears off her face as she giggled. "Really? Yay!"

I felt stronger. I felt like a caretaker. Able to hold my own tears, I could be courageous for her. She was like the child and I the mom. She needed to feel secure knowing her daughter would be there.

"Mom, I love your place. You did a wonderful job decorating it. Maybe I could come spend the night with you sometime?"

Her eyes lit up. "That would be great!"

Mom needed me to lead the conversation. I could see a certain glaze in her eyes that indicated she was slower to think and process, and I somehow knew when it was time to redirect a conversation because she was feeling lost.

Spending a few hours with her that day, I left much stronger than the first visit. But it was still gut-wrenching to witness her decline. It was heartbreaking to see her lose her mind and dignity, even if she didn't know it. She had a strong beautiful body on the outside, yet her brain was shutting down.

Another difficult moment was leaving her behind locked doors. Leaving could be tricky, but thankfully, a caregiver knew when I had to go. They redirected her as I said goodbye, sparing us any separation anxiety. For several months, I would have to fight the guilt of leaving her there, and that feeling never really went away. That spirit continued to stalk me, only this time it wasn't self-pity; it would be guilt and resentment of the disease.

As I left, I asked Macy if she was participating in the Alzheimer's walk that weekend.

"Yes, a bunch of us are. Are you?"

"I am. It's totally last minute, but the three friends who helped me during Mom's placement are doing it with me. And Mom's best friend, Ginny! You know, the one with the doughnuts last week?"

"Oh, yes, I know Ginny! How could I forget her? And she loves your mother so much. I hope to see you all there—we'll look for you."

I ARRIVED AT THE HOTEL Friday afternoon around 4:00 and met Little Ginny, Carie, and Jennifer. After chatting for a bit, we decided to head downstairs for dinner. As I changed my shoes, we heard a knock on the door that connected our room to the one next door.

"What?" Carie said.

"Hello?" I looked at Jennifer, puzzled.

There was dead silence. Nobody said a word.

Hearing the knock again, my heart pounded as I turned to Carie.

"I don't want to open that," I said, my eyes huge. "Umm, who's there?" Silence.

Jennifer said, "Hello?" Again, silence.

Jennifer began to unlock the deadbolt. I stuck out my arm. "No, don't open that! We don't know who—are you crazy?"

Terror paralyzed me as Jennifer turned the handle. We had nowhere to run.

Then Jennifer said, "Oh, hello!" As she pulled the door open, this big purple thing came around the corner.

I shrieked and jumped backward.

It was Malaise, one of my best friends from Austin, wearing a large, purple feathery headdress and a purple feather boa around her neck.

She came dancing toward me, saying, "We're gonna walk tomorrow! I'm walking with you, babe!"

I wrapped my arms around Malaise and wept on her shoulder. I couldn't believe she had driven from Austin to surprise and support me.

As I cried, she said, "I knew you wouldn't open the door. I told them you wouldn't do it!"

I wept while they all laughed their heads off.

Malaise, Jennifer, Carie, and Little Ginny pulled out all sorts of purple goodies—purple being both my favorite color and the color representing the fight against Alzheimer's—after Malaise's surprise arrival. Jennifer had purple monogrammed cups loaded with jumbo gumballs, also purple. Boas, headdresses, sparkly bracelets, necklaces, and tattoos for our cheeks—all purple. I couldn't believe the number of items they had stored next door. I had no clue.

Finally we headed for dinner. While waiting for a table, we asked a bystander to take our picture.

As we lined up, our arms around each other, I heard a familiar voice say, "Everybody get in the picture!"

Nicole, another friend from my college years, was walking towards me.

I let out another scream when I saw her. Sitting back on my heels, with my head buried in my hands, tears rolled down my face.

My friends, God. My friends.

Nicole knelt down and tapped my shoulder. "Sarah, don't cry."

I stood up and gave her the same hug I had given Malaise.

"I can't believe you are here."

"Why? I live down the street!"

Though Nicole lived in Dallas, I had never thought to ask anyone to walk with me except the three who had helped place Mom. It meant the world to me that Malaise and Nicole showed up.

Malaise grinned. "That's it, Sarah! No more surprises."

As our dinner of steak, laughter, and memories drew to an end, I proposed a toast: "To my friends, who have made me feel so loved today: Thank you for supporting me, and thank you for walking in honor of Mom tomorrow." Once again, I began to cry.

"Words can't express how grateful I am to you for showing up and carrying me through tomorrow. It won't be easy, and clearly I am very emotional, but I know I can do it with each of you by my side. I love you. You are the best."

TWENTY-FOUR

MAKING BROKEN THINGS BEAUTIFUL

October 1, 2016

--•❊•--

THE NEXT MORNING, WE WERE up early. Locking myself in the restroom, I clicked on a devotional app in my phone to set my mind on God.

The first paragraph of *Jesus Calling* read,

> "Worship me only. I am King of kings and Lord of lords, dwelling in unapproachable Light. I am taking care of you! I am not only committed to caring for you, but I am also absolutely capable of doing so. Rest in Me, My weary one, for this is a form of worship."

Form of worship. Rest in Me. I am taking care of you!

While brushing my teeth and changing my clothes, I prayed silently for God to take over my morning. God already had the day before when my friends appeared. *Form of worship.* I realized my walk that morning could be a form of worship. I didn't want to be sad, confused, or conflicted. I wanted to be grateful, celebrating His ability to get me through anything, especially Mom's disease.

Suddenly, my phone exploded again with text messages. Friends were sending prayers and words of strength. I had twenty text messages arrive in less than an hour. God was taking care of me through friends, and I knew it.

We went downstairs and walked to the grassy area by Reunion Tower. A stage had been set up, music blasted, and people were everywhere. It was a warm, sunny day with excitement and love in the air. I hugged strangers as if we were family going through this horrific disease together.

Wearing a white fedora hat with purple feathers, Big Ginny walked up. I ran into her arms, and when our eyes met, Ginny, known for holding it together, couldn't avoid the tears.

"I can't believe we are doing this, Sarah. I just can't believe she has Alzheimer's." She started crying on my shoulders. "I love your mother so much."

"I know, Ginny, I know. I can't believe we are doing this, either. She loves you so much. She would be so proud of us today. Thank you for being here for her and for me. You're like a mom to me."

Ginny never cried in public, and although it was heartrending, it made my own tears feel justified. I knew I had to dig deep today, and I gave myself permission to dance, celebrate, and have fun in the fight against the incurable disease stealing away my precious mom.

I faced a choice. I could either focus on what was good, or I could let that dark, self-pitying spirit stalk me again on that beautiful, sunny Saturday.

Focus on Me, Sarah. I am a good Father. Do this in honor of your mom and Me.

Before the festivities began, we each received a flower spinner that would twirl in the air as we walked. With a silver sharpie, I wrote on each petal something that represented Mom. One said, "Barrel-Racer Becky," a nickname Thad had given Mom when we first married because she used to barrel race. Another said, "Beauty," and another read, "Mom." On Big Ginny's I wrote, "Rangerettes forever," "College roommates," and "Best friends forever." Each friend had a spinner that said different things about Mom and their relationship with her.

We all wore our "God is Good" T-shirts, headbands with purple feathers, and purple beaded necklaces. Carie, Big Ginny, and Little Ginny wore purple-laced gloves with the fingers cut out.

A lady approached our group asking if a few of us would go on stage when it was her turn to lead the dancing and exercises for the warm-up. Every one of the girls pointed to Big Ginny and me.

I turned bright red. "No way. I am not getting on that stage."

Nicole yelled back at me, "You have to, Sarah! You *have* to do this for your mother."

Malaise chimed in. "Don't let us down! You better get up there and show 'em how it's done."

Little Ginny turned to her mother. "Mom, *seriously*? When have you *ever* turned down front-row, center-stage attention? You better do this for Becky. You and Sarah together, come on."

Big Ginny looked at me. "Well, I guess we don't have a choice: We've got to show these people how it's done. Former UT cheerleader and former Rangerette? They won't know what hit 'em! Let's get up there and shake our booties for Beck."

We all died laughing, and I agreed. I didn't want to do it and was nervous to be on stage in front of hundreds of people, but at that point, why not? If I could have the chance to dance next to my mom's best friend and college roommate the way *she* used to dance next to her, why not make her proud? *Form of worship, Sarah. Form of worship.*

As we waited backstage, I walked to the right side of the stage so I could see my girlfriends. There they were, front and center, decked out in purple, laughing and smiling and dancing away to the DJ's tunes. Chills went down my spine and I couldn't control my tears. My body started shaking, my chest got warm, and my lips quivered.

Oh, God. Thank You for my friends. Thank You for this day. Be with us, Lord, as we honor Mom, and I honor You. Thank You for Your overwhelming love.

Looking down to compose myself, I continued to ask God to help me. Just as I did, Big Ginny said, "You have to stop crying. You know

I am a private crier, and I've already broken down once—I can't do it again. Let's have some fun, my dear. You can cry later!"

The DJ started playing "Whip Nae Nae" once we were onstage. The exercise leader's goal was to warm everyone up for their walk, and we, her backup dancers, were to motivate the crowd.

Big Ginny didn't hold back. There she was at the front of the stage, rolling her hips in slow motion and rotating her bottom from left to right, drawing screams and laughs. She turned in a full circle, with her arms and hips moving in all directions. Her gigantic blue eyes worked the crowd, and she looked like a seventy-year-old woman with twenty-one-year-old moves. If only my mom had been there to see it.

When Ginny took center stage, my worries slipped away. I pictured Mom right next to her, engaging the crowd and shaking her own hips. I grabbed Ginny's hand, and we danced together, side by side, without stopping. The DJ played another song, and we stayed with the beat. I was having *fun*. I was dancing next to my mom's best friend and partner on stage, as Mom had done fifty years earlier.

In those brief moments, I felt carefree. No worries, no fears, no anxieties, and no guilt. He lifted me up as I danced and rejoiced with love by the grace of God.

WAVING OUR FLOWER SPINNERS HIGH in the crisp fall air, the girls and I walked together, taking photo after photo to document every step.

As I walked across the finish line, I wanted to find Mom's caregivers. I had been looking for them throughout our walk but never found them. There were too many people—thousands of people from different backgrounds, ethnicities, and ages coming together to raise awareness and find a cure for Alzheimer's disease. It was a beautiful sight, and we all felt like family.

An emcee was announcing the names of the different groups and teams walking across the finish line.

"Thank you, Team CC Young!"

"Way to go, Team Boyd!"

Then I heard the words: "Here we have The Tradition caregivers! Way to go!"

I took off running, pushing through hundreds of people to reach the finish line.

"Macy, Macy! Patrice!" I yelled.

"Oh my gosh, Sarah! We've been looking for you."

Mom's earthly angels were there with me at the finish line, and it was perfect. We took our picture together. It's one I will always cherish.

"Macy, I'm dying to see Mom today. Do you think it's okay if I pop over there? Is it too soon? I know I just saw her Tuesday, but I am dying to see her."

"Absolutely. Go see her. Your mom is doing great, and you can see her whenever you want. You are a wonderful daughter!"

God knew the desires of my heart that day, and He was fulfilling them.

The girls and I lunched together at the hotel, and I couldn't believe what we had done. I couldn't wait to show Mom the video of Ginny dancing on the stage. Mom wouldn't know why she danced, and I wouldn't tell her, but she would laugh and laugh and laugh. I wanted to see her gap-toothed smile, her ugly laugh-cry face with the squinty nose, and the tears of happiness that would run down her face. That is *exactly* what Ginny had done. She'd brought happiness, joy, tears, laughter, and fun throughout the entire day.

That afternoon, I went straight to see Mom. I had to hug her. I had to tell her how much I loved her and thank her for all she had done for me. Even if she didn't remember anything I said the following day, I would know in my heart I had told her and would have no regrets.

My heart was on fire and full of love. Although my heart was broken, it was being restored by God, my friends, and the choices I was making to find joy and rise above the pain. I refused to let that dark spirit stalk me. The moment it tried, I would seize it and pray.

. . .

THE NEXT FEW WEEKS, I saw Mom five days a week. My mission became loving on her, and as I did, I began to fall in love with every resident on her floor. They were becoming my friends, too. The more I saw of them, the more comfortable I felt staring into their eyes and telling them how much I loved them. As I touched their shoulders and hugged them, I told them God loved them, too.

Mom would ask, "How do you know all of these people?"

I'd respond, "Well, Mom, I come here all the time to see you, and they've become my friends, too." Mom would smile, touch my hand, and kiss me on the cheek. Deep down I knew she loved seeing me serve others because that was what she had done her entire life.

I was serving a purpose, which was to love others no matter what I was going through. Jesus bore the cross for me while in deep agony and pain. He was my example. Why couldn't I pour out love through my pain and suffering? It was nothing compared to His.

Several people had texted me for updates on the walk. Deciding to send an email, I wrote in the subject line, "Making Broken Things Beautiful."

The Alzheimer's walk was indescribable. It was a twenty-four-hour tidal wave of emotions. I was struggling with the sadness while also seeing that I wasn't alone. There were thousands of others around me who were either going through or had gone through the same heartbreak. I didn't think I was ready to walk for Mom because it would make me face her disease and accept it even more; yet, of course, I wanted to honor her.

I was overwhelmed with how God showed up those twenty-four hours. He showed up through my friends who surprised me at the hotel the night before to walk with me the next morning and through other friends who planned things behind my back! He gave me joy to dance onstage with my mom's college roommate, to know the incredible joy my mom had with her back in the day. He even showed up at the finish line when I ran into Mom's caretakers after looking for them the entire morning. It was an absolutely beautiful day.

There is nothing sweeter than the love I see in my mom's eyes. I am so grateful for the past few years I have had with her. Mom has poured her (God's) love on me my entire life, and to love her back and give her my time . . . there is just nothing sweeter. She wasn't perfect. I'm not perfect. There were mistakes made along the road, and there were things Mom said and did she wished she could take back. Don't we all have things we have said and done that we wish we could take back? The great news is He offers forgiveness along with His grace and mercy. Make time for those you love because if you don't, you miss out on so much love that He wants to pour over you! Friendships and relationships become meaningless if we don't give Him and one another our time.

The Lord has given me all I could want. I see pain, but He sees purpose, and I am finding His will and purpose in my life through this. To love better. To serve better. To give Him glory in all things. All I know is because He is alive, I can be courageous. He can make the broken things beautiful.

Thank you beyond words, and may He reveal His love to you today in an amazing way. He is a good, good Father!

XOXO, Sarah

The responses I received from that email were astonishing. People were inspired and empathized with me about their own circumstances. One friend said, "Don't focus on what is lost, but build on what remains."

There are blessings inside the pain. The scripture that kept coming to my mind over the next month was Joshua 1:9: "Have I not commanded you? Be strong and courageous. Do not be afraid; do not be discouraged, for the LORD your God will be with you wherever you go" (NIV).

God had a tight grip on me, and my eyes were opened enough to see that He loved me no matter what I was going through. He could and would give me the strength and courage to march forward. This journey was going to be difficult, but if I trusted Him and poured my heart into Him, He would provide for my needs.

TWENTY-FIVE

LIFE'S A DANCE

October to mid-November 2016

--•❉•--

TOOK MY DAUGHTERS TO SEE Mom for the first time since her placement. They couldn't wait to see Beauty. Emery, however, was nervous. She was afraid Mom wouldn't remember her. It had been nine weeks.

"Mom, will Beauty know who I am?"

"Oh, Emery, yes, she will know who you are. Now, is it possible she'll forget your name, yes. But she will know the moment you hug her and look into her eyes that you are her granddaughter who loves her deeply."

Emery nodded without saying a word. She was scared and sad, but she also knew she'd had more quality time with me those nine weeks than over the past year.

"Just be yourself," Frensley told Emery. "Mom is right. Beauty loves us no matter what happens or what she loses. We just need to love her the same."

I kept both hands on the steering wheel as I looked into the rearview mirror at Emery's big brown puppy eyes and Frensley's huge hazel ones. My two precious daughters on the journey with me, fearing the unknowns of Alzheimer's disease—yet their experience was different, because it was through the eyes of a child. I couldn't relate to how they felt, so all I could do was pray.

Oh God, thank You for Frensley and Emery. Please be with us today and help us radiate Your love. Be with the girls as they go through this difficult time of confusion and mixed feelings.

The moment we walked into Mom's room, her eyes lit up and she stretched out both arms.

"Oh, Emery! Frensley! Come here, give me a hug!"

The girls hugged Mom. Emery was hesitant and reserved, but Frensley hugged her with confidence.

"Hi, Beauty!" Frensley said. "I've missed you. I love your place!"

Mom rolled her eyes. "Ohhh, come on in. It's little."

"Yeah, but I like it. You and Pop don't need a big room. It's just the two of you!"

Praise You, God. Thank You for giving Frensley Your words and wisdom today.

Emery chimed in, "I like it a lot, Beauty! You look so pretty today."

I could see the pain in Emery's eyes. But she showed courage and strength I had not seen before. Emery and Mom were close, and I knew Emery missed her silliness. She stepped up and loved *big* on Beauty.

Mom gave the girls a tour of her new place, so we walked around the hallways. Mom was happy but kept getting lost, and every time she saw a caretaker or resident, she would say, "I don't even know who that is." By the end, Emery was laughing. I felt thankful to see their bond was still intact.

We were in the sitting area outside Mom's room when we heard "Sugar, Sugar" by The Archies come over the speaker. The next thing I knew, Mom was moving her shoulder forward and backward. She gave Emery a wink, nudging her to dance with her.

"*Uh-oh*, Beauty wants to dance!" Emery yelled.

Mom started laughing, kept moving her shoulder, and then finally stood up and starting shaking her hips.

"Beauty! Oh my gosh, Beauty!" Emery couldn't stop laughing.

I said, "Emery, go on—dance with her!"

"No! Frensley, you dance. Go dance with Beauty!"

Frensley gave Emery a sassy look. "I'd *love* to dance with Beauty."

And there they went, Frensley and Beauty dancing back and forth to "Sugar, Sugar." I walked over to the sound control panel on the wall and cranked up the volume, and before we knew it, we had a full-blown dance party.

Emery became our videographer after I handed her my phone. Mom and Frensley and I danced together, getting lost in the music.

Suddenly, I felt a tap on my shoulder, and turned to find Emery dancing behind me.

"Yay, Em! Come on, get in the circle with us."

The four of us danced to three songs in a row. It was the most beautiful time with my mom and daughters.

Thank You, God. A dance party. Only You could orchestrate a dance party on the girls' first day with Mom. You are so good.

OVER THE ENSUING SIX WEEKS, I spent as much time as I could with Mom. Dad went more often, and I'd show up when he needed to leave. We had a tag-team system because it was easier on Mom for Dad to leave if I was there to replace him. She would forget minutes later that he had even been there.

Mom and I attended the facility's chair exercise class together, and anytime a fun song came on over the speaker, she would look at me, wink, move her shoulder forward and backward a few times, and then look back up at me with a smirk. That was her signal. It didn't matter where we were—we danced on the outdoor patio, in the dining room in the middle of dinner, and while others watched television in the room next to us. Mom and I were in our own world.

Louie, the caregiver who'd dressed up as Billy Bob the first day Dad and I visited, had stolen Mom's heart from the beginning. He loved to dance and had a passion for bringing joy and smiles to every resident. He danced with Mom so much that they had their own routine. I knew he had danced with her when we weren't there because Mom knew what to do. Louie was consistent, dancing with her daily, and she began to feel comfortable and move on her own without missing a beat. She trusted and felt safe with Louie. The moment he walked in the room, she would nearly jump out of her seat.

Louie came in the dining room one afternoon during snack time. "Hey, Becky! Is my dance partner ready?"

"'Course!"

Louie went over to her seat, pulled out her chair, stuck his arm out to help her up, and walked her to the open area. They held hands, doing the twist together. They had this move where they would jump back two or three times while holding each other's hands, then he would twirl her around. Mom never took her eyes off him. He led, and she followed. By the time the song was over, Louie had sweat dripping down his face and Mom was out of breath.

I loved watching them dance because it was also great exercise for Mom. She was using her legs and glutes, and she was forced to listen to the beat of the music and try to dance to the rhythm. I didn't want Mom to lose her rhythm. She was a dancer at heart.

They made me want to dance, too. I love to dance, even though I sometimes feel embarrassed and self-conscious. But, I asked myself that afternoon, why be embarrassed? These new friends of ours loved watching people dance. They wouldn't remember how I had danced; they would simply have joy in their hearts.

There is no greater gift than loving someone, especially someone in need, slowly dying from a chronic illness. I wanted to put my faith into action and care for the sick and visit all the residents, not just Mom.

THAT EVENING, I BEGAN TO think about ways our children could serve. Our kids attended a classical Christian school, where they would sing hymns and recite poetry to all the parents and grandparents in November.

Why not bring the hymns and poetry to the residents? The hymns were traditional, which most of the residents would recognize, and as the staff had told me on more than one occasion, music brings back memories for those with Alzheimer's and dementia.

I kept telling myself, *Emery's classmates and their moms may not want to do this. Their schedules are so busy.* I went back and forth. It seemed like a wonderful idea, but I didn't like imposing.

A few days later, I received a text from my friend, Betsy, who had a daughter at school the same age as Emery. She had lost her mother to Alzheimer's disease.

"Sarah, a thought keeps coming to mind. It may or may not work, but if it did, I thought it would be fun to take a group of girls to sing at your Mom's memory-care facility during the next couple of months. We did that with my older daughter years ago, and it was such fun. Plus, the residents loved hearing old hymns and seeing sweet faces. You know best whether this would be appropriate. I'd be happy to help coordinate."

I responded almost immediately.

"I just told my dad that idea the other day. I want to cry. Absolutely we should plan it. Such confirmation from God, you have no idea!"

God knew I needed Betsy. I needed her messages to encourage me and assure me that it would not only be a gift to Mom and the residents, but also a gift to each of us who participated.

Macy was so excited about the idea that we set a date within twenty-four hours of our conversation. Friday, November 11, was it.

Sending out an email the next day, I couldn't believe the responses. People were overwhelmingly excited. Almost every mom replied, "We are in."

NOVEMBER 11TH ROLLED AROUND, AND I couldn't wait to see the fifth-grade girls in their uniforms stand up and sing old hymns to the residents. I anticipated the looks on their faces and how the music would move them. I did not anticipate, however, my emotional reaction as they sang.

The girls' first song was "My Hope Is Built on Nothing Less." As they sang, I saw one of the residents tapping her hand on her wheel-chair. Another resident began to grunt to the beat. The girls' voices filled the room with peace, love, and comfort, and their sweet faces brought smiles to everyone.

Mom took in every single note and word, despite her deteriorating mind. Tears streamed down my face as I watched her.

She was one of the residents moved by music, one of those who wouldn't remember after the kids had left why their heart was full of joy.

Gloria, a caregiver, belted out the chorus with her rich African accent. She loved Jesus, and it gave her an opportunity to sing praises to His name.

They then sang "O Great God" and "In Christ Alone," and the louder they sang, the more movement I saw from each resident. A foot tap, a hand clap. A few had their eyes closed but their heads were moving, and some were mouthing the words. It was astonishing! The music was moving their souls.

The girls recited the Lord's Prayer in sign language. They had prac-ticed all fall and were going to recite it for their parents and grandpar-ents the next Friday, before Thanksgiving break.

Kneeling next to Mom during the Lord's Prayer, I put my arm around her as she began to say some of the words out loud. I could hear her voice, and I could tell she was searching for words she once knew by heart and prayed daily. I heard another resident join in the prayer, and then another resident: "For thine is the kingdom and the power and the glory forever and ever. Amen."

The moment they finished, I heard Louie yell, "Woo-hoo!" I could feel the presence of the Holy Spirit moving all the hearts in that room— the residents', Mom's, the girls', their parents', the caregivers', mine.

The last thing the girls recited was Matthew 6:20–34. The final verse says, "Therefore do not worry about tomorrow, for tomorrow will worry about itself. Each day has enough trouble of its own" (NIV).

That verse had long been embedded in my heart and mind, but now

I heard it while sitting next to my mom, who was dying of Alzheimer's disease. God spoke to me again that day. As I held Mom's hand, I knew He had her in His hands. He was reminding me not to worry about what the next day would bring, or even the next year, but to focus on that day because that day was a gift from Him.

The room broke out into applause and cheers when the girls finished. It was such a beautiful presentation of God's love poured over them by those precious girls.

After their presentation, the girls snacked on chicken fingers and funnel cakes while Louie prepared the room for bowling.

The girls had never seen a blow-up bowling ball and pins before. The excitement on their faces was priceless. Louie lined the pins up and gave each girl a chance to roll the big, bouncy bowling ball towards them.

Emery went first.

Louie cheered with excitement, "All right, Emery, show us what you got. On three, roll that ball and knock over every one of those pins."

Emery smiled and blushed from the attention.

"All right, everybody, let's see if she can do it!" Louie shouted. "Yell with me: One! Two! Three!"

Emery rolled the ball and hit every pin except one.

"You get one more chance to get a spare! Are you ready?" Louie challenged playfully.

All the girls yelled, "She's ready!"

"Yell with me. One, two, *three*!"

Emery hit the last pin. A spare!

Each girl bowled with another resident. For those in wheelchairs, Louie helped them roll the ball.

We spent a blissful hour and a half serving on the fourth floor. I knew this was only the beginning. There was a reason Mom was there. God had a purpose. It was up to me to choose each day how I would face her disease.

Every day I dodged bullets. Every day, I was mentally exhausted. Every day, I would return to memories of Mom and me, from my childhood on up. Nearly every day, I felt broken, but by God's divine intervention and power, I was beginning to feel inspired, encouraged, and enlightened. God would pick me up and carry me through the next day. I was weak, but He was helping me become strong.

TWENTY-SIX

LIVE THE LIFE

Christmas 2016

···•❊•···

A FEW WEEKS AFTER THE GIRLS' program, I received several phone calls from mothers telling me their daughters were begging to go back before Christmas break. In the midst of holiday parties, finals, homework, and extracurricular activities, these girls were eager to entertain Mom and the residents again. I couldn't pass up the opportunity to spread Christmas cheer.

One friend bought twenty gingerbread house kits and bags of candy. We took a combination of seventh-grade girls from Frensley's class and fifth-graders from Emery's class to sing Christmas carols and traditional hymns. Spreading out among the tables, they helped the residents decorate the gingerbread houses, some of them going from table to table, hugging people and wishing them merry Christmas.

Mom was so happy, she couldn't sit still. She wanted to entertain everyone and play. She, too, went from resident to resident and hugged each one, telling them how much she loved them. In a day full of laughter, joy, and holiday fun, I knew the best was yet to come.

Dad and I had booked the private dining room downstairs for a Christmas dinner with all of our family. We couldn't wait to bring Christmas to Mom, to have her feel like she was "hosting" Christmas as she had done in the past. Of course, she couldn't cook anymore, and she couldn't go out to buy her favorite pies—which was pretty much every flavor.

Dad and I met with the chef of the facility, who told us about his passion for his profession. All I could think about was the list of dishes I wanted him to prepare. I wanted Mom to feel like she had the best Christmas ever, surrounded by the husband, children, and grandchildren she loved with all her heart.

"Chef, it's my heart's desire that Mom feel she is hosting her family with her own decorations in the room and that she chose the menu. Daddy and I both want her to feel like she is at home."

He smiled from beneath his tall, white chef's hat. "I also want her to feel at home, and I think this is a beautiful thing that you are doing for your wife, David, and your mother, Sarah. I will do whatever I can to make it the best Christmas for your family."

My eyes filled with tears as I smiled with gratitude and I grabbed Dad's hand. He tilted his neck up with a closed smile, doing everything he could to stop that knot of emotion in his throat from giving way to tears.

The chef asked us about the family's favorite Christmas foods.

"I would say "Green Bean Supreme," as she called it, with the fried onion rings on top. Definitely a turkey with homemade gravy and dressing, and she loved sweet potato casserole with marshmallows and pecans. What else, Sarah?"

I chuckled. "For sure that fruit salad with all the stuff in it! I don't know what it's called, but she loved that—Grandma English always served it, too."

The chef wrote notes quickly on a white piece of paper. "Oh, yes! The residents love that fruit salad with grapes, chopped apples, a little pineapple and maybe some watermelon, nuts, a little whipped cream. I've got you covered."

"Oh, and she loves a basket of croissants or warm rolls with butter. I think some brown-sugar ham slices might be nice, too. Beck didn't love it, but someone in the family always wanted it, so she would cook it anyway," Dad said.

"Tell me about desserts," the chef said. "Does she like sweets?"

Dad and I exploded with laughter. *Does she like sweets? Oh Chef, little do you know!*

"Can you make every pie possible? She's obsessed with pies during the holidays. She would order three or four ahead of time, and then walk in the door two hours later with about eight or nine," I said.

Dad chuckled. "I always knew who would be eating the leftovers—I could not take the weight off for weeks after Christmas."

But then I pictured Mom trying to scoop gooey pecan pie onto her fork and spilling it on her blouse as she tried to eat it.

"Chef, Mom has a very difficult time now using utensils. How can we make her favorite desserts easy for her to eat to prevent a mess? It's important to us that we protect her dignity."

He nodded in agreement. "I have the perfect solution. We simply make bite-size pieces, mini pies instead of regular pies. I will bake an assortment of her favorites and perhaps add brownie or cheesecake bites, and then something for the kids, like cookies?"

The chef knew exactly how to resolve our worries.

This will be incredible. Thank You, Lord, that we aren't alone. Thank You for a chef who understands our concern and our hearts. He, too, wants to give Mom and our family the best. I love this place so much.

THE SOUTH DAKOTA CLAN ROLLED into town earlier than expected. Our kids are the same ages, and seeing how close the cousins had become, even living so far away, was heartwarming. God knew what he was doing as each child bonded with another.

My older brother, David, hadn't seen Mom since a few months before she was placed. He was the oldest, and Mom had been hard on him for many years.

David loved Mom deeply, but he harbored pain from words said over the years that had penetrated his heart. All on our own journeys in life, I knew my brothers would handle this differently than I had. Though

I had no expectations of what the week would bring, I had prayed fervently for months that David's time with Mom would be meaningful and a time of reconciliation.

THAD AND I HAD INVITED both my brothers and their families over for dinner the evening after their arrival. Gabriel and his family came from nearby Rockwall. We all hoped Dad would be there, but he was going to play it by ear after spending the afternoon with Mom.

Then Dad texted me. "Hey there. You have enough food for me and Mom?"

What? He and Mom? Bring Mom to my house? She hasn't been here since we placed her!

I texted back, face flushing as my heart beat faster. "Are you saying what I think you are, Dad? Bring Mom with you? Here? To my house?"

"Yes. She wants to come, and I'm ready to get her out of here. What do you think?"

What do I think? Yes! No? I don't know. What if she doesn't want to go back? What if she wants him to drive her to their house? I don't know what to tell him, but I would love for Mommy to be here. God, help! What do I say?

Quickly, my thumbs typed out, "YES! Moment by moment! Day by day! God will help us get her home tonight. I'm so excited, Daddy. Thank you!"

Putting my phone down in shock, I looked over at Thad and the others.

"Y'all aren't going to believe this. Dad is on his way right now with Mom. This is amazing!"

David and Gabriel, calm and collected, smiled their approval.

Light the candles. She loves candles. Shoot, what about wine? I need to hide the wine.

Again I addressed the family. "We all know about Mom's drinking problem. I suggest we be as discreet as possible with the bottles of wine sitting out, as I don't have any nonalcoholic to offer her."

Gabriel put his arm around my shoulder. "Sissy, don't worry. It's going to be a great night. Don't worry about things that haven't even happened yet."

Instantly, a favorite scripture jumped to mind. Philippians 4:6–7: "Do not be anxious about anything, but in every situation, by prayer and petition, with thanksgiving, present your requests to God. And the peace of God, which transcends all understanding, will guard your hearts and your minds in Christ Jesus" (NIV).

Around 6:00 that evening, the doorbell rang.

"Mommy! Come in, come in. Hey, Daddy!"

The kids ran in. "Beauty! Pop!"

Everyone was home for Christmas, but this time, it didn't matter where the house was or what city we were in. It was like Christmases past.

Thad came over to help me, then kissed me on the forehead. "God is good, sweetie."

Looking up at him, I said, "He sure is, honey. All the time."

The adults sat around the dining table and the kids at the breakfast table. Their silliness, laughing, and yelling filtered through from the kitchen. As I looked across the table, I noticed Mom staring at me. Sitting with her hands placed gently on each side of her plate, her eyes spoke to me. *Thank You, God. Thank you, Sarah.*

She then looked over at David as he talked to Gabriel, and I saw it again. *Thank You, God. Thank you, David Jr.*

Going around the room, her eyes were speaking to each person. *Thank You, God. Thank you, Gabriel. Thank You, God. Thank you, David.*

It was several minutes before she even touched her fork or picked up a piece of bread. She was living in a dream and peace was written across her face. She didn't seem to want to eat. She simply wanted to stare at her three children and their spouses and be in the moment. Her heart touched, she was emotionally, mentally, and spiritually immersed in love at that moment.

For an instant, I didn't see anyone around the table except Mom in her lavender dining chair. She was an angel, sitting at our table, encouraged by the love in our family and our oneness in Christ.

What transpired that night was unbelievable. Mom and Dad had come over, we had a delicious dinner and visited by the fireplace, then they returned to Mom's new home without a glitch. Only by the grace of God could this have happened, and we had felt His grace. And my dad had the best night in years.

THAT NIGHT I WENT TO sleep sobbing. In awe of God and His wonder, I cried until 2:00 in the morning. My mom had come home. I had missed her so much, and being together with our extended family was perfect. I couldn't have prayed or wished for anything better. It was the unexpected amazingness of God.

About 4:00 a.m., I awoke to Elijah tapping me on the shoulder. "Mommy, I am itchy all over."

I walked him quietly back to his room and rubbed some soothing ointment over him. I tucked him back in, then returned to our bed. Thad was making the little sounds he occasionally does when in deep slumber. The house was especially quiet, and I could not go back to sleep. I dwelled on the private dinner we were planning at Mom's place—the decorations, place settings, and where to put the gifts.

Making a cup of coffee, I spent some time alone with God. Then I headed to the attic and collected some of Mom's Christmas decor and put it by the back door.

At 7:00 a.m., while everyone else in the house slept, I loaded the car and headed to Mom's. *If last night was that great, I can't wait to see what God does tonight!*

Pulling up to the front, I grabbed a cart and took the decorations inside. Trish, my sister-in-law, had been so sweet to help me with decorating the day before, but I wanted it to look even better. Like my mom, I wanted the best for everyone. I wanted to surprise even Trish.

I decided to make a "Longhorn" tree in honor of my older brother, who had played football at the University of Texas. If it weren't for

David, we wouldn't be such die-hard Longhorn fans. Following his example, Gabriel and I both attended UT. David had done so much for me at UT, and our few years together in Austin strengthened our bond. So a tree with burnt-orange-and-white Longhorn ornaments was what our family needed.

After decorating a three-foot Christmas tree on the entry table, I placed gifts under and around the tree, along with a favorite picture of Mom and Dad. Mom's tall Christmas nutcrackers stood on the buffet table, and the main dining table had a beautiful flower arrangement surrounded by candles. Her favorite Christmas linens and fine china completed the table.

Mom's favorite children's plates, depicting Rudolph and Santa, were on the kids' table. It was truly our Houston dining room, just like the Christmases we'd treasured from years before.

LATER THAT DAY, THE FAMILY gathered on the fourth floor to spend "happy hour" with Mom. Happy hour consisted of live music, cheese, fruit, popcorn, soda, and nonalcoholic wine.

As I walked through the door, I heard the piano. Looking up, I saw Big Ginny, her two precious granddaughters, Amber and Jade, and Little Ginny dancing with Mom. They had started a dance party on the fourth floor.

At the piano was Denny, a self-taught and incredibly talented pianist from Cuba. Mom was mesmerized, listening to him as he played songs the residents knew—everything from Elvis to hymns to "Que Será, Será," one of Mom's and my favorites.

Trish whispered in my ear, "Remember how you wanted to hire him for our family Christmas dinner? The wonder of God!"

I did not expect to run across Denny this day at the memory-care residence. *Oh, God. You are amazing. There is no such thing as coincidence.*

I turned to Trish. "This is incredible."

"Yes, it is. And it's also divine."

We hugged and held each other's hands as we watched Mom dance. I was exhausted from the night before, but I got a surge of energy watching Denny play and Dad grab Mom and twirl her around.

Dad looked so handsome. He had on my favorite color, purple, and Mom was wearing a silver top. They were two lovebirds enjoying the moment, sharing their love while shining God's light throughout the fourth floor. Life was a dance, and they danced like there was no tomorrow.

Heading downstairs to the private dining room, Mom asked David Jr. if he was hungry.

"Yeah, Mom. I'm real hungry."

"Let's eat then. Can you whistle? I need you to whistle."

He chuckled. "No, Mom. You were the whistler. I can't whistle like you."

Childhood memories flooded back. When my brothers and I were several blocks away, we would hear this loud whistle with two tones, then run home knowing it was dinnertime. In high school, I'd be warming up for a basketball game, and Mom would let out that loud whistle. Then she'd wave and give me a thumbs-up for luck. When I was in college, Mom and Dad had seats near the cheerleaders for football games. Taking a water break between cheers, I'd hear her whistle. Looking up in the stands, there she was with two thumbs-up and a wave.

Mom's whistle was her trademark. At any sporting event, special occasion, or family gathering, she could grab our attention. My heart fell when she'd tried the whistle a year and a half ago, and it was half as loud as it was in her prime. Now there was no sound at all.

I turned to Mom. "Hey, Mom, Ginny can whistle. Let her do it for you." Ginny and her family had come down to see the private dining room but weren't staying for dinner.

"Ginny, I need you to whistle," Mom said.

Ginny complied. Within seconds, the entire room fell quiet and all eyes were on Mom. Everyone thought *she* had whistled.

Taking charge, she hosted dinner as if she were at her old place.

"I want to thank you for here. For coming. You be joy, and you're all . . ." She paused and smiled, then couldn't speak. She had a difficult time getting her words out now, but we knew what she meant.

She continued, "You bring joy. Thanks for coming. I love you. All of you. David and I thank you."

And with that, Daddy said, "Let's hold hands and pray. Come on, kids. We need you to close the circle."

After prayers, Ginny and the others left. As Mom sat down, she grabbed her fork and exclaimed, "*My* napkins!"

She'd noticed! I was so happy. She'd recognized her beautiful Christmas linens. She noticed her Santa and her candles, as well as her fine china from her wedding. She even knew the kids' place mats and plates.

Looking up at Dad, she said, "Thank you. This is wonderful, isn't it? Look at them."

He kissed her on the cheek. "Yes, it is wonderful, Beck. We are very blessed."

AFTER DINNER, DAVID JR. HAD a surprise for us all. He asked if we would go into the room around the corner because he wanted to play something on the piano for Mom.

My brother had played the piano since he was ten or eleven. He'd wanted to play the guitar, but Mom said, "If you want to play the guitar, you need to learn to play the piano first." So he took piano lessons for years. David stopped playing after college, but when he and Trish had children, he began to play again. Their children now loved music and were taking cello, harp, and piano, with guitar lessons to come.

We all found a seat around the piano. Mom sat close to David Jr. so she could see his hands hit the keys and watch his fingers.

As the melody began, I began recording video with my phone, knowing this would be a time to remember.

As David Jr. began to play, Mom put her left hand over her heart.

Looking over her shoulder, she smiled at Dad, then she shook her head as if to say, "David, look at our son. Is this not beautiful?"

She faced David Jr., her eyes so peaceful.

Suddenly, the song picked up, and we realized the tune was Coldplay's "Viva La Vida," Spanish for "Live the Life."

Tears poured down my face even as I recorded the video. As I looked to Dad, he stepped back, rubbing his eyes and nose. He was doing everything in his power to keep his emotions under control.

Then I zoomed in on Mom's face. The more David played and the louder the song, the more she shook her head, mesmerized. Her eyes locked in on his hands, and, with her left hand still over her heart, she became almost still. Her reactions and body language were the most beautiful things I had ever witnessed, and this moment was the most meaningful I'd experienced with my family.

She didn't need to say a word. You could see it in her eyes, the subtle movement of her face, and the way she fixated on her son's music. David had touched her, and he had touched all of us. One word summed up the picture in my mind: "forgiveness."

CHRISTMAS MORNING CAME, AND THE kids wanted to run downstairs to see what Santa had brought. Before they did, Emery said, "Mommy? Daddy? Are y'all ready to read our verses?"

Smiling with delight, I hugged her tight. "Emery, I love you. Thanks for leading our family and making sure we stick to tradition and remember why we celebrate Christmas."

Thad retrieved the Bible as I gazed at our three children. I was so proud of and thankful for them. They were in their pajamas, Elijah with his Pillow Pet and "doggy," Frensley in her robe and slippers, and Emery in her Christmas sweatshirt and fuzzy boxers.

Thad passed the Bible around, and the kids took turns reading the

Christmas story. When they finished, they sang "Happy Birthday, Jesus," as always, before running down the stairs.

I prayed silently as they sang. *Happy birthday, Jesus. May You be encouraged and loved and praised today. Thank You for all that You have done for our family this Christmas. You are so good. I will forever praise Your name. Amen.*

While egg casseroles baked in the oven, I fried bacon and warmed up the pumpkin–chocolate chip bread.

David, Trish, and their kids arrived about 10:00, along with Beauty and Pop. We gathered in a circle as Dad prayed, thanking God for His son, Jesus, who came to save us from our sins. As he prayed, I peeked at the family holding hands with Mom on Christmas morning. Closing my eyes, all I could do was thank Him for this miracle.

Lord, thank You that Mom is here with us. I never, ever thought she would be home for Christmas. This year has been terrible and painful. God, there has been so much suffering and heartache and confusion and fear of the unknown. You have provided for us as You promised. Thank You for Your faithfulness to our family and for carrying us through Your journey. I am forever grateful for Your gift—Your Son, Jesus Christ—and for my mom this Christmas Day. Amen.

Brunch was delicious, and once again Mom looked around the dining table, staring at each of her children. I didn't want it to end. This was the best Christmas I could remember. How was that possible? How was it possible that amid the pain and suffering of Mom's incurable disease, I was thanking God? It was possible because of prayers and the power of His love. God does the unthinkable, the unexplainable, the unexpected. He thrives on doing those things for us and showering us with His grace. We don't deserve Him and His love. But that is His heart. His heart is love. Unending love.

As David and Trish were walking out the door, the house empty and quiet, I pulled David aside. "David, I need to tell you something." I paused from a knot in my throat. "I'm sorry. I just . . . I get so emotional."

He stared at me, waiting patiently.

"I wanted to tell you on the night you played the piano for Mom, but it wasn't the right time." I started tearing up. "I have to tell you in person."

My voice trembled. "When you played that song for Mom the other night, I saw forgiveness. You have been on your own journey. I know the things you've shared with me the past few years about the hurt you have endured because of Mom. I don't know what you felt as you played, but what I felt and saw was forgiveness, and I want to say thank you. Thank you for sharing the gift God gave you with our family and doing it for Mom."

David smiled calmly at me. "You are right, Sarah. My intention was to show forgiveness. I love you very much, and this has been a very special Christmas."

After we hugged goodbye, I ran upstairs, closed my bathroom door, and sobbed. God had restored a relationship between a mother and son in the most unimaginable way—through a disease. What was even more beautiful? He had allowed our entire family to witness His grace, forgiveness, and mercies before our very eyes.

None of us would have chosen this journey. It's His journey, chosen for us. I am on it, and it's the path of life He has chosen for me.

It was the best Christmas ever.

TWENTY-SEVEN

QUE SERÁ, SERÁ

December 30, 2016, to January 1, 2017

--◦✕◦--

FOR THE PAST TWELVE YEARS, Thad, the kids, and I had traveled with his family after Christmas through New Year's. Usually, we went to Mexico. This year, however, I couldn't leave my dad in Dallas. The thought of him alone during the holidays pierced my heart.

"Honey, I don't think I can travel. I need to be in Dallas with Mom and Dad. Would you be okay with that?"

Thad smiled, "Of course, honey. This has been a rough few months, so take it easy and enjoy some quiet time at home. You need the rest. Your dad will be happy to have you here."

Thad was my rock. His support for me throughout our marriage, especially since his sobriety date, kept me going. He knew I was emotionally raw, and he knew I couldn't do it all, so he carried some of my burdens. He shopped for groceries, ran errands, and even washed and filled up my car with gas. He participated more in evening soccer carpools for the girls and took Elijah to almost all of his activities. Patient and tenderhearted, Thad knew this was a personal journey, and he didn't want to get in my way.

Thad also brought me flowers every Friday, and that November, he started taking Mom "Friday flowers" every chance he had. They had a special relationship, making each other laugh all the time, and Thad was the only person besides Carie who could make Mom zip her lips before she started trouble. Over the fourteen years of our marriage, Thad had invested much of his time with my parents. He loved my dad. Thad would tell me, "I hope I can be a father like your dad one day. He is so humble and loving, and he has so much wisdom. He is a gentle soul. I'm incredibly grateful to have him as my father-in-law. I want the special bond you and your dad have for Frensley and Emery and me."

Thad and the kids left town two days after Christmas. Exhausted by the whirlwind of events, I must have slept twelve or thirteen hours that night.

The next morning, I got a text from Big Ginny.

"Hey! Can we please go to dinner while you are here kid-less? You and I have never been to dinner, just the two of us, and I would love to be with only you, Sarah. This has been so hard for me seeing your mother go down like this."

As I read her text, I realized that it had rarely been just the two of us together. Maybe a few times in New York City, but that was back in college when I visited for long weekends. Over the past several months, we hadn't had a chance to talk without being rushed. This was a fabulous idea.

"Let's do it! How about Friday? By the way, would you want to spend New Year's with Mom and me? I've told Dad I would spend New Year's Eve with her, and the pianist, Denny, is playing with a band. I thought it would be fun if you, Mom, and I were together dancing the night away. Let me know."

She immediately texted me back.

"Friday is perfect, and yes, I am in for New Year's Eve. Go buy Beauty a cute blingy top, and let's get all dolled up and make it a party!"

I was so excited, I jumped out of bed, threw on my clothes, grabbed a coffee to go, and hit the stores!

Heading to Chico's, I checked out their "blingy" tops and bought three. One was cherry red with silver trim, another was navy blue silk with gold around the neck, and the third was gold and white, trimmed in gold around the collar. All elegant yet fun.

Over the next few days, I spent a lot of time with Dad. I stayed overnight several times, and we enjoyed our morning coffee together before seeing Mom each day. Having so much time on my hands gave me room for workouts, quiet times, and hours and hours with my parents. No responsibility other than loving on Mom and Dad—there was no greater gift my husband could have given me.

GINNY AND I CHOSE A favorite steakhouse in Dallas. We hadn't had a juicy steak in a long time, so we splurged on a four-course meal.

The packed restaurant was loud, and the staff wove through the maze of tables. Ginny and I were seated in a back corner where we could hear each other talk.

After our waiter poured us some wine, we lifted our glasses for a toast.

"To Ginny, cheers! Merry Christmas and happy New Year. I love you like a second mom, and I am thankful to God we are together tonight. Mom would be so happy to know we are together."

Ginny's eyes began to water. "Cheers, Sarah. I love you like a daughter, and I love your mother so much. She is the bestest friend I could ever have."

We talked about the last year and a half since Mom and Dad's move and all the changes for Mom since then. We discussed how Dad had begun to age before Mom was placed. We broke down every little thing we remembered that preceded placing Mom.

The conversation deepened as we discussed Mom and the trials and sufferings in our lives. I shared with Ginny that Mom had been praying for her for fifty years. It was hard for her to believe.

"Your dad told me that several months ago," she said. "He said your mother had prayed for me nearly every night before bed for years. It's really true, isn't it? Why? Why did she pray for me so much? It's really amazing, the depth of her love and friendship."

I leaned in closer. "When I would come home during college, she would pray for you when we prayed together. Mom worried about you. You know, when Mom married Dad, her life changed. Her faith grew stronger, and she had three kids. You, on the other hand, married, had

Little Ginny, and then your husband left—with *no* warning. Do you know how much that devastated Mom?"

Ginny's eyes filled with tears. She tapped the table with her fingers and began to reflect.

"It's true. He flat out left me. He left me to raise our precious Ginny all on my own. There I was, in Dallas, living the life, with this beautiful little girl. He was successful, we were financially secure, and we had a ton of friends. Then one day he tells me he doesn't love me anymore and doesn't come home. I was a baby, Sarah. I was so young. I didn't know what to do. He left me for another woman."

"I can't imagine. That had to be terribly painful. You are an amazing mother. I can't believe what an incredible job you did raising Little Ginny."

"Well, it wasn't easy. But the fact that your mother prayed for me all of those years just makes me feel so . . . so . . . I don't have the words." She dabbed her eyes with her black linen napkin. "Deeply loved."

My heart was pounding. I wanted to tell Ginny more about how and why Mom was able to love her so well. I knew why, but I wasn't sure Ginny understood.

"Ginny, she prayed for you because she wanted you to experience what she had, and that was Jesus. I don't know how else to tell you, but she wanted you to *know* Jesus. She prayed you would understand who He was and how much He loved you, and she wanted you to have a better life that was more meaningful. A life that wasn't focused on material things and money. When you moved to New York City when Little Ginny was six, you had to survive. And the way you survived was seeking things that were meaningless. Money and material things lead us nowhere. They fill us up for a while, but that sense of satisfaction doesn't last. The one thing no one can take away is our faith. Do you see what I'm saying?"

She looked down and paused before speaking.

"Yes, I do. Look at me now. I'm seventy-two, and I still don't have a husband. Oh, Sarah. Where did I go wrong?"

A tear rolled down Ginny's face.

"You didn't do anything wrong! You did everything you knew to do and to the best of your ability. Your daughter is *amazing*. I love her—she's my soul sister. You raised her unbelievably well considering your circumstances. Don't beat yourself up, Ginny."

"Well," she said, laying her napkin neatly in her lap, "I have to agree with you. I do have the best daughter in the world. I don't know what I would ever do without my Ginny. We are so close."

"I know you are. Believe me, I know."

Ginny took a sip of her wine. I wasn't sure what to say next but felt like my mom was saying, "Sarah, please share Christ with her. I have tried, but it's your turn. I need you to do this for me because I can't anymore."

But it was Ginny herself who opened the door. She reached across the table and grabbed my hands as tears streamed down her face.

"Sarah, how can I get that love your mother has? How? Please tell me. I need to know, and I want to feel that. I want to *know* it."

My palms began to sweat. I knew it was time for God and Mom to take over for me.

"All you have to do is ask Jesus to be Lord of your life, to commit to following Him. It's not just about voicing or believing He is the Son of God. It's about accepting Him into your heart and life and believing He will forgive you of your sins and make you new again. He can change your life, I promise you. He's changed mine. He's changed Thad's. He changed Mom's."

I gazed into her big blue eyes as I squeezed her hands.

"It's very simple. All we have to do is ask. He promises that if we ask *in faith*, we shall receive. I'm happy to pray with you right now, right here. Do you want me to pray with you?"

"*Yes*. Please. I want my life to change. I want to feel that kind of love like never before. I will do *anything*, Sarah."

Ginny was desperate and hurting inside. She had questions she couldn't ask her best friend anymore. I could hear the regret in her voice. But I had the part of Mom in me that Ginny wanted to be with that evening.

"Ginny, close your eyes and repeat after me."

I said the Believer's Prayer with Ginny, and she repeated every word.

She asked Jesus into her life, to be Lord of her life, and she thanked Him for loving her despite her sins and faults.

After we prayed and opened our eyes, a peace came over Ginny. She smiled and laughed, and she grew more radiant as the night progressed. We shared things with each other that neither of us had shared with anyone else before.

I told Ginny on the way home how much I loved her, God loved her, and Mom loved her. I also told her that now that she had accepted Jesus into her life, it was up to her to pursue a deep relationship with Him. In other words, spend time in the Bible, read devotionals, seek fellowship, and pray.

On reaching home, I fell to my knees and cried. I cried, wanting Mom to be with us. I wished Mom had witnessed our evening together. Fifty years of prayer, and then God used *me* to share the gospel with Ginny.

Though shocked, I was elated over what had happened. Staying in Dallas to be with Mom and Dad had been my plan. But God knew all along that Ginny and I would share that impromptu dinner.

Our conversation was not by chance, and the dinner, no coincidence. It was divine intervention. Mom had prayed for Ginny, and God heard her, and in His time sent Ginny His saving gospel. He knew, and He was glorified that night.

THE NEXT MORNING, NEW YEAR'S Eve, I called Dad.

"Daddy, you won't *believe* our dinner last night! You're not going to believe how amazing it was."

"Really? I'm so glad y'all had that time together."

"Dad, Ginny accepted Jesus last night!"

"What?"

"We were talking about Mom and how much she loved Ginny and how she had consistently prayed for her over the years. One thing led to the next, and I really felt like Mom was speaking to me and wanted me to share Jesus with her."

"Well, I'll be," Dad said. "Your mother has prayed for her for as long as I can remember. I can't believe it. That is wonderful, Sarah."

"I know, Daddy! She was so happy last night. We had the best time. I will never forget last night, ever."

"I'm going to see Mom soon. Do you think it's okay if I tell her? Or do you think Ginny will want to tell her?" Dad asked.

"I think Ginny would love for you to tell her. Who knows if tonight will be the time, with all their New Year's Eve activities. You might explain it to her better in a quiet space, where she can take it all in."

"All right then. I can't wait. She's going to be so happy. Even though she won't remember, I know this is going to bring a peace and joy Mom hasn't felt in a long time."

A deep thought came over me. "Do you remember what I told you after we placed Mom? I said that if Mom knew this disease would lead even one person to Christ, she would accept it a thousand times over again. And little did I know that one person would be her best friend. I'm speechless over the whole thing. It's truly unbelievable."

Dad spent all day with Mom, knowing that when he left, he would feel at peace that they had been together. Ginny and I would be with Mom for New Year's evening.

Dad told me later that when he told Mom, she had the sweetest smile on her face. Putting her hand over her heart, she said, "She did? Wow. She really did it. He answered my prayers, David."

"God heard you, Beck. It took a long time, but you were persistent and never gave up. Isn't it amazing He used your own daughter to pray with her?"

"Yes," Mom said. "It is."

WHEN GINNY AND I ARRIVED for New Year's Eve, we found Mom looking beautiful in the gold-and-white sweater with the gold trim and beading. Her tan pants complemented the gold in the sweater, and her makeup looked angelic. Once again, her face looked soft and beautiful with her brown eyeliner, mascara, and her favorite red lipstick.

We had reserved a three-top table downstairs. Carol, the social director, had decorated the tables with party hats and gold-and-black headbands that read, "Happy New Year!"

I put headbands on Mom and myself, while Ginny chose a gold hat. At the kitchen bar, I poured Mom a glass of nonalcoholic wine, while Ginny and I shared our own wine from home.

The three of us clinked glasses and cheered. After a cheer and a toast, Ginny said, "Becky, let's show these old people how to dance!"

Mom was in heaven. She laughed so hard with her two favorite gals. In that instant, life couldn't have been better for me. *This is going to be my second best New Year's ever, the first being with Thad fifteen years ago.*

On piano, Denny began the music along with his guitarist, drummer, violinist, and a singer. Mom smiled from ear to ear. It wasn't long before Ginny grabbed Mom and twirled her around the dance floor. As he played, Denny looked over his shoulder and laughed as he watched them dance. It wasn't the first time his music had popped Mom out of her chair to dance. Taking another video, I soaked it all in.

With her arm around Ginny's waist, Mom lifted her left leg at a ninety-degree angle, touched her left foot back on the floor, and then kicked it out again. I knew what was coming—she was trying to do her Rangerette kicks with Ginny. Though they were not perfect by any means, Mom still had them in her! There they were, two best friends in their seventies, still Kilgore College Rangerettes at heart, kicking the night away once again.

Through the evening, we danced, sang, laughed, and pulled others onto the dance floor. We lived like it was our last night on earth. With my arms around Mom as we swayed back and forth in our chairs, we sang the words to "Que Será, Será." I know that whatever will be, will be. I know that the future is not ours to see. Que será, será.

As I sang those words, I was struck by the truth behind them. In that moment, the words became a reality for me. The future wasn't mine to see, nor anyone else's. Whatever happened from that night on didn't matter. I knew I had that night with her, and 2017 would be a new year for me. I would take each day moment by moment, not worrying about what the future held for Mom or anybody else. I would go forward, knowing truly that whatever will be, will be. Que será, será.

TWENTY-EIGHT

YOU ARE LOVE

January to April 2017

-•◦❊◦•-

A NEW YEAR, A NEW ME. Over the next several months, I craved time daily with Mom, as well as with the residents. She was fun and childlike, and every day was a new adventure. Although she was losing her speech and her mobility was slowing down, she could still smile, walk, dance, and laugh. I would pop in as often as I could, but I was committed to every Wednesday and Friday for our delightfully alcohol-free happy hour.

Denny now played every Wednesday downstairs and every other Friday on the fourth floor. On the off weeks upstairs, I would take Mom downstairs to hear the entertainer for that Friday. Mom loved the music to the point that she figured out the door code and tried to take another resident downstairs to hear it.

Dad couldn't believe that when Macy told him.

"How did she get the code? She can't even remember something minutes later!"

"I don't know. But she realized if she went straight down the middle of the keypad, the door unlocks," Macy said. "It's not a huge deal, but I would suggest you not take her downstairs every morning for hot chocolate. She's getting so used to going downstairs with you and Sarah that she feels comfortable enough to go on her own. Maybe you could go a few days a week instead of every day?"

Although a little disappointed, Dad agreed to cut back.

For Valentine's Day, I took the kids to see Mom. We brought her and the other residents some heart-shaped crafts, macarons, and pink heart cookies. Thad brought her a beautiful bouquet of flowers. The day before had been my birthday, but this year I wasn't sad that she didn't remember. I now saw every day with Mom as a celebration.

Pulling Macy aside one afternoon, I asked, "Do you think it's okay if I take Mom in the car with me? Like to carpool or to Starbucks or something?"

Without hesitation, Macy said, "Of course you can."

"Really? It won't be a problem bringing her back here? What if she asks about her house and wants me to drive by it or something?"

"Honestly, Sarah, I don't think she will ask that, but if she does, just tell her 'another time.' But I would not recommend driving down streets that may trigger thoughts of home."

I promised Macy I'd have her back in time for dinner at 4:30 whenever I took her.

The next day, I picked Mom up. I couldn't wait to do the things we had missed the previous spring. Here we were, a year later, and I was able to take her to carpool again. God had answered my prayers.

Mom got in the car as if it were only yesterday that we had run errands together.

She asked, "Where we gonna be?"

"We are going to grab your favorite drink at Starbucks and head to the carpool line."

"Oh, okay. What's Starb . . . Star . . . What's it called again?"

"Starbucks. There is a drink there you love!"

"There is? I've never heard of that place before, but okay. Whatever you say!"

Never heard of Starbucks. All right then, I will pretend it's her first time every time.

As Macy suggested, I took a different route as Mom looked out the window, gazing at the trees, homes, and traffic.

"So many cars. Too much, Sarah. I don't know where I am."

"I know, Mom. You are right. There is a lot of traffic. But it sure is a beautiful day, and you don't have anything else going on, so who cares?"

She smiled. "That's right! I'm happy to be here, Sarah."

Standing in line at Starbucks, Mom wanted every treat she could get her hands on.

Picking up a KIND Bar, she showed it to me. "I want this! What is it?"

"It's a KIND Bar. It's delicious. They are healthy, and you love a mix of nuts and chocolate."

"I don't have my money. Daddy didn't give me money."

"Oh, Mom, please. I have money. You can pay me back."

Mom usually wanted to pay for anything and everything, but if I told her she could pay me back, she would quickly agree and move on.

She grabbed a bag of popcorn. "What's this?"

"It's popcorn. But I have your KIND Bar, so let's get that and our drinks."

"A KIND Bar? What's that?"

Here we go again. Patience, Sarah.

"It's this bar you picked out with chocolate and mixed nuts."

I noticed other people in line staring at us. Feeling anxious, I felt the need to protect Mom from others knowing something was wrong with her. But it was too late for that.

Mom grabbed a bag of coffee. "What's this?"

"That's a bag of coffee. We don't need that. You and Dad have plenty of coffee at your place."

The line moved, and it was our turn to order.

"I'd like a grande iced soy chai and a grande dirty iced almond chai, please."

Mom grabbed a chocolate bar and a small bag of almonds at the counter.

"What's in here? What are these?"

As I paid the cashier for the drinks and the KIND Bar, Mom insisted, "Sarah, I want these, too."

Looking at the cashier, who seemed a little impatient, I said, "We'll get the almonds as well, please. And that will be it."

As I swiped my credit card, I heard Mom say, "What's this?"

Pretending not to hear her, I guided her to a table outside where I showed Mom her snacks.

Pushing them away, she said, "I didn't get those. You eat them. I'm not hungry."

A few seconds ago she was grabbing everything as if she were hungry, and now she doesn't even remember picking these out? I don't want them.

Mom took a sip of her drink. "Mmmm, this is *so* good. Wow!"

Mom didn't remember our Starbucks runs nor her favorite drink. So why was I doing all of this? Why was I taking her to Starbucks and the carpool line? Was it for her or was it for me?

I longed to be with Mom and do the things we had done before. I wanted things to be normal again, but they never would be. She was happy being out, but Mom would have been happy if I were visiting with her anywhere. All she cared about was being with me.

We sat in the carpool line for thirty minutes and could see the football field from our lane. Emery was playing soccer with her friends, and we watched her run, her two long braids bouncing off her shoulders.

"She's so pretty, Sarah," Mom said.

"Thank you. She's your Mini-Me, Beauty. She looks just like you."

As I gazed out the window and felt the crisp air on my cheeks, I turned to hold Mom's hand, but she was sound asleep. Her head was down, tilted slightly to the right and leaning on her seat belt. Her drink was tipping over in her hand, so I placed it in the cup holder.

Things were different now. There would be no long conversations in the car, blowing of bubbles, or listening to podcasts. Mom was in a different phase, and I had to accept that. But I still loved being with her. I felt at peace knowing my mom was sitting right next to me.

The kids were so happy to see their Beauty.

As the door opened, Emery yelled, "Beauty! You're here!"

Then Elijah: "Beauty! Wait, what? Beauty?"

Elijah was excited to see her but confused. The last he knew, Beauty couldn't leave her new place.

Frensley was the last to get in the car. "Hi, Beauty! Wow, this is a nice surprise."

All three kids hugged Mom before they buckled their seat belts. Watching them with their grandmother made every anxious moment at Starbucks worth it. Even sitting in the carpool line while she slept was worth each quiet second.

We dropped Mom off at 4:00 without a hitch. When she walked in, she blurted out, "Ahhh, home sweet home!"

As I held her hand and we walked to the elevator, I felt a sense of gratitude and relief that she had called it home.

OVER THE WEEKS TO COME, Mom and I had a blast together. We drove through Chick-fil-A, to Starbucks for more drinks and chocolate bars and almonds, waited in more carpool lines, and we even went back to Tona, her hairdresser. We danced at happy hours, and others danced with us. We sang "Que Será, Será" together. The joy that filled our hearts and the love that poured out of us was indescribable.

The week before Easter, the girls took friends from school to paint wooden crosses with Mom and the residents. They wanted to share the meaning of Easter with them and sing a few hymns. That spring, the opportunities for our family and children to serve were endless. Frensley and Emery's friends begged to go back.

One afternoon in April, I received a call from Macy.

"What's up? Everything okay?" I asked.

"I wanted to talk to you about our annual caregivers appreciation lunch at the end of the month, and I am calling to ask if you would be willing to speak at the luncheon?"

I paused, a little confused.

"What do you mean?"

"Well, we all agreed we would like you and your dad to speak. You have both been so involved here, and you know many of the caregivers. We love you, your dad, your mother, and your family so much, and we would be honored if you would be our guest speakers and share your journey with us."

I couldn't believe the words she was saying.

"Yes, of course I will speak! I would love to show appreciation to the caregivers. They have done so much for Mom and our family. I'm nervous to speak, of course, but I can't turn down an opportunity to publicly thank those who have poured their hearts and souls into my mom and the other residents. Did you already ask my dad?"

"Yes, I spoke to him this morning, and he agreed to do it. This will be great, Sarah. I mean it when I say we love you all very much. You don't realize the impact you have made on each of us, watching your love for your mom and watching your dad take care of his wife. We have never seen anything like it, and your family is very special to this community. So thank you. Very much."

I felt strange, hearing this. *Impact? Watching your love for your mom? Never seen anything like it?* I wasn't sure I fully understood what she meant, but I was humbled and honored that the facility's staff thought of us this way.

Over the next several weeks, I prayed God would write the speech for me. I wanted the caregivers to know how thankful and appreciative we were, and I wanted them to know that God's grace in us was the only reason we were able to love the way we did. It was not because of our ability that we were able to face Mom and her disease each day. It was truly God's grace, strength, and courage that carried us through this difficult time.

Little did I know that the entire luncheon would be about Mom. It was about the love story of a man and a woman, married fifty years, and the journey the husband and daughter were taking with this woman they deeply loved. The director wanted the caregivers to understand Mom's origins, how she met Dad, and how she had arrived at The Tradition.

Each resident had a story, and the director wanted her staff to know their roles in each of those lives.

Dad brought a DVD I had made for their forty-fifth wedding anniversary. The video was a combination of pictures of Mom and Dad as babies and children, their courting days in college, their wedding, and their grandchildren, all set to their favorite songs.

After the DVD played, Dad stood up to speak. He started by telling them how he and Mom met.

"It was a beautiful fall afternoon in Denton three or four days before class began, and I was relaxing on the couch in my apartment, watching TV. My fourth year of college at North Texas State—this year began differently. I was staying off campus with my best friend and roommate, Don Vest, to resist the temptations of checking out the freshmen girls and partying with friends and fraternity brothers. I had no goals, ambitions, or anything of the sort during my time there. As young people in college say, 'I just wanted to have fun!'

"Then it happened—the event that changed my life. As I lay on that couch, I heard giggling just outside our picture window. To my surprise, there was a beautiful girl standing there, peeping in the window. With long, dark hair, a big smile that showed her pearly-white teeth, and gorgeous dark eyes, she stood there in tan khaki shorts and a white top.

"As soon as I caught her peeking, she ran back to the car where another beautiful girl, a blonde, was waiting. After realizing I had seen them, they sheepishly walked up to the front door. Having never seen either one of them before, I had no idea what they were doing there.

"Giggling, they admitted they were looking for my roommate. Kathy, the blonde, had met Don the previous summer and found out where he lived. She had sent Becky, the brunette, to peep into the window to see if Don was home."

My dad grinned. "That was the first sighting of the girl I would marry one year later, although at the time I pretended to be disgusted that these two girls were stalking my roommate. They both left, rather embarrassed over being busted."

The room chuckled listening to Dad.

"About a week later, I was sitting in my anatomy class, with well over one hundred students seated in alphabetical order. The girl seated next to me during the previous class was absent. Suddenly, I looked up to see Becky, the same beautiful brunette from outside my apartment a few days earlier! She had her books and was coming toward the vacant seat."

Dad's face lit up. "After she was seated and had placed her other books on the floor, she calmly pulled out a black ballpoint pen, reached over, and scribbled 'Hi' in my open textbook. I was stunned! Would I be able to sell my book with ink marks in it? Then my next thought: 'I wonder if she'll go to lunch with me after class.'"

The audience laughed. They were loving this.

"She did go to lunch with me," Dad said. "I'll never forget that day. I had a burger with barbecue sauce, and she had a burger with chili and cheese. This became our routine after each anatomy class for the remainder of the semester. The two of us sitting in the car, eating a burger, and talking about life and our families. We both realized something was happening. We fell in love and were married one year later."

I had never heard Dad tell the story quite like this, and I, too, sat in rapt silence. He went on to talk about things they had done together, the life they had built, their kids, and, eventually, her diagnosis. He said he tried everything he knew to keep her home, that he did not want to place her, but in the end he had no choice.

"Fifty-one years have now passed since that day she peeked into my window," he said, "and we still have a burger about once a week while sitting in the car. It's much different now. I pick her up here, and a plain meat hamburger has replaced the chili and cheese, as she can no longer control her hands well enough to prevent the chili and cheese from dripping. It's important for her she retain her dignity, and she has done that very well. As we sit together in the car, it seems like nothing has really changed that much. But she has forgotten most of the events from our fifty-one years together, so we just eat our burgers and smile and laugh at each other."

I could feel myself choking up. While this part of their story was sad, their love was beautiful at every single moment.

Toward the end of his speech, Dad said one thing that touched every heart there. "I have given you my most prized possession. I've given you everything I have left. Thank you for taking care of Rebecca, and I hope you remember how important she is to me as you show up each day."

His words were profound. I had never heard him say anything like that before. He showed the staff appreciation, and yet he also let them know she was his most valuable asset in life, and he trusted them to take care of her in his place. It was the most beautiful statement I had ever heard.

It was my turn to speak. I looked around the room into each person's eyes. I told them I hoped the things I shared with them would inspire them, encourage them, and even more important, make them feel loved before they left the room that day.

"When Mom was first diagnosed, Dad had a difficult time keeping the news to himself. He wouldn't tell us the test results because he promised Mom he wouldn't. I didn't understand at the time, but he wanted her to be the one to tell us, as it was her diagnosis, not his. This was painful because Dad was hurting. Mom was good at covering things up. As many of you in this room know, she can be a little sneaky and tricky, and she is a very smart and strong woman!

"The last thing Mom wanted was to be treated differently by anyone. But the one thing she and Dad did not know, and could not have known because they had never gone through this before, was that 'keeping a secret' meant they had to go through it alone for quite some time. When Dad finally shared the news with me—because I basically begged and persuaded him, in a loving and respectful way—he was able to release some things that were burdening him and finally feel a little freer.

"You see, that's the thing in all walks of life. We are all going through something. And if you aren't going through a trial right now, you either have gone through one or you will go through one. We can't go through these trials alone. I'm not saying we have to tell the world, but it's impossible to go through them alone. We can release those burdens and experience freedom in our sufferings if we will share.

"Our story is about an unexplainable love. It's about a love that's unimaginable. And it's about a love that's unthinkable. It's God's love. He has given us hope, and whether you believe it or not, He has used each one of you here today. He continues to bring us hope on this very day through your hearts, your hands, and your feet."

Some of the caregivers wiped their eyes, and I heard sniffling around the room. I felt the presence of God; He was speaking to each of them.

I continued to share our journey and what it was like for us to reach a place mentally where we could move Mom from the comfort of her own home to a memory-care facility. I shared with them the events of the painful day we placed her at The Tradition. So many of them had no idea how Mom had arrived there—the Valium and the wine.

"You took over for us. You rose to the occasion. Some of you probably lost sleep over it. Some of you worked overnight. Precious Macy was constantly texting me updates. *You showed up.* I am sure some of you did not want to deal with my mom. You had the courage to show up. Daddy and I are forever grateful to each one of you.

"Fast-forward to where we are now. God is so good. When here with Mom, I still meet caregivers I have not seen who say, "Hey Becky!" I'm in awe of how you all know my mother. It goes back to your hearts. You genuinely care to know your residents, and my mom feels loved.

"You need to know something: When you give hope, you restore every heart that is broken. You have restored my broken heart. My heart still breaks, but He continues to restore it through each one of you in this room. The courage you have shown me makes me want to face this disease with my head held high. The strength you have shown me makes feel like I can do anything. The patience you have shown me helps me love even more. You build me up when I am down, just by your smile.

"Romans 5:1–5 says this: 'Therefore, since we have been justified through faith, we have peace with God through our Lord Jesus Christ, through whom we have gained access by faith into this grace in which we now stand. And we boast in the hope of the glory of God. Not only so, but we also glory in our sufferings, because we know that suffering produces perseverance; perseverance, character; and character, hope. And hope does not put us to shame, because God's love has been poured out into our hearts through the Holy Spirit, who has been given to us.'

"God has given me peace and hope, not only because of my faith but because of your courage, strength, patience, kindness, gentleness, and love toward my mom. I thank God and thank you from the bottom of my heart for your hard work, the hours you put in, and for showing up each day.

"I pray for you. I pray that if you are going through a difficult time at home or in your personal life or even here at work that you remember how much God loves you.

"At church this past Sunday, I heard a woman say, 'God permits what He hates to accomplish that which He loves.' I don't think God wanted Mom to have early-onset Alzheimer's. But I know two things to be true: First, my mom used to tell everyone about Jesus. She has a heart for the Lord. If she knew this disease would lead one person to Christ, she would accept this disease a thousand times over. Second, I can now boast in the hope of the glory of God and I can now glory in my own suffering as I lose my mom and watch her slowly slip away.

"He loves all of us. And He wants us to feel loved no matter what we are going through. It's up to us to choose to accept His free gift of grace and march forward through difficult times. In this we identify with Him through His sufferings and experience the glory and love of God that brings peace and hope to all.

"Each one of you is beautiful. Each one of you is radiant. Each one of you is courageous. Each one of you is strong. Each one of you is His. And there is nothing you can't do with Him by your side.

"I often ask myself, 'What is the big picture?' Is it that my mom's dying? Is it that she may forget who I am? Is it that my dad may be a widower? Is it that my kids won't have Beauty, their grandmother, in their lives anymore? What is the big picture?

"For me, the big picture is glorifying God in all that I do and sharing the love He has shown me through Mom's disease. And much of the love He has shown me has been through you.

"What is the big picture in your life?"

With that, I surprised Dad by asking him to stand with me. I wanted the two of us to look out at each "angel," to take in their beauty and to note the love that exuded from their smiling faces.

I then said, "I have to give a shout-out to one of the *best* caregivers I know. He's standing right here next to me."

Daddy smiled with embarrassment and gave me a big hug.

"Daddy, you are love. You are joy. You are peace. You are patience. You are kindness. You are goodness. You are faithfulness. You are gentleness. You are self-control. You embody the nine attributes of a Christian according to the apostle Paul's letter to the Galatians. We call those nine attributes the fruit of the Holy Spirit, and I am honored to be on this journey with you. I can't imagine my life without you. I love you so, so much."

Daddy and I hugged again and both cried. As I wiped my tears, I looked out to see almost everyone in the audience crying. God was so good that day. He spoke clearly and made each and every one of the staff feel immeasurably loved.

I closed with prayer.

Dear Heavenly Father, I thank You. I thank You for the sufferings in my life. I thank You for these beautiful men and women in this room who have taken such amazing care of Mom these last eight-and-a-half months. I praise You for Mom's new home and the staff who pour out their hearts to make all of the residents and their families feel loved. I pray that You be with each caregiver in this room and continue to give them strength and courage to walk through these doors each day. Renew their minds daily and remind them of the big picture. Our hope is in You, God, and You alone. I thank You for sending Your Son, Jesus, to be Lord of my life. I thank You for this opportunity today to thank Your earthly angels and bring glory to You. Thank You for giving Dad, me, and our family hope through them so that You can restore our broken hearts.

In Your holy name I pray, amen.

When the luncheon was over, I couldn't count how many caregivers came up to us, tears flowing from their eyes, thanking us for speaking. They hugged me tightly. Moved by how touched they were, I wished I could have thanked them even more. We had a connection, a bond that no person could rend. It was the bond of love.

TWENTY-NINE

HAPPY MOTHER'S DAY, MOM

May 2017

--⊶✄⊷--

"**H**EY, BEAUTY!" I CALLED AS I opened her door. "I'm here. It's happy-hour time."

It was Wednesday, and I had dropped the kids off at home and driven straight to Mom's place. May was a busy time for us, being the last month of school, but I would not let anything interfere with our Wednesday and Friday happy hours. Not to mention there were assisted-living residents downstairs awaiting our arrival because they loved to watch us dance!

A month prior, I had begun contemplating what to do for Mom for Mother's Day. I knew, though, that whatever I did, she wouldn't remember it. It was painful to me to think she would not remember our time together.

In a cycling class in mid-April, I had a vision of Frensley and me, along with other mothers and daughters, riding in a class together. The more I thought about it, the more excited I became. After class, I asked the instructor, Aaron, if he ever led "private rides."

"Absolutely! I do them often for brides and their bridesmaids or birthday parties. Let me give you the contact number for booking."

That evening, I mentioned it to Frensley, and she loved the idea. Within twenty-four hours, God had placed on my heart the idea of having a mother-daughter spin class to honor Mom on Mother's Day. Although Mom wouldn't be spinning next to me, I was riding for her, and Frensley would be giving *me* a special Mother's Day gift at the same time.

Calling the contact number, I explained to the woman about Mom's early-onset Alzheimer's and my desire for a special Mother's Day class for friends who had been a part of our journey. We booked a private ride, calling the event Pedal for a Purpose. She said that 100 percent of the proceeds would go to the cause of my choice, and proceeds from the sale of any retail item or cycling package purchased that day would also be contributed. This was a no-brainer! Mom's gift from me would be a donation in her name to the Alzheimer's Association.

The email invitation I sent read:

"Zyn22 Park Lane invites you to Saddle Up for a Mother-Daughter Pedal for a Purpose Ride in Honor of Rebecca 'Beauty' Bearden. One hundred percent of the class fee will be donated to the Alzheimer's Association."

The invitation included two beautiful pictures of Mom and me taken a few months before. It was purple, the color representing Alzheimer's.

Emails poured in over the next several days, and within three weeks, forty-seven out of the fifty spin bikes were booked. Frensley and I couldn't believe how quickly our friends had dropped their busy May plans to help us honor Mom.

Online, I ordered glow necklaces, bracelets, and flashing rings, and at a wholesale store, I ordered personalized cups as party favors. Preparing in the days leading up to our event could not have been more fun for Frensley and me.

I called my dad to share the fun news.

"Daddy, you won't believe it. Almost every single bike is taken for our ride this Saturday. We are so excited we can't stand it! I wish y'all could be there."

"That's so neat, Sarah. Y'all will have a great time. How special for Frensley to see her friends come support her grandmother's disease and be there for her. Y'all really do have some special friends."

"We really do. God has been so good to our family. Do you think you can stop by at the end so everyone can see Mom?"

"Well, I don't know. It depends on her mood. It's hard to predict. I'll do my best to have her there, but I can't make any promises."

"No pressure. I thought it'd be neat if she could be there. We can all take a picture with her when we finish. You be the judge. I'll understand if it's too hard that day."

SATURDAY CAME, AND FRENSLEY AND I arrived early at the studio. We set out the party favors: six cups and cellophane bags tied with purple ribbons. A staff member helped me light the glow necklaces and place them on each bike handle. The music was blaring, and Aaron was ready to start the party.

As everyone showed up, we hugged and Aaron helped them set up their bikes in the studio. A woman at the front desk brought in a big sign in purple and white that read "Pedal for a Purpose," and we took a group photo while holding it.

Then Aaron dimmed the lights and yelled into his microphone, "All right, moms and daughters! Who is ready to ride?"

The class was amazing. Beginning in a dark studio, Aaron turned the lights to purple then hot pink, and some songs had strobe lights.

Aaron's playlist consisted of current pop music, and several of his songs were about mothers and daughters. One song was John Mayer's "Daughters." He had put so much thought into his playlist. Looking over at Frensley pedaling next to me, I became emotional. Being around dear friends and my own daughter was the best Mother's Day gift to *me*, especially knowing each minute of our class was in honor of Mom.

Little Ginny and her two daughters were next to Frensley and me in the front row. All the women who had prayed for our family over the past year were there. And the few who couldn't be there, though disappointed, were there in spirit.

During class, girls screamed and whooped, pumped up by Aaron's music and the things he said. Everyone felt inspired, determined to finish the class strong.

Everyone loved the hour of fun and camaraderie. The women and girls kept each other going, despite the difficulty of the class, just as they had kept me and Frensley going all year through the pain and difficulty of our circumstances.

During the last song, Aaron had us focus on pedaling as fast as we could. He was yelling out motivations to help us finish strong.

Suddenly, Big Ginny burst through the door and started dancing across the classroom floor. Though trying to pedal faster, I couldn't help but laugh aloud. Putting my head down, chin to my chest, I prayed as tears began to roll down my cheeks. *Of course Ginny would come in dancing, just as Mom would have done. You are so awesome, God. Her best friend showed up. Thank You, Jesus, for the perfect ending to this class. Greatest gift ever!*

When class was over, we were breathing hard and cheering. How amazing it felt, having this class together. Aaron said a few things, and I walked onstage to thank everyone, knowing it would be emotional.

"Thank you, our dear friends, for being here today. This was the *best* Mother's Day gift, not only for me, but also for my mom. Mom loved to give generously, and I am forever grateful to each of you that I can give generously to the Alzheimer's Association in her name."

As I choked up, I grabbed Aaron's hand.

"Aaron, thank you for making this special day happen for all of us."

As the lights brightened, I saw each sweaty face clearly.

"This ride will never be forgotten. You have prayed for my family and me for several years now, especially this past year. I could not have made it through without each of you. Thank you for coming!"

Everyone clapped and cheered. Some of the girls high-fived.

As we walked out of the studio, Mom and Dad were standing there. I did everything I could not to sob the moment I saw her.

"Mommy, you made it!" I turned to my dad. "Thank you so much, Daddy."

The young girls who had been serving Mom over the past seven months—and some who had known Mom from her attendance at their sporting events—ran up and embraced her.

"Beauty! Hi, Beauty!"

I watched as Mom gazed at each girl. Looking absolutely beautiful, she was smiling so big that she glowed. Wearing a coral-and-white outfit, her hair parted on the side, with makeup as becoming as ever, she smiled radiantly. Mom felt *so* much love that day. She didn't understand what was going on, but she knew she was loved, and every girl wanted to hug her. Dad wiped his eyes as Mom, in the middle of the room, stood surrounded by twenty girls.

I hugged Dad. All he could do was smile and hug me back. I knew by the look in his eyes he was saying, "Thank you, Daughter. Thank you."

We had pictures taken around Beauty, one of the girls holding the "Pedal for a Purpose" sign. As they scattered to retrieve their belongings, I told my mom that every person there had helped raise money for an organization that helped the sick—a donation made in her name for Mother's Day.

Mom's jaw dropped to the floor. She stared at me for what felt like a full minute, processing what I had said.

"Really? For me? Wow. That's so nice!"

She didn't fully understand, but I knew she grasped that money was being given to help others, and that was all she needed to hear.

"Yes, Beauty. For you. Happy Mother's Day. That is my gift to you."

As everyone began to leave, they urged us to do it again next year.

Joyfully I said, "This can be the first annual mother-daughter ride! We will make it a tradition."

Later that evening, I received a text from my dad.

"I love you, Sarah. I can't believe all your friends, who love Mom so much, came out to support this. What an honor to share our lives with them. If Mom knew what you and your friends had done today, she would be so proud of you!"

I cried myself to sleep that night. Not tears of pain and sadness, but tears of joy. Tears full of gratitude, appreciation, honor, bliss, pleasure, and triumph. Through God's grace, I was an overcomer. He was helping me overcome.

"QUE SERÁ, SERÁ" PLAYS CONSTANTLY in my mind. Wherever I go, I hear those words. Mom and I sing it together weekly, holding each other's hands and staring into each other's eyes as we sing. There is something in it that she understands. She can't express it, but she comprehends "whatever will be, will be."

I've learned a lot about my mother through this disease. There really is more there than I know. Her brain can't connect the thoughts with the words, but if I ignore the words and look at her facial expressions and her heart, I know what she is thinking and what she wants to say. I could easily convince myself she's clueless, but that would be untrue. Mom isn't clueless. She's perceptive and feels things, even when she can't express them.

And it's not just Mom. It's every resident on that fourth floor. They feel. They know love when it knocks on their heart. If I can spread love and bring happiness to their hearts, even a few hours a day, then that is worthy of my time. Spreading love is a gift, a privilege, and an honor. Why keep it to myself?

It's possible one day Mom may just stare blankly at a wall, but even then I *know* she will feel the presence of love when I am sitting next to her. Eventually, she may not recognize my face, but she won't forget she loves being with me. She may completely forget who I am, but she won't forget she loves me and I love her.

I look back at my life, and I've missed out. I've been selfish with my time, and I've chased things that don't matter. Now my only desire is to chase after more love. Love from God. He is everything. Alone, my love for others will *never* have the depth of love God can give through me.

God and I are a team. We are friends. We are partners. He abides in me, and I in Him. He guides me, He leads me, and He gives me strength, comfort, and courage when I am weak. He's taught me how to love better and bigger and how to serve. He's taught me to let Him take the wheel and walk the steps *for* me to Mom's front door. He's given me rest when I needed it most. He's taught me perseverance and discipline and given me faith and trust during my fears and through the unknown. He's given me hope beyond understanding and taught me what "moment to moment" really means—to live one day at a time, hour by hour, following *His* lead.

He's taught me about friendships. True friends are honest and faithful. They show up during difficult times. They make time for others in a busy and distracting world. My true friends have never left my side and reach out consistently. They've shown me by example how to be a better friend. Being encouraged by friends is amazing, so why wouldn't I want someone else to experience that feeling, regardless of that person's mental state?

He's shown me the hard work of caregivers. Caregivers pour their hearts and souls into serving individuals who can't give back. I know because I am one! Many days I have given up everything for Mom, only to leave feeling empty because she can't give me anything in return.

But then I ask myself: Am I doing this for her or for me? Or am I doing this for God? I've chosen to do it for Him because He has given me everything: my parents, my husband, and my children. Everything I have is His. There is no doubt in my mind every caregiver who takes care of Alzheimer's patients has a calling from God, because there is no other way they could do this job. Yes, there may be a few who do it because they *have* to, but I would guess most are caregivers because they *get* to. With special gifts from God, they have been chosen to use them to spread His love.

God longs for our hearts. Our hearts are what He values most, so if I use my heart to love others, then I am glorifying Him by sharing with others what He treasures most. Caregivers glorify God whether they realize it or not.

In 2 Peter 1:5–8, we read, "For this very reason, make every effort to supplement your faith with virtue, and virtue with knowledge, and knowledge with self-control, and self-control with steadfastness, and steadfastness with godliness, and godliness with brotherly affection, and brotherly affection with love. For if these qualities are yours and are increasing, they keep you from being ineffective or unfruitful in the knowledge of our Lord Jesus Christ" (ESV).

I pray these qualities increase in me. I want to be fruitful and effective for God. He has been faithful and never left my side. I want to give back to Him. Though I will fail sometimes, He is a forgiving God. He will help me get back on the path.

Daddy and I and our family have had to accept this was God's plan all along. I will love Beauty to the end. Dad will make sure she is loved, honored, and cherished to the end. Even in Mom's present state, she makes our lives better, whatever the circumstance. All we are capable of is love, and we know now that Alzheimer's disease can *never* stop the love.

EPILOGUE

-»•‡‹•«-

BEAUTY'S MIND HAS BEEN DAMAGED and doesn't work properly. Though disrupted by this change, Mom has a way of bringing pleasure to my heart through her disease. Her mind may be fading away, but her spirit is the same. She is light, even in brokenness, and her light shines brightly upward and outward.

People often ask me, "How is your mom?" My answer, as of today, is "She's safe, and she's happy, and that's all our family can ask for." I'm also asked, "How's your dad doing?" Though Dad has accepted this as God's plan all along, it has been devastating beyond words for him. He used to think "through sickness and in health" meant that he should only take care of her from home, and that placing her outside the home meant he was a failure. But those were lies he believed. The reality is that having her at home nearly killed him, though it broke every part of his heart once she was placed. He has shown us, his family, what true love and commitment look like. And he encouraged us and others to seek help when we needed it and not to believe those same lies. He never gives up. A strong and loving man, he will love her to the end. He promised her when she was diagnosed that he would keep her safe and protected, and above all else, maintain her dignity. Dad follows God's lead, which is always the best for Mom.

Beauty doesn't know our children's names anymore, and it's difficult to hear her ask, "Where's the boy?" when looking for Elijah. As Thad sits across from us visiting with another resident, Mom leans in and asks, "Are you two married?" I painfully answer, "Yes, we are married! Sixteen years now!" And with a smirk on her face, she says, "GREAT!" It is in those moments I know she's happy for me, and that she can't get enough of our presence even when she can't recall our names.

This disease is rough, and living with it each day is tiring and challenging. Our family's lives are constantly uncertain, and we are learning, in our spiritual beings, how to interact with Mom. We take her on outings, and we include her in our home for the holidays. She goes to the salon weekly and looks forward to Wednesday "happy hour" musicals. However, we all know these special times can end with a fall or broken bones. It feels like we are playing roles in a heartbreaking drama, even while knowing our interactions with Beauty are guided by trust in God. He has been our rock and He has been the source of all the blessings through Mom's disease. As God gave me strength to roll out of bed during overwhelming weeks of distress, He was and is the massive rock that's firm, dependable, and doesn't change. I believe He's prepared me to see the beauty through the pain and also allowed me to appreciate this difficult, yet divine, experience.

As Mom continues her journey through early-onset Alzheimer's disease, I've learned to live in the moment and live in her world. If she tells me an apple is orange, then by golly that apple is orange! If she thinks Frensley is my friend and not my daughter, then for that moment in time, Frensley is my best friend!

I don't want to live with any regrets. I will continue to look into her heart, and eyes, and facial expressions, and will do my best to co-labor with God in her new world each day, being grateful that He is allowing me to shine light during this strenuous and laborious time. Mom is a human being with a name, and although this disease is a mystery and I want it to be cured, her life and my relationship with her are important, significant, and worthy of attention.

Note from David Bearden
(Sarah's Father)

THERE IS NO WAY TO properly express my gratitude to my daughter Sarah for all the things she has done for her mother and me. During a time of sadness and grief for our family, she has taken the lead position to keep us going, while continuing her role as a wife and mother of three wonderful children. She also encouraged me to document the events that were happening daily in order to help and share with others who were facing this long, hard journey. After realizing that it was hopeless to have me write anything, she again took the lead and wrote this book.

Sarah's relationship with her mother actually began more than two years before her birth. Our second child and first girl, Jessica, was stillborn after a full-term pregnancy. When Sarah arrived, it was as if Beck's love for both daughters was poured into Sarah. That began a beautiful mother-daughter relationship that continues to this day. Their roles have reversed, but it is still an amazing relationship to observe. I mention this so you, the reader, will have a better understanding of the extreme difficulty that Sarah faced when placing her mother in memory care.

There are many people affected by this cruel disease, and I hope this book will offer encouragement to the families, friends, and caretakers of the victims.

To the men and women who are struggling to determine if placement is the right thing for their loved ones—may you have a better understanding of what can happen after a decision is made. You can continue to be a part of their lives and give them a small amount of joy by visiting them regularly. I've discovered that a big laugh or smile from one who has Alzheimer's gives me more joy than going to a sporting event, a nice restaurant, or a movie.

To the friends of a victim of Alzheimer's—don't be afraid of visiting your friend for fear of not knowing what to do or say. You will be amazed at what resides in their damaged brains, and the more you are around them, the more joy both of you will receive. After what began as an arduous journey to visit my wife in a memory-care facility, I now look forward to arriving each day. It truly is a new world every day for the patient and the caretaker, and it can be fun and exciting if you will just allow it to happen.

Statistics tell us that more women have Alzheimer's than men. Recently, I've realized that the women caring for men with Alzheimer's may be the worst victims, due to the strength and violence of men. My heart goes out to those thousands who are in this situation and don't have the financial resources to place them in a memory-care facility. If you know someone in this situation and can help, please do so.

Rebecca and Ginny taking a break and having fun in 1965.

Lieutenant Becky English preparing for the
1965 Cotton Bowl halftime performance.

Rebecca and David on their wedding day, September 10, 1966.

Rebecca and David running to their getaway car after their
wedding reception, September 10, 1966.

Beauty and Pop dancing at a wedding in August 2002.

Sarah and Beauty on the Disney World monorail after a
full day at the park in Orlando, Florida.

Big Ginny and Beauty on New Year's Eve, January 31, 2016, at
her memory care facility. That same evening, Ginny received
Jesus in her heart while praying with Sarah over dinner.

Sarah and Beauty in February of 2017,
6 months after Beauty's placement.

ACKNOWLEDGMENTS

WRITING A BOOK WAS NEVER a dream of mine. A stay-at-home mom driving an SUV, aka "shuttle bus," I carpool kids to and from school, soccer, flag football, lacrosse, basketball practices, games, and tournaments. My husband and I go on weekly date nights so we can continue to "date" in the midst of our busyness. As I became a caregiver to Mom, God began drawing me closer and closer to Him through my pain and sorrow.

I must thank God first and foremost because the truth is, I would not be an author if it weren't for the undeniable and unexplainable things He revealed to me during a time of grief—for weeks leading up to Mom's placement and several months after. As much as I questioned Him and tried to run away from this call on my life, God continued to push me out of my comfort zone and teach me how to trust and walk by faith and help others through our journey. As 1 Timothy 1:12 reads, "I thank Christ Jesus our Lord, who has given me strength, that He considered me trustworthy, appointing me to His service" (NIV).

To my dad, or as I still call you, "Daddy," thank you for all of your support, love, and encouragement. You knew God was working on my heart, and you never stepped in His way. You simply said, "Well, then journal. Write things down and take it day by day, and He will guide you. All you can do is listen and trust, and He'll take care of the rest." Thank you for showing me how love can fill the heart. Your presence in my life has been the greatest present you could ever give. You are the definition of spiritual legacy, as you told me, "It's all about your relationship with the Lord. The stories of your past and present walk with Jesus into the future. These stories acknowledge the bad times, but are combined with the good that God creates in and through you." You have shown your family and the world what true love and commitment really are, and you are a better man and husband because you chose to follow God's lead.

I'm so proud of you, Daddy, and I thank you for making it possible for us to share our story with the world.

Thank you, Thad, my husband of sixteen years. You have been my rock. Not once did you question my ability to write. Quite the opposite, actually. You encouraged me to try something new and "venture out." You knew my heart's desire to help others in this situation, or in any difficult trial, and in my times of doubt, you reminded me of Philippians 4:13, "I can do ALL things through Christ who strengthens me" (NKJV).

Frensley, Emery, and Elijah, our precious three children whose hearts were broken when they heard of Beauty's disease—thank you for all of the hugs and kisses during the times you saw me crying. Thank you for making me laugh and smile and see Beauty's disease through the lens of a child. We strengthened each other together, and I know Beauty's disease has shown you that life isn't easy. Life is difficult and full of pain, and sorrow, and sometimes devastating news, but we don't give up. Life matters, and you have had the honor and privilege of seeing the beauty in the brokenness and the hope available to you through Jesus Christ. He is faithful, and you can and will get through the hard times. The life lessons you have learned along this journey are priceless, and I'm so proud of the young ladies and young boy you have become these past several years. You have been light and examples to your friends and family. You are all three overcomers. Daddy, Pop, and I are so very proud of you! And, Beauty would be also, if she knew all that you have done for her this side of heaven in the world around you, through her brokenness.

Gabriel, you know how close Mom and I have always been. Thank you for supporting me as I walked this road. David and Trish, the deep conversations we have shared over the years, and the love and encouragement you passed on weekly and monthly kept me going. What an honor and blessing it has been to see you both travel, often from another state, to spend time with Mom, dance with her, play piano for her, or even read a Bible story to her. You rose above things of the past, and you put love first.

Thank you to Thad's family, my "Smith" in-laws, for your love and prayers throughout this journey. And to Joan and Steve, for building the teepee in Colorado—be careful what you pray for! Big things happen in the "tent of meetings," as I love to call it. I love you Smiths, Becks, Muellers, and Kochs.

To "Big" and "Little" Ginny and Carie—the world sure is a brighter place with you girls in it! Thank you for all of the "laughs-so-hard-we-could-cry," and for the hours of dancing we've had together in assisted living and memory care! Big Ginny, thank you for being that one friend who never left Mom's side. You did your best to help alleviate the stress in our lives and offered your time. Little Ginny, I'll never forget that gut-wrenching day we placed Mom. I don't know how I would have survived without you. I asked a lot of you that day and without hesitation, you agreed to do the inevitable. I know it was a painful day for you, also, and I thank you for carrying me through. Carie and Ginny, our friendships runs deep and wide, and I love that they began with our mothers.

Jennifer, thank you for the hundreds and hundreds of boxes you helped me unpack! God has given you the ability to carry people through difficult times, and somehow, you were able to make me laugh *and* get stuff done! I remember our walk and your words, "Well, everyone has a story!" You are loved, Jennifer. I see you. God sees you.

Mom's caregivers over the past several years—thank you for your patience and love and not giving up on her stubborn personality! You know what you are doing, and I'm grateful that, because of you, my dad is sleeping through the night more (because he knows she is safe).

Thank you, Christine, for saying to me, "You gotta do it!" I shared my heart and fears and was clueless how to start the writing process, but you shared every resource you could think of to get me started. You gave me names and numbers and said, "Just call them! You never know!" Those words reminded me of Mom. It was as if she was speaking through you during our three-hour lunch. Thank you for being one of my biggest cheerleaders.

Bree, thank you for the coaching and teaching me how to write! You challenged me to dig deep and not be afraid to be vulnerable. With each new chapter I brought to the table, you got more and more excited. Your energy and positivity made me more courageous. I absolutely loved working with you. Lorna and Linda, thank you for your edits and excitement to get our story out.

Selby and Stephanie, who knew that summer in Aspen that I would be asking you to "edit" my manuscript?! You both were not afraid to give me honest feedback. You, also, were vulnerable when writing comments on the pages. Thank you for fervently praying for my journey and this book. Your faith in the Lord is inspiring, and your belief in me helped me knock on all kinds of doors. And Selby, "the Connector," I thank you for being an incredible mentor in my life. This has been quite the adventure, and a simple "thank you" will never be enough. I love you to heaven and back!

Lee, thank you for going back to difficult memories of you and your mom and sharing them with me. At a time I was lost and confused, you made me feel supported. Thank you for reading my manuscript and your beautiful endorsement.

Ron, thank you for the beautiful foreword. We really are the *same kind of different!* Your wisdom has taught me much, and I thank you for the time you have taken to help guide me along the way.

John and Eric, thank you for *Breakpoint* (daily commentary and podcasts) and *The Eric Metaxas Show*. Your emphasis on a biblical worldview and your perspectives on American culture are impactful and powerful, not to mention funny. Thank you for valuing life and sacrificial love.

Thank you, Vince, for introducing me to the amazing Greenleaf team! Thank you to Justin, Dan, Sally, Nichole, Kimberly, Sam, Olivia, and Kristine. Working with the Greenleaf team has taught me so much. Corresponding with each of you, and learning about your unique gifts and talents has blessed me tremendously. I will never forget this experience, and I pray that God continues to go before each one of you and that you feel His love daily throughout your lives.

To all doctors, researchers, nutritionists, and therapists specializing in Alzheimer's research—THANK YOU for helping find a cure.

And lastly, thank you to my "prayer warriors"—my dear friends and the "Yayas" who prayed for me often—especially the times I sent a text beginning with, "I'm so sorry to ask this of you, but can you please pray for . . . " You made me feel my prayer requests weren't a burden, but rather an honor and a privilege. I found out who my true friends were as I battled heartbreak and was filled with grief. Instead of chasing after things of this world, like popularity or fame, you put God first, others second, and yourselves third. Your friendships are real and authentic. You don't hide from shame and aren't afraid of being vulnerable. Thank you for showing me what true friendship looks like and being there in every way possible. I needed you, God knew I needed you, and I am forever grateful for His timing and that He brought each of you into my life.

Reading Group Guide

1. How much of *Broken Beauty*'s power came from the fact that it was a memoir? Would the story have been more—or less—impactful if it were written as fiction?

2. What lessons did you take away from the story of Sarah's life? Discuss why is it important to you and your particular life situation.

3. How did the book affect you? Do you feel changed in any way? Describe what the change means to you.

4. Some memoir authors feel they have to portray themselves in a positive way, but Sarah shares all of her experiences—both good and bad. Do you think this helped the story? Did it change how you viewed her? Were you able to connect with her better because she was honest?

5. *Broken Beauty* begins with Sarah discovering her mom trying to eat broken glass. This was one of Sarah's most troubling experiences during her journey of caring for her mother. How does this one scenario frame the rest of her journey? Was it a powerful way to start her memoir?

6. What was the catalyst that caused Sarah and her father to finally find a place for Rebecca? Was there one experience in particular that you felt was the turning point?

7. Sarah's faith guided her through her journey with her mother. Discuss the role religion and faith played in this memoir.

8. When Rebecca learned of her disease, she didn't tell Sarah. Why do you think she didn't? Do you think she was trying to shield Sarah from what the future might bring? Or was it because Rebecca didn't want to face the truth? Do you think it would

have been better for everyone if she had told Sarah sooner? How would you handle this situation?

9. Sarah had a great support group while going through everything. Discuss how some of the people in Sarah's life helped her and what would have happened if she had not had their support.

10. In what moments did Sarah experience God's presence most strongly? How did it help her in those moments?

11. What were some of the more powerful moments in this book, both good and bad? Why were they so powerful or emotional?

12. The title, *Broken Beauty,* refers to Rebecca's broken mind, but also to the fact that there can be beauty in something that is broken. Discuss some examples where this is reflected elsewhere in the book or in your own life.

AUTHOR Q&A

Q: You are very honest about your struggles—from learning about your mother's illness to caring for her. What was it like for you to revisit these painful memories and experiences as you wrote the book?

Writing this book was almost more painful than the experiences we went through! The reason I say that is when you are walking through a journey, you don't realize the burden and stress and heaviness you carry. You do what you need to do, and I think your mind goes into protective mode and you are almost blind to what is really happening in front of you. As I wrote the book, there were times I had to take several days or weeks off because it was so gut-wrenching to not only relive the journey, but to realize how bad it really was. I internalized so much that tears poured out of me as I wrote the story. I honestly had no idea it would be that intense and difficult, but I am thankful it affected me that way, because it was also therapeutic.

Q: What inspired or compelled you to share your journey with others?

I was compelled to share my journey with others because at the time, there was not enough information on early-onset Alzheimer's. I was in my thirties, and I didn't have one friend who could relate to my situation. They may have had a grandparent with dementia or Alzheimer's, but it is different when it is your young, fit, and healthy parent and best friend. It's a terrible disease no matter the age! I was grateful to have found Kimberly Paisley's book about her mother, and I loved reading Still Alice, *but other than those two "stories," it was hard to find material on EOAD. As far as inspiration, I can only say it was from God. I was a happy stay-at-home mom of three, wife of an amazing husband, and driver of kids to and from sports, school, and activities. I never in a million years thought I would or could write a book! God continued to press it on my heart, and after many "signs" that I simply could not deny, I couldn't turn my back on Him and went for it! God was my true inspiration.*

Q: A lot of memoir writers believe that they need to portray themselves in a positive way, yet your memoir is very honest about the struggles you faced. Was it hard for you to write about your flaws so publicly?

The most difficult part wasn't being honest about my struggles. The hardest part was feeling vulnerable throughout the process. It's easy to worry what others may think, and for a while, I was concerned about even my own family members passing judgment about things that I shared publicly, but at the end of the day, feeling vulnerable is exactly what I, personally, needed to learn. I didn't want to hear, "It's so hard, I'm really sorry." I wanted to hear what may happen, things she may do, some sort of time line, and so on. It is so important and healthy to be completely honest and vulnerable. Why pretend it's "okay" when it's actually not? Why not say my mom started wearing Depends and share how devastating that day was? It's the reality of the disease, and if it helps even ONE person, Mom would want that. Unzipping your heart and being completely open draws more people in, and I believe it allows a person to be more open and honest with themself and their own situation. There should be no shame. It's life, and life is hard.

Q: Did you discover anything new in the process of writing the book? As you revisited past memories, did anything surprise you? Were there any connections you hadn't made before, or did you see any elements of your life in a new light?

My biggest discovery throughout this entire writing process was how much my mom truly loved and loves me. In my early years, teenage years, and even in my young adult years, Mom could be tough. I thought she was hard on me because I wasn't good enough, or she had to have control! But, what I learned was that her love was SO grandiose for me, it was SO big, that anything less was not enough for Sarah! She wanted the very, very best for me. Mom lost a daughter at birth. Jessica is her name. She is a few years older than me, and she died during labor. Dad always said the reason Mom carried me on her hip all of my toddler years was because she didn't want to lose another daughter, and I was double the blessing. So, whether it be the best coach in gymnastics (hence many hours of traveling in the car to be under the training of Olympic coach Bela Karolyi), tennis, a boy I dated, or a particular job I wanted . . . whatever it was, she just wanted the best for me because she LOVED me. I saw her love in a whole new light when writing this book. And, as hard as this is to say, I am thankful, in a way, for this disease, because I know in the deepest part of my heart and soul how much Mom loves me, and I will keep that forever and ever—even when the good Lord takes her home. I'll never go back to thinking she was controlling or I wasn't enough. I was enough, and she knew it, so she did everything she could, because of her love for me, to make me the best person I could ever be.

Q: What was the most rewarding experience you had through this journey? What has been the most important or beneficial lesson you have learned from writing your story?

Well, this is going to sound so strange, but my most rewarding experience was in Colorado finishing my book in our family teepee designed by my mother-in-law. For me, this teepee is my "tent of meeting." Moses pitched a tent and called it the "tent of meeting," and it says in Exodus 33:7 (NIV) says that "anyone inquiring of the Lord would go to the tent of meeting outside the camp." It's hard to put into words my experience in this "tent of meeting," but I truly felt the manifestation of the Holy Spirit when I hit the "period" on my last sentence of the last chapter. The entire teepee began to shake and the fabric around the teepee whirled like a huge gust of wind had come through. I was in such shock that all I could do was look up and around and watch. I had chills all over my body! But what I haven't mentioned is that right before I typed that last sentence, I had prayed to God that He would please let me know if there was anything else He wanted to say in the book. I was afraid to "finish" it before making sure God was finished, too! After I prayed, typed the last sentence, and hit the period on the keyboard, the entire teepee started going crazy. It felt like an eternity, although it was probably only thirty seconds! It was a perfectly calm day that day, and I had been in that teepee writing for three hours. Then, after the shaking stopped, it continued to be a perfectly calm day! I even sat in the teepee for another forty-five minutes to see if the wind would blow again! I know this all sounds bizarre for some, but even as I type and share this personal story with the world, I have tears because I know what I felt, I know what I saw, and I can only attempt to explain the unexplainable! I choose to believe it was the manifestation of the Holy Spirit, and therefore, it was my most rewarding experience throughout this entire process! The most beneficial lesson I have learned is to write from my own heart and not what others want me to write. If it's going to be truth from my own experience, then let it be truth. You can't please everyone, and you never will, so I did what I felt pleased God and honored my mother and father.

Q: What advice would you give readers who are also affected by early-onset Alzheimer's?

Live in the moment, agree with them (most of the time!), and listen to your doctor. Dad fought meds for Mom for a long time. Neither of them believed in medication. She refused it, and he complied because he didn't really like it anyway. But, one of the biggest mistakes he made was not convincing her to take meds sooner. It's a game changer, and it's necessary. It's also important to re-evaluate the meds frequently as the disease progresses. Living in the moment is crucial. It's hard to get used to it because the loved one knows what is happening, but at some point doesn't know or understand what they are losing. But the caretakers always know and try to live in their world and LOVE on them as much as possible. And lastly, do your best to not hide the diagnosis from others. Though some will treat your family member differently over time, you will need support. It's crucial. Hiding is very lonely. You need a supportive community to live with this disease.

Q: What do you consider to be the most important thing people should know about caregivers for early-onset Alzheimer's?

Caregivers for early-onset Alzheimer's have one of the most difficult jobs in the world. I always thought being a Mom was the hardest job, but I am not sure I can say that anymore. Perhaps they are equal. It's mentally and physically exhausting, depleting, and debilitating. You begin to feel empty. Caregivers need adequate time away from the situation or they can eventually make the situation worse. Early-onset caregivers will have moments of retreat or withdrawal and need to step away from the loved one. Caregiving is also a mindset. Do you go down the road of bitterness, anger, frustration, resentment, despair and self-pity, or do you savor the moment, live in the moment, show love even if you may not feel love in return, sacrifice your time and serve others, and choose happiness regardless of what the disease says through the person who is sick? The disease is exhausting, but the person you love is still inside. When the disease takes over and speaks ugly words, and its actions are volatile, it is important to remind yourself it's the disease and not the person you love and who loves you. Happiness is a choice. It takes a ton of discipline to renew the mind. If you get in the habit of renewing your mind daily, you will find you can rise above the pain. Early-onset caregivers can't do this alone. They need support, too!

Q: What do you hope readers will take away from this book?

It's my hope that for one, readers will feel the power of love. Love trumps all suffering. Secondly, there is hope in God. No matter the disease, struggle, or difficult circumstance, you are loved and can get through anything with

God. Thirdly, for anyone going through early-onset Alzheimer's, I hope they feel that this book gave them an authentic glimpse into the power of the disease and what is to come, and that no matter what they may tell themselves, they are not alone and there is no shame or guilt for any of the feelings they feel. It's normal, and it's okay. And lastly, show up for your loved one if they need to be placed. The more love that shows up each day for them, the better their quality of life. It feels good to be loved whether healthy or sick, and the more they feel love, the better they feel. My dad, at one point thought by placing Mom, he was breaking their vows. I want readers to see true love, "through sickness and in health," doesn't mean it's only at home. Placing Mom was a very hard pill for dad to swallow. He felt like a failure. He would tell you now he is loving her better than ever because he has the rest he needs, she has the help she needs that he couldn't provide, and he is there every single day. He loved her fully without the disease, and he loves her fully with the disease. Alzheimer's can't stop the love.

Q: What was the most difficult part of the writing process? Was there an "easy" part? Was any part of the experience enjoyable?

For sure, the most difficult parts were the two chapters on placing Mom (Abandonment Day, Parts 1 and 2). It actually took me a few weeks to get through those, if not longer. I had to set aside time on days when I knew my kids were carpooling straight from school to sports and I had a babysitter for our youngest. It was beyond emotional, and I had no idea it would be that way. God took me back like I was walking in those shoes all over again, and I don't ever want to go back to that day again! It was terrible, terrible, terrible. I still see things so clearly in my mind: Dad's face the morning we left, Mom picking up the pecans, the color of her nail polish, her lovely turquoise outfit, the powder in her wine glass, and her leaning over a woman in a wheelchair when I turned my back on her and left. Worst experience ever, and the most difficult chapters to write. The "easiest" chapter was the caregiver appreciation lunch! Caregivers need to be appreciated every single day of the year!

Professional caregivers are underappreciated. They have my heart. They are amazing. It was an easy chapter to write because I meant every word of my speech at that luncheon, and I would say those words all over again. The most "fun" chapter to write was the cycling class! Big Ginny walking in not knowing she wasn't supposed to just barge into the class like that. She just took over and danced in front of the instructor and did what she does best: make everyone smile, laugh and cry! I love that woman!

Q: Did you have a favorite chapter to write in *Broken Beauty*?

I think chapter 24, "Making Broken Things Beautiful." The Walk to End Alzheimer's was a very difficult day for me, yet it turned into so much fun. I was anxious in the days leading up to it, and when my friends showed up and surprised me at the hotel the day before, it was love showing up for ME. I felt so loved, and it was encouraging, uplifting, and invigorating. It nurtured and strengthened me during a time in which I felt delicate, frail, and weak. I don't think Big Ginny and those girls will ever truly know how special that weekend was for me. And to top it off, I saw many of Mom's caregivers at the finish line, which was liberating! I was heartbroken, but the entire day turned into one of the most beautiful moments of my life.

Q: One thing that stands out in your book is that while there are many challenges and struggles with being a caretaker for someone with Alzheimer's, there are also some beautiful moments. Can you share one of your favorite moments spent with your mother?

One of the most beautiful moments spent with my mother was the first time the fifth-grade girls came to visit Mom and the other residents, singing hymns and reciting scripture and the Lord's Prayer with sign language. I remember so vividly putting my arm around Mom and watching the girls say, "Therefore I tell you, do not worry about your life, what you will eat or drink; or about your body, what you will wear. Is not life more than food, and the body more than clothes? Look at the birds of the air; they do not sow or reap or store away in barns, and yet your heavenly Father feeds them. Are you not much more valuable than they? Can any one of you by worrying add a single hour to your life?" (Matthew 6:25–27, NIV). I did everything I could to not fall down on my knees in front of the kids and Mom. The girls were not only speaking to Mom and the residents, but they were speaking to me! I turned and looked at Mom, and she just smiled and leaned her head into mine and squeezed my other hand. I believe she knew in that moment that everything would be okay, and that we were there for her and would never abandon her.

Q: Your relationship with your mother had to change very suddenly, and it was a change that she never realized or remembered. It was also something you had to adjust to alone, without her input. How did you handle this? What was the hardest thing about this change?

Truthfully, I was in complete despair. It's a miracle I got through it all without an antidepressant. I fell into a state of depression, and I did my best to hide it and continue to be strong, but I wasn't. The kids went to school, and I lied to my husband about working out and running errands. I was at home in bed, crying for hours and hours. I went from talking to my mom on the phone nearly every day, when she lived in Houston, to her finally moving here and me getting to see her every day. Then overnight, I couldn't speak to her or see her for over six weeks. It was like she died. My dad looked like he had lost the love of his life, and I felt like I had lost my mother. It's hard to explain. The only thing I could do was cry and lean on God. I prayed every single day for hours. If it wasn't for God, I don't know how I would have made it through everything. I look back and wonder how in the world I got in the car and drove carpool—after crying for hours—pretending I was okay! It's amazing, the power of the mind; how we can be so determined and pretend we are okay when we really aren't. I was very alone, and I should have been more open about what was really happening so I could receive the help and support many people offered to give. But I refused it, and pretended I was okay.

Q: Can you share any specific goals or intentions you had for this book? Do you feel you accomplished them?

My goal for this book is to finish the race and help people, although I know my race isn't really "finished" until God calls me home. There were many times I would think to myself, "What am I doing? This is crazy to think I can write a book!" And it IS crazy, but God was by my side. He's the only reason this book is complete. My goal was to honor God, and my parents, and help others through their suffering. And if it leads one person to Jesus, then mission accomplished! That's what Mom would want, and as I said in the book, she would accept this disease a million times over if she knew it led one person to faith in Jesus.

Q: At one point, you said that being with your mother was emotionally exhausting, yet you knew the time with her was priceless. Do you think you have reached a balance about these feelings? What advice would you give others dealing with similar situations?

My advice on getting through the exhaustion is to focus on the renewal of the mind. It is crucial. Find time to meditate and pray; exercise or go for a walk; and, throughout the day, renew your mind by seeking God's will. The mind is a powerful thing, and it takes a lot of discipline to direct your thoughts towards positivity and God in this exhausting situation, but trust me, it can be done! I am proof! I overcame despair as love took a hold of me. I'm a new person! Also, there are three things a loved one with Alzheimer's responds to: sweets, music, and affection. I believe if caregivers were aware of this, it would enhance their lives and give them peace in times of despair.

Q: Has your relationship with your mother changed after writing this
   book? Are you more at peace with the choices you made?

*My relationship with my mother has changed quite a bit. It's a unique love,
because she is like a child, and I am now the parent, and she depends on Dad,
her caregivers, and me for all of her needs. Before, she was a very independent
woman. She was a strong leader and would hardly accept help from anyone
(wonder where I got it, ha!). She also gave a lot of advice, some wanted and
some unsolicited. While our love is deeper and our bond is stronger, I also miss
her unsolicited advice. Most of the time, that advice was because she loved me
so much, though I didn't realize it then. The most difficult part is not being
able to call her all of the time. I told her almost everything, and even if I
didn't like her input, I still wanted her "motherly" advice! I don't have that
anymore. She was easy to approach with things, because she was so outspoken.
We always teased her because she couldn't keep her mouth shut and "nagged,"
but I miss that more than ever now. She just didn't know how to channel it
very well, and I sure miss it when I am down about something and she can't
give me advice. She can, however, simply rub my arm, hug me, and say, "It's
okay, Sarah. It will be okay." And that is all I need—for my mom to tell me
it will be okay. I'm at peace with everything. She is where she needs to be, she's
safe, and she is so loved. That's all that matters.*

Q: Can you describe your writing process? Did you keep a journal when
   going through this experience with your mother?

*I didn't begin journaling until a few days after I placed her. During my
time of despair, I felt like I needed to document all of my feelings. God
really pressed it on my heart. I didn't want to, but it was an overwhelming
feeling, and I began typing things on my laptop. I had also been emailing friends updates even before her placement, and some of those emails
read like a blog. Many friends and family members encouraged me to*

keep writing. They wanted to be a part of the journey and appreciated the authenticity, rawness, and vulnerability. During the writing process, my walk with God grew stronger and stronger. I wholeheartedly believe the reason He pressed it on my heart was to help me overcome the pain, hurt, depression, and suffering. I channeled my emotions through writing and dumped them on God when I lost it emotionally! It was therapeutic to write, and it revealed a lot of things about myself, my family, and my relationship with Mom. It also revealed who my true friends were, and that was hard. Some I thought were close didn't show up. I hardly received a call or text from them during the hardest time of my life, as if they disappeared. It revealed people's true colors and deepened my walk with God. The writing process has been difficult, exciting, adventurous, demanding, and exhilarating. It's been challenging, and it most definitely was out of my comfort zone! I wouldn't trade this experience for the world, though. I'd never felt such love from God, Mom, Dad, Thad (my husband), our children, and friends. Those who showed up these past several years know who they are, and I am forever grateful for this journey.

Q: Can you tell us how going through this experience has affected your relationship with your father? Have you learned anything about him that you did not know before?

Going through this experience with my father has pulled us even closer. I have always been a "daddy's girl." Yes, Mom and I have always been close, but I'll always be a daddy's girl! Dad and I communicate very openly. We don't hold anything back, and he doesn't hide things from me he thinks will upset me. He's open about how he is emotionally, physically, and mentally. Our bond is so tight, and our love for God is strong. One thing I learned about him that I didn't realize before was HOW much he loved Mom and how truly humble he is. I sometimes used to think he was slow in making decisions, but as I've grown older and gone through this experience, I've realized how wise my father really was and is. He is slow to make decisions because he is very patient and he waits on the Lord. He is the closest human being on this earth I can compare to my Father in Heaven. He is forever and always will be my daddy.

About the Author

SARAH BEARDEN SMITH is a housewife, mother of three, and a woman of deep faith, who has lived in Texas all her life. Sarah's childhood was anchored by her family's faith and their participation in church activities. She was a gifted athlete and reached elite status in competitive gymnastics by the time she was thirteen years of age. Sarah was born and raised in the Houston area, and remained there until her departure for the University of Texas at Austin, where she was a speech communications major and varsity cheerleader, and a member of Tri Delta Sorority. Following graduation, she remained in Austin, working in the software and high-tech industry. After her marriage to Thad Smith in 2002, the couple moved to Dallas, Texas. Through their years in Dallas, Sarah and her husband have served on various boards and committees, including the Greer Garson Gala, the Presbyterian Hospital Healthcare Foundation, East-West Ministries, AWARE Dallas, and the Providence Christian School of Texas. They actively serve with their children in assisted living and memory care facilities and support organizations such as Council for Life, the Alzheimer's Association, the Women's Alzheimer's Movement, and Community Bible Study. Sarah and her family are members of Watermark Community Church.